William Barrows

Oregon

The struggle for possession. Third Edition

William Barrows

Oregon
The struggle for possession. Third Edition

ISBN/EAN: 9783337015930

Printed in Europe, USA, Canada, Australia, Japan

Cover: Foto ©ninafisch / pixelio.de

More available books at **www.hansebooks.com**

American Commonwealths.

EDITED BY

HORACE E. SCUDDER.

American Commonwealths

OREGON

THE STRUGGLE FOR POSSESSION

BY

WILLIAM BARROWS

THIRD EDITION

BOSTON
HOUGHTON, MIFFLIN AND COMPANY
New York: 11 East Seventeenth Street
The Riverside Press, Cambridge
1885

, 1883,
By WILLIAM BARROWS.

The Riverside Press, Cambridge:
Electrotyped and Printed by H. O. Houghton & Co.

TO THE ONE

WHO SUGGESTED THIS VOLUME,

AND

GAVE UP THE AUTHOR

TO ALCOVE STUDIES AND FRONTIER WANDERINGS FOR IT;

WHO HAS BREATHED THE HOME INSPIRATION

THAT MAKES LIFE A JOY AND WORK A DELIGHT:

TO MY WIFE,

THIS BOOK IS DEDICATED,

BY

HER HUSBAND.

THE AUTHORITIES ON THE STRUGGLE OF FIVE NATIONS FOR OREGON.

[It has seemed best to name these in summary, in order to avoid burdening the text with very many references, and to afford aid to any who may wish to study this topic more at large.]

Astor, John Jacob, Letter of, to the Hon. J. Q. Adams: Agreement for the Sale of Astoria, and Account of the Capture of Astoria, in Greenhow's History of Oregon and California. Appendix G.

Bancroft, George. History of the United States.

Barrow, Sir John. Chronological History of Voyages into the Arctic Regions. London, 1818.

Belcher, Edward, R. N., etc. Narrative of a Voyage Round the World. London, 1843.

Bent, Silas. Gateways to the Pole, or Thermal Paths to the Pole. 1872.

Benton, T. H. Thirty Years' View. From 1820 to 1850. 1854.

Brougham, Lord. Speech on the Ashburton Treaty, or Treaty of Washington, April 7, 1843.

Browne, Peter A., LL. D. Lecture on the Oregon Territory. 1843.

Butler, Capt. W. F., F. R. G. S. Great Lone Land. London, 1872.

Calhoun, John C., Speech of, on the Treaty of Washington, in the Senate, August, 1842.

Carver, Jonathan. Travels throughout the Interior Parts of North America, 1766–1768. 1813.

Congress. Congressional Reports, House of Representatives; Linn's, June 6, 1838; Poinsett's, Secretary War, 1840; Pendleton's, May 25, 1842; and Report of March 12, 1844.

Executive Document No. 37 of the 41st Congress, 3d Session, Senate. February 9, 1871.

AUTHORITIES.

House Document No. 38 of 35th Congress, 1859.

Journals of both Houses of Congress and the Abridgment of Debates, for the years covered.

Message of President J. Q. Adams. With accompanying Documents. December 28, 1827.

Papers relating to the Treaty of Washington, Berlin Arbitration, Foreign Relations of the United States. 3d Session, 42d Congress, 1872–73.

Senate of the United States: Documents, 1837. On the Transfer of the Louisiana to the United States.

Territory of Oregon. 25th Congress, 3d Session House of Representatives. Report No. 101. By Caleb Cushing. February 16, 1839.

Cook, Capt. James, F. R. S. Voyage to the Pacific Ocean. Third Voyage. Dublin, 1784.

— Coxe, William, A. M. Russian Discoveries between Asia and America. 1780.

Curtis. Life of Daniel Webster. 1870.

Cushing, Caleb. Treaty of Washington. 1873.

+ De Smet. Oregon Missions.

Dunn, John. History of the Oregon Territory and the British North American Fur Trade. 1845.

— Falconer, Thomas. The Oregon Question; or, A Statement of the British Claims to the Oregon Territory, etc. London,
+ 1845. Strictures on the Above. By Robert Greenhow. History of Oregon and California, pp. 1–7.

— Farnham, Thomas J. Travels in the Great Western Prairies and Anahuac, and Rocky Mountains, and in the Oregon Territory. 1843.

Fitzgerald. Examination of the Hudson Bay Company. London, 1849.

-| Frémont, J. C., Brevet-Captain. Report of the Exploring Expedition to Oregon and North California in the years 1843–44. Washington, 1845.

Frobisher, Martin, Three Voyages of. Hakluyt Society. Voyages toward the Northwest. London, 1849.

— Gallatin, Albert, Letters of, on the Oregon Question. Washington, 1846.

Gayarré, Charles. History of Louisiana. The French Domination. 1854.

AUTHORITIES.

- Gray, W. H. History of Oregon from 1792–1849. 1870.
- Greenhow, Robert. History of Oregon and California. 1845.
- Harmon, D. W. Journal of Voyages and Travels in the Interior of North America. 1820.
- Hearne, Samuel. Journey to the Northern Ocean. London, 1795.
- Hines, Rev. Gustavus. Oregon: Its History, Condition, and Prospects. 1851.
- Irving, Washington. Astoria. 1836. Rocky Mountains and Adventures in the Far West. From the Journal of Capt. B. L. E. Bonneville. 1837.
- Life of George Washington. 1857.
- Jeffrey. History of the French Dominion in North America.
- Kelley, Hall J. Emigration to the Oregon Territory, A Society for Promoting. Hall J. Kelley, General Agent. 1831.
- Lewis and Clark, History of the Expedition of. By Paul Allen, 1814.
- Long, S. H., Major. An Expedition from Pittsburgh to the Rocky Mountains, 1819–20, by order of John C. Calhoun, Secretary of War.
- Mackenzie, Alexander. Voyages from Montreal, through the Continent of North America to the Frozen and Pacific Oceans. London, 1801.
- Martin, R. M. Hudson Bay Territories and Vancouver's Island. London, 1849.
- Monette, John W., M. D. History of the Discovery and Settlement of the Valley of the Mississippi. 1846. Harpers.
- Parkman, Francis. Pioneers of France in the New World; The Jesuits in North America; The Discovery of the Great West; The Old Régime in Canada; Count Frontenac and New France under Louis XIV.; History of the Conspiracy of Pontiac; The Oregon Trail; Prairie and Rocky Mountain Life. 1865–1877.
- Pike, Major Z. M. Expeditions to the Sources of the Mississippi, Arkansas, Kansas, and La Platte. 1807.
- Pilcher. Narrative of Travels in the Missouri, Columbia, Assinniboin, etc., 1827–29. A Document accompanying the Message of President Jackson, January 23, 1829.
- Porter, Robert E. The West: From the Census of 1880.
- Robinson, H. M. Great Fur Land. 1879.

AUTHORITIES.

Selkirk, Lord. British Fur-Trade in North America, A Sketch of.

✝ Simpson, Sir George, Governor in Chief of the Hudson Bay Company in North America. Narrative of a journey Round the World. London, 1847.

Small, Hugh. Oregon and Her Resources. 1872.

— Townsend, J. K. Narrative of a Journey across the Rocky Mountains to the Columbia. 1839.

— Twiss, Travers, Professor of Political Economy, Oxford. Oregon Question Examined. London, 1846.

✝ Victor, Mrs. F. F. River of the West. 1871.

Walker, Charles M. History of Athens County, Ohio. 1869.

Wallace, Edward J., M. A. Oregon Question. London, 1846.

Webster and Ashburton. Correspondence between Mr. Webster and Lord Ashburton, on the McLeod Case; on the Creole Case; On the Subject of Impressment. 1841–42.

Webster, Daniel, Private Correspondence of. Edited by Fletcher Webster. 1857.

Wilkeson, Samuel. Notes on Puget Sound: A Reconnoissance. 1869.

Westminster Review. The Last Great Monopoly. July, 1867, and in Littell, August 10, 1867, No. 1210.

— Wyeth, J. B. Oregon: or, A Short History of a Long Journey, 1833.

CONTENTS.

		PAGE
I.	The European Powers in America	1
II.	Spain Enters the Struggle and Fails,	5
III.	France Sells her Claims	17
IV.	Russia Declines the Struggle	22
V.	English Explorations and Ambitions	27
VI.	The Hudson Bay Company	33
VII.	English Monopoly of the Frontier	48
VIII.	Astoria; Its Founding and Failure	57
IX.	Face to Face; America and England	64
X.	American Speeches, English Steel-traps, and Diplomacy	71
XI.	Western Men on the Oregon Trail	77
XII.	The Great English Mistake	87
XIII.	Four Flat-Head Indians in St. Louis	103
XIV.	"A Quart of Seed Wheat"	114
XV.	A Bridal Tour of Thirty-five Hundred Miles	121
XVI.	Whitman's "Old Wagon"	140
XVII.	Anxiety and Strategy of the Hudson Bay Company	147
XVIII.	Whitman's Ride	160
XIX.	Oregon not in the Treaty of Webster and Ashburton	179
XX.	Is Oregon worth Saving?	189
XXI.	Titles to Oregon	205
XXII.	The Claims of the United States to Oregon	212
XXIII.	History Vindicated	224

		PAGE
XXIV.	Two Hundred Wagons for Oregon	239
XXV.	The People Discuss the Question	255
XXVI.	Immigrants Settle the Oregon Question	263
XXVII.	"Fifty-four Forty, or Fight"	272
XXVIII.	At Last a Treaty	282
XXIX.	What did the Treaty Mean?	297
XXX.	The Emperor William and Arbitration	315
XXXI.	The Whitman Massacre	320
XXXII.	The Oregon of To-Day	330
XXXIII.	Conclusion	349

OREGON:

THE STRUGGLE FOR POSSESSION.

CHAPTER I.

THE EUROPEAN POWERS IN AMERICA.

In 1697, the year of the Treaty of Ryswick, Spain claimed as her share of North America, on the Atlantic coast, from Cape Romaine on the Carolina shore a few miles north of Charleston, due west to the Mississippi River, and all south of that line to the Gulf of Mexico. That line, continued beyond the Mississippi, makes the northern boundary of Louisiana. In the valley of the lower Mississippi, Spain acknowledged no rival, though France was then beginning to intrude. On the basis of discovery by the heroic De Soto and others, she claimed up to the heads of the Arkansas and the present famous Leadville, and westward to the Pacific. On that ocean, or the South Sea as it was then called, she set up the pretensions of sovereignty from Panama to Nootka Sound on Vancouver. These pretensions covered the coasts, harbors, islands, and fisheries, and extended themselves indefinitely inland, and even over the whole Pacific Ocean, as then limited. These stupendous claims Spain based on discovery, under the papal bull of Alexander VI. in 1493. This bull or decree gave to the government of the discoverer all newly discovered lands and waters. In 1513 Balboa, the Spaniard, discovered the Pacific Ocean, as he came over the Isthmus of Panama, and so Spain came into the ownership of that body of water! Good old times those were, when kings thrust their hands into the New World, as children do theirs into a grab-bag at a fair, and drew out a river four thousand miles long, or an ocean, or a tract of wild land ten or fifteen times the size of England!

At the Ryswick partition of the world, France held good positions in America for the mastery of the continent. Beginning on the Mississippi, where the Spanish line crossed it, that is, where Louisiana and Arkansas unite two of their corners on the Father of Waters, the French claimed east on the Spanish boundary, and north of it to the watershed between the head streams dividing for the Atlantic and the Mississippi. Their claim was bounded by this highland line, continuing north and east, and still separating Atlantic streams from those flowing into the Great Lakes and the St. Lawrence. Where this line reached the springs of the Penobscot it followed its waters to the ocean. It was the proud thought of France, that from the mouth of the Penobscot along the entire seaboard to the unknown and frozen Arctic, no European power divided that coast, and the wild interior back of it, with her. So France claimed indefinitely north to the farther rim of Hudson Bay, as now known, and all lands drained into that Bay, and wildly west to the heads of the Mississippi and Missouri, and thence down to our two corners of Louisiana and Arkansas. This gave to France even the western parts of Virginia, Pennsylvania, and New York, and a large northern portion of New England, as we now name those sections. Certain vague doubts hung over those French claims in the great north land after the convention of Ryswick, but they were claims of little worth.

Russia had no possessions in North America at the date of this survey, 1697. But as Peter the Great, her emperor, had at that time his plans matured for gaining interests in the New World which afterwards resulted in Russian America, and as that nation entered the list of competitors for Oregon, it seems best here to outline her position on the field of struggle.

The Russians came into possession on the northwest coast of America through their ardor in the fur trade. Within a few years after the Treaty of Ryswick, the Russians had subdued all Northern Asia in the interests of this trade, and Siberia became the great game preserve of the empire. When once on the Asiatic shores of the Northern Pacific it was natural and not difficult, in the chase for the sea-otter and other valuable furs, to push off to the Aleutian Islands and then to the American mainland of Alaska. So through the enterprise of his widow, Queen Catharine, and of his daughter, Queen Elizabeth, the wish and vision of Peter the Great were realized in a commercial conflict with the Spanish and French and English on that coast. Among the distinguished leaders in this Russian enterprise was Bering the Dane, who, in his third voyage, gave up his life on the desolate little granite island that bears his name and his grave. In after years the narrow passage between the two continents, through which he had twice sailed without discovering the Straits, but supposing himself to be in the broad Arctic, was honored with his name.

Having outlined the claims of these three leading

powers in North America at the opening of this narrative, the English possessions are obvious as the small remainder. They constituted the long, narrow Atlantic slope, extending from the Spanish Cape Romaine, north of Charleston, to the French bounds on the Penobscot, and inland up that river and along the watershed of the Alleghanies and of the French claim, down to the east and west Spanish boundary, and on it to Cape Romaine again.

Under these claims, France and Spain held much more territory on this continent than the entire area of the continent of Europe; an estimate of the Russian possessions has been given; the narrow English belt, hugging the Atlantic, was hardly equal in area to Missouri.

Of course these outlines are stated only approximately, and somewhat guessingly, because of the dark geographical ignorance that shrouded North America at the opening of the seventeenth century. The pretentious claims of royalty, of the papacy, and of the rival favorites of the different courts, overlapped each other like bogus mortgages, and they ran far and wide as liberally as astronomical spaces.

Thus stood the foreign ownership of the New World at the conclusion of the Treaty of Ryswick, 1697. At this date and our starting point, England was at her minimum and France at her maximum of claims in North America, and Spain had come down from grandiloquent assumptions to sensible pretensions.

CHAPTER II.

SPAIN ENTERS THE STRUGGLE AND FAILS.

The claims of Spain in North America have been marked off. A notice of the vast shrinkage in her pretensions, prior to the Treaty of Ryswick, will prepare one to trace, in this chapter, her weakening and final departure from the contest for Oregon.

"To prevent collision between Christian princes, on the 4th of May, 1493, Alexander VI. published a bull in which he drew an imaginary line from the north pole to the south, a hundred leagues west of the Azores, assigning to the Spanish all that lies west of that boundary, while all to the east of it was confirmed to Portugal." [1]

Since Spanish navigators had explored somewhat the Atlantic Ocean and coasts as far as Newfoundland, Spain claimed, by this papal authority, and under the name of Florida, "the whole sea-coast as far as Newfoundland and even to the remotest North. In Spanish geography Canada was a part of Florida. Yet within that whole extent not a Spanish fort was erected nor a harbor was occupied nor one settlement was planned." And when St. Augustine, Florida, was founded, the bigoted Philip II. was proclaimed monarch of all North America.

More surprising it is to see such pretensions set forth at a much later day. The archbishop Lorenzana, in his

[1] Bancroft's *History of the United States*, Author's Last Revision, vol. i. p. 9.

history of New Spain, published in 1770, at the City of Mexico, says, "It is doubtful whether the country of New Spain does not border on Tartary and Greenland, by the way of California on the former, and by New Mexico on the latter." The bishop was poor in geography, and was in the error then still lingering, that America was made up of big islands, extending west and ending in the East India Islands, and that one could sail through, somewhere, from Newfoundland to China.

When the French began their discoveries and settlements in Canada and the other northern provinces, the Spanish gradually, but under bloody protests, withdrew their claims toward the South. After the Jamestown colony was established, and parts of New England occupied, they consented to make the southern boundary of Virginia the northern boundary of their Florida. This was about 1650, and when the royal province of Virginia had about fifteen thousand white inhabitants and three hundred negro slaves.

Then followed the English grant for the Carolina plantations; and the Edict of Nantes, that expelled so many Protestants from France, furnished many colonists with other adventurers. The Spanish remonstrated against the encroachments, but the English would not acknowledge a claim both unwarranted and unused. At length, about 1690, the Spanish quietly contracted the limits of their shrinking Florida, and agreed to the line already named, being a little north of Charleston, and running exactly west from Cape Romaine to the Mississippi River.

Having set bounds, mutual and somewhat permanent, on the seaboard between themselves and the English, the Spanish already began to feel the encroachments of the

French, down the Mississippi from the St. Lawrence and the Great Lakes. Vague and fascinating rumors had gone up from time to time, among the scattered and frozen settlements of the St. Lawrence, about great rivers that never froze over, and plains and warm valleys toward the South Sea and the Gulf of Mexico. As early as 1658 French fur traders had wintered on Lake Superior, and two years later the devout Ménard had gone up there, to a death that he knew must soon come from the Indians, that he might plant the Cross on the barbarous border. More and more, trader and Jesuit, forgetful of all toil and danger, threaded the Indian trails to the head waters of rivers that disappeared in the mysterious southwest. The almost social waters, as if talking of better homes in more sunny climes to which they were hastening, tempted these Indian merchants and preachers to the bold venture. So with only blankets and food for a few days they pushed their frail canoes into the jolly waters, saying: Where shall we land? In the Sea of Virginia? In the South Sea? In the Gulf of Mexico? In China? In Cathay?

In 1670 the spirited La Salle, a Jesuit priest in France, a fur trader and feudal colonist in Canada, and an ardent dreamer of the Straits of Anian, opening somewhere from the Atlantic to the Pacific, floated in his birch canoe south as far as Louisville. In 1671 St. Lussen, with his fifteen whites, and swarming red men of fourteen tribes, chanted the Vexilla Regis at the Sault Ste. Marie, the outlet of Lake Superior, and took possession for Louis XIV. of all the country bounded by the seas of the north and of the west and of the south. It was a wonderful occasion in that deep interior wilderness in North America. On that leafy morning in June, and on an eminence at the foot of the rapids, the civilians in showy armor and the Jesuits in their robes surrounded the wooden cross and chanted and offered prayers. The Indians, crouching and gliding and gazing on all sides, watched the pompous ceremonials while a large part of North America was made over to Louis the Grand. A volley of musketry, a *Vive le Roi*, and the yelping of the savages closed the marvellous scene. Mr. Parkman in his " Discovery of the Great West," — a captivating volume, where true and pure history makes the highest romance, tells the story with fascination.[1]

Two years later we find Marquette and Joliet at the mouth of the Arkansas ; and in 1682 La Salle appears again, and now at the mouth of the Mississippi. With what daring and romance and grand expectations these early voyageurs and the first of white men must have glided into and through those primeval solitudes ! Twenty-five hundred miles they pushed off into the unknown, among savages and wild beasts. Now they take the broad stream midway, and now under its dark forest banks. One timid deer is shot from the grazing herd, and no sound like that has ever waked echoes in that stillness of ages. The calm evening comes over the prairies, and then the cheery camp-fire, venison, vespers and sweet sleep.

Shortly after the Treaty of Ryswick the French began to occupy, and with energy, that portion of the great valley that was recognized as their own. As early as 1705 Kaskaskia had become a populous and happy French post, and seven years later it was constituted the capital of the Illinois country, having a population of two thousand, a monastery and a college. It was a

[1] Parkman's *Discovery of the Great West*, 40–42.

marked frontier town, and had the vicissitudes of Indian, French, and English wars. In 1778 Colonel Clark, by one of those heroic and romantic movements that have so signalized our frontier and stored it with material for an American Walter Scott, took possession of it for the young republic.

In 1682 La Salle spread French claims over the lower Mississippi, and three years after he annexed Texas to the realm of his king, and established a trading post and fort on Isle Dauphin, between which and Quebec a lively trade sprang up. Thus early the active and progressive French opened a way into the very interior of indolent New Spain, and were transporting not only peltries and furs, but grain and flour and other agricultural products down that mysterious river.

The same persistent discoverers, the trader and the Jesuit, also opened the Ohio, Illinois, Wabash, and Kaskaskia. The bold and far-reaching plan was adopted to connect the Great Lakes with the Gulf of Mexico by a cordon of military posts. About 1720 the first of them, Fort Chartres, was founded on the eastern bank of the Mississippi, and about forty-five miles below St. Louis. It became the French headquarters for Upper Louisiana, and continued for a long time their western centre of life and fashion, intrigue and ambition—the Paris of the Great West. So active were the French that in 1730 they had planted one hundred and forty families and six hundred converted Indians on the Illinois alone, and five years later they founded Vincennes on the Wabash, as a military and rallying centre.

Such was the colonizing activity of the French in the upper Mississippi, thus overshadowing and making timid the Spanish below. But in Lower Louisiana the encroachments were still more annoying and alarming. In 1699 D'Iberville made a settlement near Ship Island, and proposed French control over the whole coast and region from Pensacola to the Rio Grande. He surveyed the Mississippi for about four hundred miles, to the region of Natchez, and caused an exploration of Red River for a thousand miles from its mouth, and the Arkansas up to Little Rock, while the Washita and Yazoo were not neglected. The Missouri he explored up to the entrance of the Kansas, and the Mississippi to the St. Peter's. Waters now made familiar by steamboats and crossed by railroads the light canoes and pirogues of D'Iberville glided over, like waterfowl, shooting rapids, making "carries," and submitting to no obstacles. No white man had ever before much disturbed these hidden recesses of nature.

In 1710 the entire population of Lower Louisiana amounted to only three hundred and eighty souls—a small village to-day. The men were ignorant, indolent, and vicious; negro slaves and Indian girls did the most of the work, and the loose, arms-length government was supported by a hundred and seventy-five soldiers.

The Spanish governor at Pensacola remonstrated against these French intrusions, but as his remonstrance was able to do no more it was in vain. On the east of the Mississippi the Perdido had been accepted by both governments as the eastern line of the French and the western one of Florida. But on the west of the Mississippi all claims to territory were in a contested uncertainty. While the Spanish claimed eastward, across Texas, almost to the Mississippi, the French claimed westward across the entire province to the Rio Grande.

Nor was the struggle between the two foreign crown

confined in that Indian wilderness of the New World to the Gulf coast and the deltas of the lower valley. Spanish adventurers from New Mexico and the Santa Fé country had ranged north and east, across the upper Arkansas, to the Missouri and Mississippi, and found there also the intruding and irrepressible French. An expedition was forwarded to expel these traders and colonists, but the result was very disastrous to the Spanish. After this the French built Fort Orleans on an island in the Missouri, above the mouth of the Osage. In military connection and about the same time Fort Chartres was built, as before mentioned. The wonderful changes in the bed and channels of the Mississippi are seen in the fact that Fort Chartres, originally on the bank of the river, was washed away and then rebuilt, and of stone, far inland. The encroaching river followed and is undermining the new fort. For ten years, ending about 1750, the French were active in establishing friendly relations with the Indians between the Alleghanies and the Missouri, and from the heads of the Mississippi to Texas. This was a deep stroke of policy and involved vast labor.

By all these explorations and encroachments the French crowded the Spanish to the south and west of the following line: From the mouth of the Sabine up that river to latitude thirty-two, then due north to the Red River and by it to longitude twenty-three; thence north to the Arkansas and up it to latitude forty-two and on it west to the Pacific. This was the boundary, practically, that the French forced on the Spanish, though it was not then very formally or definitely agreed to. Indeed, it was one of those singular treaty lines, sometimes appearing in history, on which much has been settled, while they have never been run. The one in question has had a peculiar history.

When, in 1762, France secretly conveyed her western portion of Louisiana to Spain she made this its limit on the southwest. But it was only descriptive, having never been run or traversed by either party. When Spain reconveyed the same to France in 1800, it was limited by the same boundaries and in description only. In 1803 France sold this territory, the Louisianas, to the United States, "with all its rights and appurtenances as fully and in the same manner as they have been acquired by the French Republic." To this extent, and on a line unrun, and not very definite, the United States were now bounded on Spanish territory, and for sixteen years there was negotiation, and at times unpleasant struggle, to locate and run the line. Then, when, in 1819, the United States purchased Florida, an article was inserted in the treaty restating this line, but it was drawn only by diplomats in sentences, and not by engineers on the ground. The treaty called for a survey, but various delays prevented the setting of metes and bounds, till we acquired New Mexico in 1848, when the line became unnecessary, because we became owners on both sides of it, and so it has never been run. It is a singular fact that this line of three august conferences and treaties, one war, and much diplomatic intrigue and correspondence was never anything more than imaginary and declared.

We have thus grouped the facts, that it may be seen in summary how France crowded Spain on the southwest, and compelled a continuance of the shrinkage in her boastful claims on the New World.

Now, it is important to notice that the old Spanish

claim extended from Panama, on the Pacific, to Prince William's Sound; and of course covered the Oregon of our narrative, that is, the Oregon, Washington Territory, Idaho, and British Columbia of to-day, up to 54° 40'. According to the decree of Pope Alexander VI., the Spanish had granted to them exclusive privileges in all lands and seas which they might discover in the Pacific. On this basis they founded the audacious claims of sovereignty over the American shores of the Pacific.

When, therefore, the English, profiting by Cook's discoveries, that ended with his death in 1778, and by the enterprise of others, sought to open the fur, seal, whale, and other traffic, on the northwest coast, the Spanish government regarded the attempt as an intrusion, and in its anxiety as to the end sought by its rival, entered strong objections. This arrogant claim of Spain to all Pacific waters and coasts and islands near to our continent is well illustrated in the case of the American ship Columbia. In 1788 she left Boston for trade in the Pacific, was damaged, and put into Juan Fernandez for repairs, and having been refitted, was allowed by the Spanish authorities there to proceed. For this the Commandant was removed under severe rebuke, on the ground that every vessel found in seas beyond Cape Horn, without Spanish license, was to be treated as an enemy, since no nation had a right to territory or trade that would require the doubling of that Cape. Russia was already on the northwest coast of America, and Spain sought to make Prince William's Sound the southern limit of Russia. This was in 1789.

At this time "no settlement, factory, or other establishment whatsoever had been founded or attempted, nor had any jurisdiction been exercised by the authorities or subjects of a civilized nation in any part of America bordering on the Pacific, between San Francisco and Prince William's Sound."[1] It is true that Spain led off in discoveries on those coasts, and afterward she had, jointly with England, France, and Russia, landed here and there, and taken possession ceremonially. But it early came to an understanding among these nations that no such pageant could constitute possession. That could be proved and maintained only by habitations and residence.

The issue between Spain and England as to sovereignty on the northwest coast was made at Nootka Sound in 1789. Each nation then attempted to form a settlement there. The Spanish captured the English vessels, and this threw the case into diplomacy between the two courts. England informed the Spanish court that she could "not accede to the pretensions of absolute sovereignty, commerce and navigation" that were claimed, and secretly prepared to back her protest by two fleets. The Spanish government was informed that " British subjects have an indisputable right to the enjoyment of a free and uninterrupted navigation, commerce, and fishing, and to the possession of such establishments as they should form, with the consent of the natives of the country, not previously occupied by any of the European nations." The younger Pitt, then in his prime of power, and with all his father's hatred and contempt of Spain, shaped the policy that ended in the famous Nootka Treaty of 1790.

The question opened so widely that France did not think it best to remain quiet; and though she seemed to maintain neutrality she took steps, at once, to increase

[1] *History of Oregon and California*, by Robert Greenhow, p. 187.

her navy to unusual proportions. Under Louis XVI. Mirabeau led this policy, and, by a semblance, assumed to mediate between the two courts. The result was the Nootka Treaty, by which England gained her full commercial demands. Five years later Spain, for various reasons, informally and quietly, and without quitclaiming her rights, withdrew from Nootka Sound, and afterward fixed the northern limit of her claims at the present northern boundary of California. When she withdrew thus to the southern limits of Oregon she could well be counted out as a competitor for the Oregon of our story, though she had owned it from 1763 to 1800.

Here, therefore, we take leave of Spain in the grand game of kings for that magnificent prize in the northwest. But we cannot do it without reflecting on the weak ambition and papal folly that grasped for so much while it could hold so little. Spain once claimed from Panama, on the Atlantic side, to Newfoundland, and on the Pacific to Prince William's Sound. At this date in our narrative all her Atlantic claims were dwarfed to eastern Florida, and at this date of writing all her vast interior and Pacific claims have gone out of her hands.

As we look back on this amazing collapse of the Spanish inflation in North America the view should not surprise us. With a few noble colonial leaders the mass of the colonists were of the lower grades, and many of them from prisons, asylums, and the streets. Any country would be benefited by the outgoing of such classes, or damaged by their incoming. After landing in the wilds of America they were more like "dumb, driven cattle" than like citizens. The Jesuitism that took charge of their education by no means crowded on them the printing-press and spelling-book; and priestly hands held back the Bible, though in Latin, and religion was much embodied in rituals and ceremonials. There was nothing in such a colonial system to produce men and women who constitute and perpetuate society.

CHAPTER III.

FRANCE SELLS HER CLAIMS.

FRANCE was only second to Spain in the extent of her inflated claims in the New World. The treaty of Ryswick conceded to her all the country whose waters flowed into the Atlantic, from the Penobscot north to Hudson Bay. This includes not only the basin of which that bay is the reservoir, but also the basin of the Great Lakes, emptying through the St. Lawrence. Down the western slope of the Hudson Bay basin there come the Red River waters of central Minnesota, and those of Lake Winnipeg, fed by the Saskatchewan and Assiniboin, that spring from the melting snows where the Rocky Mountains look down on the Pacific. So far west on the rim of that basin was the French claim conceded, in the old Dutch palace of Ryswick. There was also conceded to her all the great western valley which lies between the Alleghanies and the Rocky Mountains, and whose drainage runs by New Orleans, omitting so much as lies south of the thirty-third degree of latitude on the east of the Mississippi, and so much as feeds the head-springs of the Arkansas and territory south of it. This immense French domain in America would more than cover all the map of Europe.

The peace of Ryswick was brief. Wars soon followed between the parties in both the Old World and the New, and matters soon came again to the council-table of kings. This time it was in 1713, at Utrecht, another Dutch town, and the prominent parties present, by their ministers, were Anne, queen of Great Britain, and Louis XIV. of France. France, once so imperious, had been humbled by failure to absorb the Spanish in the French crown, and by the adverse issues of war in North America. Moreover, Louis was now seventy-five years old, and the shadows of age were falling across his brilliant court of Versailles. He put his name to the Treaty of Utrecht, but not with the bold, iron hand that had throttled kings and pushed thrones aside. The signature is the unsteady scrawl of age, as when old men, nursed and pillowed up on the dying bed, sign their last will and testament.

That signature gave back to Great Britain the Hudson Bay basin, from rim to rim, Newfoundland, and Nova Scotia — the poetic Acadia. There and then, in the old halls of Utrecht, France began to give up her chances on the Pacific by yielding those immense regions on the Atlantic. The tide had turned, and now it went out as with the rapidity with which it is wont to leave her former Bay of Fundy.

Struggles followed the concord at Utrecht, and they were between courts and cabinets, prime ministers and ambassadors, armies in Europe and armies in the new continent. The brilliant uniform of the European mingled with the feathers and paint and scalp-lock of the Indian along the forests and rivers and lakes of our then border land. More and more the destinies of battle turned one way, till that fatal September day on the Plains of Abraham, at Quebec, 1759. That was the Waterloo for France in North America; and in the settlement afterward, by the Treaty of Paris, 1763, she was humiliated to yield all her possessions east of the Mississippi. That is, she then lost the eastern slope of the Mississippi Valley, the Canadas, and New Brunswick. After much diplomatic delay — more than three years — while from time to time the hostile negotiators felt for their swords again, Great Britain allowed France to retain three little islands off the coast of Newfoundland — not the area of two Yankee townships — where she might build fishermen's huts and dry her nets. Only the assignment of St. Helena to Napoleon suggests so great a fall or equals so great a humiliation.

About one hundred days before this painful transfer France secretly made over to Spain all her territorial claims on the west of the Mississippi. Under one of those terrible pressures of war, when sometimes a strong nation is no more capable of resistance than an iron ship in an ice-pack, she parted with that half of a grand empire. She feared, and probably foresaw, that Great Britain would finally take all, and so put this beyond the reach of her grasping victor.

In her successive generations France never forgave herself for losing the ancient Louisiana. She chafed under the memories of the Plains of Abraham, and she watched to recover herself from a step, forced and inevitable, in the fickle fortunes of war. All through and following our Revolution, while she was friendly, her leading statesmen were alert and hopeful for chances that would reinstate her in that valley. The secret service of Vergennes, the bold and almost defiant intrigues of Genet, and her gold freely used between Pittsburg and New Orleans as bribes to bring about secession, are evidences of her wishes and of her endeavors.

Therefore, it agreed well with national ambition, as

well as with the gigantic schemes of Napoleon, when he recovered from Spain, in 1800, the western half of that ancient Louisiana.

The king of Spain, who owned this part of old Louisiana, married his daughter to the poor Duke of Parma, and he was not so rich in territory as his wife was proud and ambitious. Adjoining their petty domain was the kingdom of Tuscany, owned by France. To please, therefore, his spirited daughter, now a duchess in the small Duchy of Parma, the king of Spain exchanged with Napoleon Louisiana for Tuscany, and then the Duchy of Parma and Tuscany were combined into the Kingdom of Etruria for the royal son-in-law and his royal wife. So, as in so many great matters, there was a woman in the case, and half an empire in America was sold off to buy for her a wedding present.

Thus the long cherished ambition of France was realized and she again had in the New World more than St. Pierre and the Great and Little Miquelon — her three islands tethered off the coast of the Continent. It was the ambition of Napoleon to restore a grand New France in the recovered Louisiana. It was to be for France her empire of the West — the India of France, to balance the India of Great Britain. Its area and natural resources, and its openness to the commercial world, were commensurate with the daring wish and plans of Napoleon.

He framed a government for it, appointed a board of officers, and gathered an army and navy for its escort, and then waited a year to evade the watchful eye of England, and ship the whole to the mouth of the Mississippi. But the mistress of the seas was too strong and too wary for him, and he did not dare to venture.

Impatient of delay, suffering severe reverses and many anxieties, in the broadening wars of that most eventful period, and solicitous how the young France of the West might be able to keep her domains, and put on manly years, especially if old France should come into adverse emergencies, he sold the province to the United States. In the Old World trade Tuscany and Louisiana were reckoned equal, at one hundred thousand francs each, but we paid seventy-five thousand — fifteen millions of dollars, including two and a half millions of French debt due to Americans which the United States assumed. It was with reference to this and earlier ownerships of Louisiana by France that De Tocqueville, in his "Democracy in America," made his lament — the old refrain of La Belle France: "There was a time when we also might have created a French nation in the American wilds, to counterbalance the influence of the English upon the destinies of the New World. France formerly possessed a territory in North America scarcely less extensive than the whole of Europe. The three greatest rivers of that continent then flowed within her dominions. . . . Louisburg, Montmorenci, Duquesne, St. Louis, Vincennes, New Orleans, are words dear to France."

For two and a half years that magnificent region was again nominally in the hands of its ancient owner, and for so long a time France was the claimant of Oregon under the old Spanish title. As will appear by and by, the United States claimed Oregon under the old Franco-Spanish title, while Great Britain denied the validity of it, in the final settlement of the Oregon question. Here, therefore, in our purchase of the Louisianas, France disappears from the list of competitors for that Pacific prize. Only three now hold the course of struggle, — Russia, England, and the United States.

CHAPTER IV.

RUSSIA DECLINES THE STRUGGLE.

Peter the Great, shortly before his death in 1725, determined to look up the countries beyond the seas, that made his eastern boundaries. He knew that the Spanish and French and English had trading colonies in those regions, and he proposed to enter there as a rival, if not as an invader. His death came too soon for the execution of his plan, but Catharine, his widow and successor, attempted the enterprise, and so dispatched that distinguished navigator, Bering, the Dane, on a voyage of discovery, three years after Peter died. Bering established the fact that Asia and America are separated by the strait which now bears his name, and yet, strange to say, he twice passed through it without knowing it to be a strait, or that the American continent was near to him. His success led to a second voyage of discovery, 1741, in which the American shores were brought to light, and the name of St. Elias given to that eminent mountain. After this they ran about among the Aleutian Islands. At length they sought a return to Kamtschatka, and after head winds, sickness, and many casualties, they took to winter quarters on a small island eighty miles off that coast, where the vessel was afterward wrecked. Here the gallant and daring man made his grave with thirty of his men, and history has affixed his name to the island, as if a monument; and indeed it is but a pile of granite.

The survivors of the unfortunate expedition carried home with them choice furs, and made large profits on their sale. This led to individual enterprises in those hard seas, and in 1766 to the organization of companies for the Russian fur trade. While, therefore, France had been hastening through a series of reverses to quit North America, Russia was preparing to take it, and she was well established on the north-west coast by the time the United States were a nation.

Two years before the century closed the Russian-American Fur Company was formed, with exclusive rights of trapping and trading for twenty years between latitude fifty-five and Bering Strait. The Company soon occupied the American coast for a thousand miles, up and down, and also the Aleutian archipelago, with their chief traders, sailors, and native helpers.

Meanwhile New Englanders worked into the same region and lucrative trade, and ten years after the organization of the Russian Company the court of St. Petersburg made formal remonstrance to the United States, that Americans were furnishing the natives of the northwest with firearms and ammunition. In the diplomatic correspondence which followed, our minister to that court, John Quincy Adams, drew out the fact that this Russian Company set up claims to the entire coast and islands between Bering Strait and the mouth of the Columbia, and at the same time was extending its trade and monopoly down the coast. In 1812 the Russians obtained permission of the Spanish governor of California to found a trading post at Bodega Bay, a little north of San Francisco. Their ostensible object and real permission were to lay in beef there, from the wild cattle, for their northern posts and traders. In two or three years they had so multiplied and fortified themselves, that the authorities of California remonstrated, and finally ordered them to leave, when the Russians coolly replied that they had concluded to remain. They did so, and in 1820 established another fortified trading house about forty miles farther north.

In the following year, the Russian government claimed, by public decree, all the northwest coast and islands north of latitude fifty-one, and down the Asiatic coast as low as forty-five degrees and fifty minutes, and forbade all foreigners to come within one hundred miles of the coasts, except in cases of extremity. To this bold claim our Secretary of State, John Quincy Adams, objected most strenuously, as infringing on the usages and immemorial rights of Americans, and he denied, most emphatically, that Russia had any just claim on that coast south of the fifty-fifth degree. As Russia had claims on both the American and Asiatic coasts she claimed the islands between as in a close sea. Mr. Adams replied to Chevalier de Poletica, the Russian minister, that an ocean four thousand miles wide could hardly be regarded as a "close sea," and that the Americans would continue to exercise their ancient privileges in those northern waters. There the correspondence closed.

Great Britain made similar protestations. The American protests were emphasized in 1823, by the proclamation of the Monroe doctrine, so called. The substance of this noted doctrine was in these words: "That the American Continents, by the free and independent condition which they have assumed and maintain, are henceforth not to be considered as subjects for colonization by any European power."

After much correspondence it was agreed between

Russia and the United States, in 1824, that the United States should make no new claims north of 54° 40', and the Russians none south of it. Russia also made a similar agreement with Great Britain the next year, and the two were to be binding for ten years, but with the privilege of continued navigation and trade where they had been previously enjoyed. When the ten years expired Russia served notice on the United States and Great Britain of the discontinuance of their navigation and trade north of the agreed line of 54° 40'.

A compromise was effected between Russia and Great Britain by a lease from Russia to the Hudson Bay Company of the coast and margin from 54° 40' to Cape Spenser, near 58°—that narrow strip of Alaska which now lies between British Columbia and the Pacific. With the United States matters were finally adjusted to mutual satisfaction.

But England was ambitious to hold Oregon and California; and therefore those two Russian colonies in the latter were an annoyance and a check to her. The Russians had posted themselves strongly at Bodega, having built a stockade, with block-houses, the two towers of which mounted three guns each. It had only one gate, and this was protected by a brass nine-pounder. In 1836 it had three hundred men, besides sixty or more Kodiack Indians.[1] It will be noticed that, after the loose and adventurous manner of those times, the Russians were in possession both north and south of the Oregon of our narrative. Of course, they were liable to gain a footing in it, by trade with the natives, and by agriculture. They had intimated to the United States that they had

[1] Sir Edward Belcher's *Voyages Round the World*, 1836–42, vol. i. 313–15.

no rights in California, while they notified the Mexican government that they had come to stay. The English accused the Russians of infringing treaty obligations by making and holding settlements south of 54° 40′, and asked Mexico to expel them. Mexico was willing but not able, and therefore asked for the kindly offices of the United States in the matter. At our request Russia withdrew from California, and relinquished all claims and ambitions south of 54° 40′. Russia, therefore, was counted out from among the competitors for Oregon.

We started in our story with seven European powers, which might be regarded as fairly competitors for Oregon. We have seen them drop out, one by one, as in some exciting boat-race. Now one near the prize, vigorous, and well posted on both sides of it, withdraws. Only two remain for us to watch.

CHAPTER V.

ENGLISH EXPLORATIONS AND AMBITIONS.

In the last chapter we carried one thread of our narrative ahead of time, in order to dispose of one of the parties in the struggle — the Russians. Now we must return and bring up the English to the point where we just now left them, as the only competitor with the United States for Oregon.

In colony times Spain, France, and Great Britain, each in turn, looked toward the Mississippi Valley, as a new seat of empire. Soon after the eastern half had been conveyed to Great Britain, after her victory of immeasurable importance on the Plains of Abraham, she began to explore her new possessions. Leading and prominent among the explorers was Jonathan Carver, a hard soldier in the French and Indian wars, that terminated at Quebec, a rugged and daring pioneer, with a passion for forest life and all its wild adventures and thrilling incidents. In the late wars he had become inured to hardship, and he was enamored of the fascinations that lie along an unexplored border of wilderness. Carver left Boston in 1766, under the geographical delusion of the day, that North America was an archipelago, and that a sailing passage could be found, extending through to the Pacific. The leading purpose with him in his tour was to discover those mythical and always receding "Straits of Anian," as the channel was called. His head was fired with the vision of "the discovery of a northwest passage, or a communication between Hudson Bay and the Pacific Ocean — an event so desirable and which has been so often sought for, but without success." He returned in two years, having explored no farther than the present limits of Wisconsin, Iowa, and Minnesota. He claimed that he was the first white man, after Hennepin, the French missionary, to explore the Mississippi, as far up as the falls of St. Anthony. He prophesied well of the region as "a country that promises in some future period to be an inexhaustible source of riches to the people who shall be so fortunate as to possess it." He thus anticipated Secretary Seward, by about a century, in his prophecy in 1860, in his speech at St. Paul: "I now believe that the ultimate, last seat of government on this great continent will be found somewhere within a circle or radius not very far from the spot on which I stand, at the head of navigation on the Mississippi river." All this reads well of wheat fields and empire states, but the fancy is rich and very enjoyable, that sees Carver's merchantmen under full sail making their crosscut through these prairies from China to New England.

The Indians gave him much information concerning precious metals in the "Shining Mountains," as they called the Black Hills; and Carver is led to say that "probably in future ages they may be found to contain more riches in their bowels than those of Indostan and Malabar, or than are produced on the golden coast of Guinea; nor will I except even the Peruvian mines." He made many trials to get farther west, and when he asked the Indians to guide him to these mountains, they replied that white men could not enter them and live. So sadly true of poor General Custer and his men!

Carver, in his narrative, drew somewhat from his observations, but much from his memory of French and fanciful narrators. His book was published in London, and had its effect, both in England and in this country; it fascinated Great Britain with the value of her conquest, and stimulated new explorations.[1]

At this time the Hudson Bay Company had stations on that inland sea, and it had some belief, but more doubt, of the existence of navigable waters between Hudson Bay and the Pacific. Rumors had also reached the Company of a metal river to the west of the Bay. They therefore commissioned Samuel Hearne, one of their agents, to explore from the western shores of the Bay towards the Pacific, for the rumored channel and river. This was the year following the return of Carver. Hearne made three of these excursions into the northwest, west, and southwest — tours of a thousand miles each. He discovered Great Slave Lake, and identified Metal River as the Coppermine, which he traced to its mouth. So highly did the Lords Commissioners of the British Admiralty esteem his discoveries, that they kept them secret, as exceedingly important, from his return in 1772 to 1795.

Of course English statesmen, capitalists, and navigators were greatly interested in northern North America by these discoveries. Under this stimulus Cook was commissioned in 1776 to explore the north-west coast, and look for any water openings inland that might lead to Hudson Bay and, with the consent of the natives, or in the absence of any inhabitants, take possession for Great Britain of any country not already claimed by

[1] *Travels Throughout the Interior Parts of North America*, 1766-8. By Jonathan Carver.

European powers. The plan was to make his discoveries by sea meet and close in with those of Hearne by land. But the English Admiralty were then deeply ignorant of the vast spaces and distances in this country, as many are, most amusingly, to-day. Hearne may well have made those extensive tours, and yet Cook, on the Pacific coast, not be within a thousand miles of the track of the inland explorer.

Thus early after their expulsion of the French from the northern portion of the Continent the English closed in on it, by extending their line of trading posts, or "factories," from Hudson Bay and the Canadas westward. The tragic death of Cook at the Sandwich Islands, in the third year of his enterprise, terminated, for the present, the extension of English discoveries and possessions on the north-west coast. Meanwhile the English government was in a desperate struggle to hold her colonies on the Atlantic, and had little leisure or surplus force, or perhaps heart, to plant new ones on the Pacific, where they might repeat rebellion. Yet she had obtained intimations enough of the value of the region beyond the Great Lakes, and around the sources of the Mississippi and Missouri, to make her ardent and persistent for its possession.

The French had furnished much information of that wild interior. It might be difficult to tell, sometimes, whether the religious zeal of the Jesuit, or the mercantile spirit of the trader, led those earliest expeditions into unexplored lands: but one thing was sure and fortunate, the religious partners, under convoy of the *voyageurs*, made good record of what they saw, and they were good observers as well as recorders. Of course this information spread by rumor, if not by manuscript and print, and English enterprise used it.

There was also a most valuable territory between the Ohio, the Mississippi, and the Lakes, which Great Britain was quite unwilling to yield after the wager of battle went against her, conclusively, at Yorktown. She reluctantly conceded independence to the young republic, but first insisted that its domain should not extend beyond the Ohio and its head waters. During the negotiations for the treaty of peace, the British Commissioner, Oswald, pressed his demands, long and arbitrarily, for this restricting boundary. The American Commissioners, Franklin, Adams, and Jay, resisted, and claimed that, as the Colonies, when dependent, had been accustomed to have territorial sovereignty west to the Mississippi and north to the Great Lakes, they should have the same domain by their acknowledged independence. That grand section seemed too much for the mother country to yield, but the commissioners were firm, and it was finally agreed that the dividing line should be a central one, from a certain point, up the St. Lawrence, and through to the Great Lakes, and the smaller ones, to the Lake of the Woods, and thence to the head of the Mississippi, and down it to the Spanish possessions.

This was a great bar to the extension of English supremacy westward, and a sad rebuff to its ambition in that direction. The report of Carver on the northwest — published in London — was fresh and tantalizing, and this treaty boundary would not only give over a part of that tempting region to the young republic, but place the republic directly before the grand remainder, with an open door between, and no resident keepers.

The bar and the rebuff seemed to beget in Great Britain an unfriendliness, if not a lack of good faith, for she persisted in holding the posts of Oswego, Niagara, and

Detroit, and four more, that were within our lines, for ten years after she signed the treaty that gave them up. They stood within the territory that Oswald contended for, and reluctantly yielded; and appearances were that the English were waiting for some mishap to the republic, for some contingency of war, or for some adroit diplomacy that would enable her to recover that region to the crown.

The Indian wars that harrassed the border after the Revolution, and nearly to the end of the century, were known to have been instigated by English agents and emissaries in the retained posts, and on the Canadian borders. The object, as confessed by both Indian and Englishman, was to keep emigration from the States from passing beyond the Ohio. These agents encouraged the notion in the Indian mind, that the proper and permanent boundary between the whites and the Indians was the Ohio, as laid down in 1768 by Sir William Johnson, in the treaty of Fort Stanwix. It was not strange that England should be reluctant to yield the richer southern country, but by the final partition it only remained for her to make the most of her Canadas and the snow lands beyond, and press a broader and deeper extension of them into the dim and mysterious west — the great fur land of America. With the frozen north on one side and the United States on the other, the only chance for English growth in America was to lengthen her dominion into the west, and make it a long and very narrow parallelogram.

Into this wild region of woodland, river, and lake, and of treeless wolds, heaths, and downs, like South American pampas, or the steppes of Asiatic tablelands, we must now plunge, if we would keep in hand the converging threads of our narrative in their western leading.

CHAPTER VI.

THE HUDSON BAY COMPANY.

The Hudson Bay Company was chartered by Charles II. on the 16th of May, 1670. The original corporators were eighteen, headed by Prince Rupert, and hence the old name of Rupert's Land once given to that region. The first object of the Company, as named in the charter was, "the discovery of a new passage into the South Sea" —the Pacific Ocean. During its first century the Company had done something in the line of geographical discoveries in the northwestern parts of North America, and were growing hopeless of an inland channel to the Pacific.

As early as 1778 the celebrated Frobisher and others had established a trading-post or "factory" on Lake Athabasca, about twelve hundred miles from Lake Superior. Ten years later it was abandoned and Fort Chipewayan was built as its substitute, on the southwest shore of the same water. From this fort Sir Alexander Mackenzie made an expedition to the Arctic and back, following the river which now bears his name. This was in the warm season of 1789, and was accomplished in one hundred and two days. Three years later, and in the autumn, he started with a purpose to explore a route to the South Sea, the Pacific. From Lake Athabasca he went up Peace River, to its head in the Rocky Mountains. In that dreary solitude, so far from this live and warm world, he made his winter quarters, where he lay with his ten men, snow-bound, till May. How that great fur-trader must have revelled in some of those mountain scenes! On one occasion he says: "In some places the beavers had cut down several acres of large poplars." A few Indians were found on the line of travel. "They had heard, indeed, of white men, but this was the first time that they had ever seen a human being of a complexion different from their own." We could hope that these first white men did not begin to "civilize" them as they did the poor natives whom they found on the Mackenzie four years before. "We made them smoke, though it was evident that they did not know the use of tobacco. We likewise supplied them with grog, but I am disposed to think that they accepted our civilities rather from fear than inclination."

A memorable and unprecedented sight met their eyes in June of this year, 1793. They came to the divide, and saw the waters separating, some for the Atlantic and some for the Pacific. Never before had white men seen streams running from the crown of the Rocky Mountains to the great western ocean. In July they came in sight of the sea, and were soon on its shores. There, on a bold rock looking off toward Asia, this daring explorer painted in vermilion these words: "Alexander Mackenzie, from Canada by land, the twenty-second of July, one thousand seven hundred and ninety-three." This was the first expedition of white men across the continent to the Pacific Ocean. If we connect this inscription, in a historical comprehensiveness, with explorations for the Straits of Anian, and with the British fur trade in North America, and with the discussions and conclusion of the Oregon question, it will be found that few sentences written in America were more significant and full of consequence, and worthy to be put in rock.[1]

The dates of these expeditions of Mackenzie are significant. We have noticed that the treaty closing the Revolution left to the English only the wild countries north of the United States. This was in 1783. Now within ten years they had pressed exploration and occupation to the Pacific in the latitude of their Atlantic possessions.

This Mackenzie was a man of remarkable power, and he had few equals, if even one, in shaping British interests in North America to their highest attainment. He soon foresaw, in his Pacific and Arctic expeditions, what advantages could be made to come from them, and he at once recommended the union of the Hudson Bay and Northwest fur companies — for a long time fierce and even bloody rivals — a line of commerce between Canada and the Pacific, overland, and a permit from the East India Company for trade direct between both India and China and the northwest coast of America. That trade, he suggests, is now " left to the adventurers of the United States, acting without regularity or capital, or the desire of conciliating future confidence, and looking only to the interest of the moment." These sugges-

---

[1] In the return of the Lewis and Clark expedition, the Clark division came down the Yellowstone. Twenty miles or so above the mouth of the Big Horn stands a mass of yellow sandstone an acre in base and four hundred feet high, called Pompey's Pillar. About half way up is cut this inscription: —
WM. CLARK,
July 25, 1806.
It has more to do with the Republic, than Mackenzie's, and is closely associated with the signatures on the Declaration of Independence.

tions were generally and promptly adopted by the English government and by the Hudson Bay Company.

The point reached by Mackenzie on the Pacific is within the present limits of British Columbia on that coast (53° 21′), and it was the first real, though undesigned step toward the occupation of Oregon by Great Britain. That government was feeling its way, daringly and blindly, for all territory it might obtain, and, in 1793, came thus near the outlying region which afterwards became the coveted prize of our narrative.

The Hudson Bay Company was the most formidable obstacle which lay between the United States and the final confirmation of her right to Oregon. It contested, persistently, every advance of the Republic in that direction, and it was the undelegated agent and very embodiment of Great Britain in North America. It will, therefore, aid much to make a brief survey of this Company.

Its two objects, as set forth in its charter, were "for the discovery of a new passage into the South Sea, and for the finding of some trade for furs, minerals, and other considerable commodities." It may well be suspected that the first was the face and the second the soul of the charter, which grants to the Company the exclusive right of the "trade and commerce of all those seas, straits, and bays, rivers, lakes, creeks, and sounds, in whatsoever latitude they shall be, that lie within the entrance of the straits commonly called Hudson Straits," of all lands bordering them not under any other civilized government. This covered all territory within that immense basin from rim to rim, one edge dipping into the Atlantic and the other looking into the Pacific. Through this vast extent the Company was made, for "all time hereafter, capable in law, to have, purchase, receive, possess, enjoy, and retain lands, rents, privileges, liberties, jurisdiction, franchise, and hereditaments of what kind, nature, or quality soever they be, to them and their successors." The company held that region as a man holds his farm, or as the great bulk of real estate in England is now held. They could legislate over and govern it, bound only by the tenor and spirit of English law, and make war and peace within it; and all persons outside the Company could be forbidden to " visit, haunt, frequent, trade, traffic, or adventure " therein. For all this, and as a confession of allegiance to the crown as a dependent colony and province, they were to pay annually as rent " two elks and two black beavers." Cheap rent that, especially since the king or his agent must collect it on the ground of the Company. To dwell in the territory or even to go across it would be as really a trespass as if it were done on the lawn of a private gentleman in Middlesex county, England.

Such were the chartered rights of a monopoly that growing bolder and more grasping became at last continental in sweep, irresistible in power, and inexorable in spirit. In 1821 the crown granted to this and the Northwest Company united, and for a term of twenty-one years, the exclusive right to trade with all Indians in British North America, north and west of the United States, and not included in the first charter. This granted only trade, not ownership in the soil. Thus, while the chartered territory was imperial, it grew, by granted monopoly of trade, to be continental. By degrees the trappers and traders went over the rim of the Hudson basin, till they reached the Arctic seas along the outlets of the Coppermine and the Mackenzie. They set beaver traps on the Yukon and Fraser rivers, around the Athabasca, Slave, and Bear Lakes, and on the heads of the Columbia. From the adjacent Pacific shores they lined their treasury with the soft coats of the fur seal and the sea-otter. They were the pioneers of this traffic, and pressed this monopoly of fur on the sources, not only of the Mississippi and Missouri, but down into the Salt Lake basin of modern Utah. What minor and rival companies stood in the way they bought in, or crushed by underselling to the Indians. Individual enterprise in the fur trade, from Newfoundland to Vancouver, and from the head of the Yellowstone to the mouths of the Mackenzie, was at their mercy. They practically controlled the introduction of supplies and the outgoing of furs and peltries from all the immense region between those four points.

Within the Canadas and the other Provinces they held the Indian and the European equally at bay, while within all this vast unorganized wilderness, their hand over red and white man was absolute. At first the Company could govern as it pleased, and was autocratic and irresponsible. By additional legislation in 1803, the civil and criminal government of the Canadas was made to follow the Company into lands outside their first charter commonly called Indian Countries. The Governor of Lower Canada had the appointing power of officials within those countries. But he did not send in special men; he appointed those connected with the Company and on the ground. The Company, therefore, had the administration in those outside districts in its own hands. Thus the commercial life of the Canadas was so dependent on the Hudson Bay Company that the government could be counted on to promote the wishes of the Company. In brief, the government of British

America was practically the Hudson Bay Company, and for all the privilege and monopoly which it enjoyed without seeming to demand it, there was an annual payment if called for of "two elks and two black beavers."

This Company thus became a powerful organization. It had no rival to share the field, or waste the profits in litigation, or in bloody feuds beyond the region of law. It extended its lines, multiplied its posts and agents, systematized communication through the immense hunting grounds, economized time and funds by increased expedition, made many of its factories really fortifications, and so put the whole northern interior under British rule, and yet without a soldier. Rivers, lakes, mountains, and prairies were covered by its agents and trappers. The white and the red man were on most friendly terms, and the birch canoe and the pirogue were seen carrying, in mixed company, both races, and, what was more, their mixed progeny.

The extent of territory under this Company seems almost fabulous. It was one-third larger than all Europe; it was larger than the United States of to-day, Alaska included, by half a million of square miles. From the American headquarters at Montreal to the post on Vancouver was a distance of twenty-five hundred miles; to Fort Selkirk on the Yukon, or to the one on Great Bear Lake, it was three thousand miles, and it was still farther to the rich fur seal and sea-otter on the tide waters of the Mackenzie. James Bay and the Red River at Winnipeg seem near to Montreal in comparison. These distances would compare well with air-line routes from Washington to Dublin, or Gibraltar, or Quito. This power, so extensive and monopolizing the American side of the British throne — was reaching out and preparing to enfold Oregon.

One contemplates this power with awe and fear, when he regards the even motion and solemn silence and unvarying sameness with which it has done its work through that dreary animal country. It has been said that a hundred years has not changed its bills of goods ordered from London. The Company wants the same muskrat and beaver and seal; the Indian hunter, unimproved, and the half-breed European, deteriorating, want the same cotton goods, and flint-lock guns, and tobacco and gew-gaws.

To-day, as a hundred years ago, the dog-sledge runs out from Winnipeg for its solitary drive of five hundred, or two thousand, or even three thousand miles. It glides, silent as a spectre, over those snow-fields and through the solemn, still forests, painfully wanting in animal life. Fifty, seventy, an hundred days it speeds along, and as many nights it camps without fire, and looks up to the same cold stars. At the intervening posts the sledge makes a pause, as a ship, having rounded Cape Horn, heaves to before some lone Pacific island. It is the same at the trader's hut or factory as when the sledge-man's grandfather drove up, the same dogs, the same half-breeds or *voyageurs* to welcome him, the same foul, lounging Indians, and the same mink-skin in exchange for the same trinket. The fur animal and its purchaser and hunter, as the landscape, seem to be alike under the same immutable, unprogressive law of nature:—

"A land where all things always seemed the same,"

as among the lotus-eaters. Human progress and Indian civilization have made scarcely more improvement than that central, silent partner in the Hudson Bay Company — the beaver.

It is said, with an accusing comparison, that the English get along more peacefully than the Americans in their Indian policy. Let the Jamestown colony leave the Indians in perpetual quiet in their wigwams up the James, and the Pilgrims their savage and pagan neighbors back of Plymouth woods; pay them in finery and cheap fabrics for tending steel-traps; and give their emigrating sons to their tawny daughters, and you will have no troublesome Indian question, and — no United States of America. England has obtained peace in her Indian territories, and what else? Splendid dividends in Hudson Bay Company stock. The same wants and articles of exchange on both sides at the end of a century, never rising to the demand and supply of a plough as an article of usual shipment and use.

One feels toward the power of this Company, moving thus with evenness and immutability through a hundred years, much as one does toward a law of nature. At Fort Selkirk, for example, the fifty-two numbers of the weekly London "Times" came in on the last sledge arrival. The first number is already three years old, by its tedious voyage from the Thames. Now one number only a week is read that the lone trader there may have fresh news weekly till the next annual dog-mail arrives, and each successive number is three years behind time when opened! In this day of steamers and telegraphs and telephones, does it seem possible that any human, white habitation can be so outside of the geography and chronology of this world?

The goods of the Company, packed and shipped in Fenchurch Street, leave London, and at the end of the third year they are delivered at Fort Confidence on Great Bear Lake, or at any other extreme factory of the Company; and at the end of three years more the return furs go up the Thames and into Fenchurch Street again. So in cycles of six years, and from age to age, like a planet, the shares in the Hudson Bay Company make their orbit and dividends. A run of three months and the London ship drops anchor in Hudson Bay. "For one year," says Butler, in his "Great Lone Land," "the stores that she has brought in lie in the warehouse of York Factory; twelve months later they reach Red River; twelve months later they reach Fort Simpson on the Mackenzie."

The original stock of this Company was $50,820. In fifty years it was tripled twice by profits only, and went up to $457,380, while not one new dollar was paid in. In 1821 the Company absorbed the North-west Company of Montreal, on a basis of value equal to its own. The consolidated stock then was $1,916,000, of which $1,780,866 was from profits. Yet, meanwhile, there had been an annual payment of ten per cent. to stockholders. In 1836 one of the Company's ships left Fort George for London, with a cargo of furs valued at $380,000.[1]

A further illustration of this rapid increase in value should be mentioned here. Prior to 1837 men from the United States had begun to promote agriculture in Oregon by the planting of colonies. To offset this movement and hold the territory by colonies of its own, the Company, with its surplus funds, organized and put into operation the Puget Sound Agricultural Company, as another department of their work. When the English government, in 1846, conceded the claims of the United States to Oregon, property of the Hudson Bay Company was found within Oregon for which that Company claimed $4,990,036.67. The lands, buildings, and im-

[1] *A History of Oregon*, 1870. By W. H. Gray, pp. 68, 69, **83**.

provements, generally, of this Puget Sound Company, made a large item in the total amount claimed as damages. To such an extent had this company of Hudson Bay traders grown in territory, government, business, capital, dividends, and presumed damages, when called on to retire from their trespass in Oregon. In view of such a competitor it is surprising that the United States should have succeeded in recovering its original and long alienated rights in that country. Nor would it have succeeded but for its hardy frontiersmen. Our vast border of wild land has furnished, and is still furnishing, a class of people peculiar to ourselves. They disappear beyond the line of cabins and plowed fields and courts and locks to be a community and a law unto themselves. The constitution and statutes and by-laws to which they own allegiance are in their rifle and revolver and saddle. Organized law and order follow tardily under the flag, and much more tardily the Bible and the spelling-book of benevolent societies. While indispensable to our magnificent growth in settlements and American institutions, they are neglected, as beyond reach, and unworthy of attention, and a hopeless class. While we succeed, thousands of miles off, in teaching cannibals to prefer beef, we reproach these Americans three generations from a New England or any other school-house for being rough and lawless and unchristian.

One cannot but admire the foresight, compass, policy, and ability with which those English fur-traders moved to gain possession, and then keep in wilderness for furbreeding, so much of North America. Their agents gained a kind of ubiquity, wherever there could be found the beaver, the land and sea otter, the fisher and mink, the muskrat, wolf, wolverine, and the many foxes of commerce, the sable, raccoon, and rabbit, the black, brown, and grizzly bear, and the lumbering buffalo. The sale of rabbit skins in London alone in one year was ordinarily thirteen hundred thousand.

For these fur-bearing animals the hunters of this Company were almost everywhere in the wild half of North America. One could seldom travel long and far without crossing their trail or springing their steel-traps. Their birch was on the lake, or headed up to it, silent and graceful as the wild-duck; and around and over those swampy acres flowed by the beaver-dam, they glided stealthily. In that sunny nook, far up in the Rockies, where the grass is last to go and first to come, and in more north-western regions never fails, one may see the smoke curling up cliffs and blackening the snows around their cosy huts. Where wide-awake Omaha and Council Bluffs now bridge the Missouri, they were, as to-day they are in the perpetual verdure of Vancouver. They are at Fort McPherson and the mouths of the Mackenzie, where icebergs come drifting in, perhaps across the track of the lost Franklin, and they are basking, too, in a six weeks' summer on the upper Yukon, after a pack of ten months in snow and ice. When Lewis and Clark were going through our new purchase to examine it, and were fifteen hundred miles up the Missouri, they found a McCraken of this Company trading with the Indians. After they had gone into winter quarters in December, 1804, among the Mandans, one Henderson visited them. He had a Hudson Bay trading-post eight days north. It was as if that Company had picketed all the wild interior, and this watchful sentinel had challenged the advance of intruders.

Travelers tell us of an oppressive, painful silence through all that weird northland. Quadruped life, and the scanty little that there is of bird life is not vocal, much less musical. This Company has partaken of the silence of its domain. It makes but little noise for so great an organization. It says but few things and only the necessary ones, and even those with an obscurity often, that only the interested and initiated understand. The statements of its works and results are mostly in the passive voice.

It may be well to note here how far the Hudson Bay Company hindered discoveries in North America. According to its charter its first object was "the discovery of a new passage into the South Sea," but the Company put various hindrances in the way of such enterprises, as if success in this line would open a highway through their monopoly, or plant rivals on their border.

In his history of Arctic Voyages Sir John Barrow says that when the Company came into a prosperous state of affairs "the north-west passage seems to have been entirely forgotten, not only by the adventurers who had obtained their exclusive charter under this pretext, but also by the nation at large ; at least nothing more appears to have been heard on the subject for more than half a century."

When, in 1719, Mr. Knight, its governor, proposed that two vessels be sent to look up a rumored copper mine at the mouth of a river on the Arctic, the Company refused the proposal. In 1741 one Dobbs secured such an expedition from the Company, and yet they showed such indifference and even hostility to it that he says in his narrative : "The Company avoid all they can making discoveries to the northward of Churchill, or extending their trade that way, for fear they should discover a passage to the western ocean of America, and tempt by that means the rest of the English merchants to lay open their trade." Commenting on this passage, Sir John says: "They not only discouraged all attempts at northern discovery, but withheld what little information came to their knowledge." The next year Captain Middleton was commissioned by the Lords of the Admiralty to explore the northern and western waters of Hudson Bay, for any connection with the Arctic. He was openly accused of taking a bribe of five thousand pounds from the Company to make his expedition a failure, as it was. Then the government, as if struggling against the Company, offered a reward of twenty thousand pounds to any party who would make a success of it. When, in 1746, an exploring party were aground in the vicinity of Fort York, the Governor of the Company cut down the beacon, that the wreck might be made sure. In 1769 the Company, to keep up appearances, and the letter of their charter, sent one of their number, Mr. Hearne, overland, with a party to discover a rumored copper mine. He went out over twelve hundred miles, and yet made but one observation to fix latitude, and added but a trifle to the knowledge of those northern regions, though he went as far as the Coppermine River. Twenty years later they sent Mackenzie to the same vicinity, and he brought back even less information. Though the river seemed to have a tide he did not even taste the water to see whether it were salt and he near the sea. In 1790 a Mr. Duncan was sent out by the Governor to make explorations in a certain vessel of the Company. But when he arrived at the post the men there pretended that the vessel was unseaworthy, and he gave up the expedition, though they used the vessel for twenty years afterward. When he was carrying out his plan the next year his crew mutinied, encouraged by his first officer, who was a servant of the Company.

Thus it appears that the Hudson Bay Company obstructed the progress of geographical and general discovery in North America; and we shall see that it did the same as to the increase of English commerce and the growth of English settlements and civilization in the same vast regions.

CHAPTER VII.

ENGLISH MONOPOLY OF THE FRONTIER.

It required a second treaty, 1794, to bring the English to a surrender of the seven military posts within the United States, which they agreed to surrender by the Treaty of 1783. As we have already seen, they continued to hold these for Indian trade, to stimulate hostility to immigration, and as good bases for working their own interests in recovering territory beyond the Ohio, if things should go unfavorably for the young Republic. But the growing compactness of the Republic as a union of states, and its natural increase in population and general strength, held out but poor hopes for Great Britain in this purpose.

In 1751 the English, through the Ohio Company, planned to remove the French from the region of the Ohio, and after much diplomacy and fighting, here and there, they succeeded, on the Plains of Abraham, in wresting from them all their claims east of the Mississippi. "For the acquisition of this great and fertile region," says Monette, "Great Britain had contended with France for more than sixty years, at an immense cost of blood and treasure, expended in no less than five long and expensive wars, and great human suffering by sea and land."[1]

It is not surprising, therefore, that Great Britain

[1] Monette's *History of the Mississippi Valley*, 1846, vol. i. 440.

strenuously urged the Ohio as the western limit of the now independent colonies. When she reluctantly consented to carry the line to the Great Lakes and river, it was in accordance with her previous policy that she did not keep her promise promptly in vacating the strongholds in the ceded territory. England had adopted a similar course, and successfully, when France gained the Hudson Bay country by the Treaty of Ryswick. At that time she shuffled and hesitated over the stipulated surrender, and held Fort Albany, on James Bay, till her reacquisition of the whole by the Treaty of Utrecht.

In 1779 the Spanish on the lower Mississippi being in sympathy with the revolutionary colonies, moved to expel the English from West Florida, and were successful, with the exception of Pensacola, the capital. To avenge these wrongs and divert the Spanish forces from the south the English commander at Mackinaw, in 1780, organized an attack on St. Louis, the capital of Upper Louisiana — then a Spanish province. His force consisted of about one hundred and fifty British and Canadian regulars and fourteen hundred Indians. The mixed Spanish, French, and Indian town had a stockade defence with a few cannon and some light arms. The Spanish governor was not free from suspicion of dealing treacherously, and, but for the timely arrival, on express call, of General George Rogers Clark from Kaskaskia, the United States officer in charge of the Illinois country, the result must have been serious in the extreme. As it was, about sixty citizens were killed, but the attack was a failure. The year is registered in the annals of that frontier and wilderness town as *L'Année du Coup*. If the English had succeeded, their possession of St. Louis would probably have given to them Upper Louisiana in the capture of its capital. At least it would have embarrassed, and perhaps prevented, the retrocession of it by Spain to France in 1800, and so its sale to the United States in 1803. Thus, possibly, the old ambition of England might have obtained on the west bank of the Mississippi a substitute for its painful loss on the east of it.

This, very likely, would have made the Oregon question impossible; and perhaps would have left that western slope of the great valley in hands that we have seen were fast taking possession of it. If so, and the Hudson Bay Company had allowed no more settlement and civilization there than in their original field, they might now be skinning buffalo on the wheat farms of Illinois, Minnesota, and Dakota, and catching beavers and grizzlies where Americans have honeycombed the mountains for gold and silver, and built factories and cities, and stretched out railroads.

It was very clear that the fur-trade would be ruined in the northwest if immigration poured into that region. Hence the agents and servants of this traffic excited the natives against the innovating settlements, from the independence of the colonies to the War of 1812. Our entire domain beyond the Alleghanies, south to the Gulf, and north to the Lakes, was in an uneasy and critical relation to the government in 1794 and thereabout. It had no direct communication over the mountains with the Atlantic, for the transportation of its productions, and only fickle, expensive, and annoying permits from the Spanish for passage down the valley to the Gulf. It was not in easy and frequent communication with the States, and with the national administration at Philadelphia, and was both tempted to secession, and provoked toward war with the Spanish in the southwest. Within a few years of the close of the last century, and in the opening ones of this, there were four tendencies among the Americans beyond the mountains, with a chance that one or more might develop into a sectional faction: Secession and an independent government: Annexation to the Province of Louisiana: War with Spain to gain the Mississippi River: Union of the territory between the Ohio, Mississippi, and Gulf with the Province of Louisiana under a foreign protectorate. Probably Washington never showed more of the combination of the general and the statesman than when, ten years before, he made the tour of the West, and then wrote to Governor Harrison of Virginia and the father of the President: "I need not remark to you that the flank and rear of the United States are possessed by other powers, and formidable ones too. . . . How entirely unconnected with them shall we be, and what troubles may we not apprehend, if the Spaniards on the right and Great Britain on the left, instead of throwing stumbling-blocks in the way, as they now do, should hold out lures for their trade and alliance. When they gain strength, which will be sooner than most people conceive. . . . The Western States hang upon a pivot. The touch of a feather would turn them any way." [1]

As early as 1787 the Spanish authorities in the southwest took active measues to seduce sections of our domain there into secession, and lead them to join the Spanish Province of Louisiana. To this project General Wilkinson, our military head of the southwest, is strongly suspected of having given not only ear, but aid,

[1] Irving's *Life of Washington*, vol. iv. 454–459.

and to have received heavy pecuniary bribes. This suspicion and almost assurance covered him from this date to the exposure and suppression of Burr's conspiracy to draw the southwest into a revolt, in the years 1805–7.

A bundle of private letters in my possession, written about that time by one who was afterwards an eminent citizen of Missouri, distinctly asserts this suspicion. Quite lately Gayarré, the historian of Louisiana, is said to have discovered in the archives at Seville the secret correspondence of Wilkinson with the Spanish officials, showing that he and others received bribes and entered into negotiations, to annex Kentucky and Tennessee to the then Spanish dominion of Louisiana. Indeed it was with great peril that the United States maintained supremacy over her own territory in that region against the schemes of the Spanish and French.

The most serious and obvious danger, however, was English, since Great Britain, from the strongholds she retained, fed and armed and incited the Indians, who, in marauding parties, made raids upon the frontier and held in check the growth of settlement. These annoyances and dangers continued with but little cessation, and with other causes brought on the War of 1812. Tecumseh, a man of great native talent, activity, and persistance, had opposed the treaties that gave to the whites the lands beyond the Ohio. From the days of the Revolution he had stood forth as the great Indian statesman and warrior of the west. The English used him, with his brother, the Prophet, to rouse and combine the Indians all along the frontier, from the Lakes to the Gulf. General Harrison, afterward president, met Tecumseh, with a score or more of his chiefs, in council at Vincennes, 1811, for a friendly settlement of grievances. The imperious and insolent sachem broke up the conference, and Harrison soon after carried the questions to the battle of Tippecanoe, where there was a total defeat of the Indians. That battle opened the War of 1812, in which, among other issues, the English made an effort to recover the northwest, and so carry a monopoly to the Pacific, but in this they failed.

But while Great Britain, the nation, was thus struggling and failing, the Hudson Bay Company, the corporation which, practically, was Great Britain in North America, was silently coming into actual possession in the deeper wilderness between the Mississippi and the Pacific. The United States, it is true, had come into legal possession of that magnificent country, but not into occupation. The issue, therefore, between the mother country, ambitious for territory, and the growing republic was to be made in a farther west, and the national title to Oregon was to be determined on its immediate border, and within its limits.

After the Treaty of 1783, in the settlement of the Revolution, the boundary was to be run, according to agreement, between the United States and the British possessions. In attempting and at last completing this work, the same old Saxon greed for land showed itself. At first it might seem an easy and brief labor to run the lines, yet before the work was done, eighty-nine years passed by.

Both parties to the war were wearied of the strife, and were willing to guess jointly on a river head, or lake point, or mountain height, and so fix bounds, and thence run treaty lines on paper, through wild lands unknown to each. Thus the northwest point of the Lake of the Woods was assumed for one bound from which the line was to run, to the north-western point of the Lake, and thence "due west" to the Mississippi. The clause in the treaty reads thus: "to the said Lake of the Woods, thence through the said Lake to the most northwestern point thereof, and from thence on a due west course to the river Mississippi." But the head of that river proved to be a hundred miles or so to the south. So that little prominence in our otherwise straight boundary on the north is the bump of ignorance developed by two nations. The St. Croix was fixed by treaty as the boundary on the northeast, but a special "Joint Commission" was required in 1794 to determine "what river is the St. Croix," and four years afterward this Commission called for an addition to their instructions since their original ones were not broad enough to enable them to determine the true St. Croix.

Still nothing was agreed to by actual lines and bounds, and in 1814 another Joint Commission was appointed, but in an entirely new field. At this time the work was to determine what islands should belong to the United States between Florida and Nova Scotia. In the same year, however, another set of Commissioners began the running of the boundary from the head of the St. Croix, by the head of the Connecticut to the St. Lawrence, and thence through the middle of its channel and the middle of the Lakes, to the outlet of Lake Superior. After a labor of seven and a half years in mapping, naming, and dividing about one hundred and eighty islands along this middle channel, the Corps of Commissioners and civil engineers arrived with their line at the Sault Ste. Marie. Still it remained to carry the line through Lake Superior and to the Lake of the Woods, which in due time was accomplished, and in 1818 it was agreed to by the

Commissioners, though not run on the forty-ninth parallel from the Lake of the Woods to the Rocky Mountains.

Yet this was not without hindrances and anxieties. The negotiations were carried on at London, and both parties were still in ignorance of the location, in latitude and longitude, of the old bound — the north-west point of the Lake of the Woods. It was agreed, therefore, to run north or south from it, as the case might require, till the forty-ninth parallel should be struck, and then on that parallel to the mountains. The English Commissioners, still painfully reluctant to part with the coveted and long-struggled-for Mississippi Valley, endeavored to secure for English subjects over the line, a right of way to the Mississippi River, and free navigation of the same.

It was probably a fair hundred miles across the country from the nearest British territory to the upper heads of that river, where the Mississippi begins in some trout brook. Thence its waters run more than three thousand miles to the Gulf of Mexico. It was a bold, English request, that they be permitted to traverse that belt and avail themselves of that navigation, where they had no foot of land. It was a vain endeavor of course, and with a longing, lingering, and last look on that splendid valley, they turned away, and set their faces "due west" on the latitude of forty-nine.

Therefore in the London negotiations of 1818 there was a suspension of line running westward. A compromise followed, the joint occupation of Oregon for ten years was the result, and in 1827 the compromise of joint occupation was renewed, and was to run indefinitely, but terminable by a notice of one year given by either party.

Meanwhile the line between the St. Croix and the St. Lawrence remained undecided, and the Ashburton-Webster Treaty of 1842 fixed it. Four years later another Joint Commission was raised to run the northwestern boundary line from the mountains to the " middle of the channel" between the mainland and Vancouver Island. But when the Commission came to the Pacific coast they could not agree on the " middle of the Channel."

In 1871 the question was submitted to the Emperor of Germany as final arbiter on the meaning of the phrase, " middle of the Channel," and which channel it called for; and in 1872 he affirmed the claim of the United States.

Thus, under eight treaties, with fifteen specifications of work to be done, and running through eighty-nine years, this boundary question was prolonged to its conclusion.

This summary of the boundary questions between the United States and Great Britain will show with what tenacity England held to her land claims, and land chances too, and with what protesting reluctance she receded north and west before the United States. The summary will aid, too, in showing how the two nations slowly and earnestly closed in around the coveted Oregon. For fourscore years distance from the prize had kept them cool and steady in the struggle, but now the two parties, standing together and looking down on that prize from the crown of the Rocky Mountains, warmed into an ardor which could only increase till one of them should take it.

CHAPTER VIII.

ASTORIA: ITS FOUNDING AND FAILURE.

WHEN, in 1818, the Joint Boundary Commission agreed on the parallel of forty-nine, and carried it west to the mountains, and would have continued it to the Pacific, they were stopped by fur-traders, who had, practically, set up two nationalities in the territory, each of which was striving for the whole. It came about in this way.

When the Commissioners were trying, in 1794, to determine "what river is the St. Croix," Mackenzie had just returned from a tour from Montreal to the Arctic and Pacific oceans. This tour was the first sign of white men, and of a new order of things in the wilds beyond the mountains. The openings and possibilities for trade made known by Mackenzie's tours were discussed, not only at Fort Chippewa, on Athabasca, but at York Factory as well, and in London too. Unmeasured territory and untold wealth seemed to be suddenly revealed to the English fur-trade, and one company, the Northwest of Montreal, at once began preparations to enter it.

The tour of Lewis and Clark, 1804-6, made the English jealous lest the Americans should gain the advance; and in 1805, before the American explorers had returned, the Northwest Company dispatched an expedition under one Laroque, to occupy the Columbia with trading-posts. They, however, did not proceed beyond the Mandan village on the Missouri. But in the year following Mr. Fraser left Fort Chippewa, crossed the mountains, and planted an establishment on Fraser Lake. This was the first settlement made by the English west of the mountains. Other posts were soon planted by the same Company, and the region was called New Caledonia.

The return of Lewis and Clark, the next year, stimulated individual enterprise in occupying the new American purchase and magnificent fur lands. The struggles of competitors were sharp and serious at times, but were finally compromised in the organization of the American Fur Company, in 1808, with head-quarters at St. Louis. They started trading-posts on the sources of the Mississippi and Missouri, and some on the other side of the mountains. Mr. Henry, one of their agents, established Post Henry, on Lewis River, and, so far as appears, this was the first trading factory of any white people in territory drained by the Columbia.

The long-deferred contest for Oregon was now fairly opened, not by ministers of state, but by daring and frontier business men, who it will be finally seen closed the contest. They were the primaries of the two competing governments. Two overland expeditions to the Pacific, led by Mackenzie, and by Lewis and Clark, had challenged each other for the grand prize, and the two primaries stood at Fraser Lake and Post Henry.

John Jacob Astor made the next prominent movement in the direction of Oregon. Mr. Astor was a man of broad business vision and keen perception in financial lines. He had such a passion for fur that his whole nervous organization seemed to thrill with the ruffling and smoothing of some rare and choice skins. He probably never looked on a prime black beaver or one of those heavy, pulpy sea-otter skins without coveting it, and never let one slide out of his sensitive hands without reluctance.

An incident will show his eye for business. He was a German immigrant, and when first coming upon our coast in Chesapeake Bay, a terrible storm and thin ice-floes made the wreck of the ship in which he sailed almost a certainty. While thus in long and increasing perils, young Astor came on deck, to the surprise of his stricken and hopeless companions, in his best suit of clothes. His explanation was that if he escaped with life his clothes would be all he could save, and he would save his best. That habit of forethought for the main chance grew with his years, and finally placed him in the first line of millionaires in America. When I used to see him on the streets of New York he was supported between two stout men, much bowed over, so that he could not look up to see even his own merchant blocks, where every brick represented a beaver and every faced stone a sea-otter.

At the age of forty Mr. Astor was well established in his favorite business on the Great Lakes and their rivers, where this western and Pacific opening was made tempting to daring men. His quick eye saw the chances, not only for his fascinating fur-trade, in the mountains and on the shores beyond, but for a half-way house on the Columbia between New York and China, for his general Asiatic trade. The scope and verge of the new field opened fairly to the compass of the man, who had a continental grasp in his business hand. His general plan was to build a substantial and fortified trading-post at the mouth of the Columbia, as a place of deposit for goods and their exchanges with Indians, trappers, and small traders. To this post he would, with the co-operation of government, open a comfortable and protected overland route to facilitate general traffic and settlements westward. From the post he would trade up and down the Pacific, and thence to Canton and on the old line of commerce to London and New York. It was a plan of excellent strategy, even if designed only to take possession of Oregon for the United States, and such a government as patronizes an East India or Hudson Bay Company would have so regarded and used it.

But the old east of the United States has never measured and appreciated and anticipated the new west. "When they gain strength, which will be sooner than most people conceive." Washington said that of the west, after his tour through the region, and its truth holds yet. The growing strength of the new country is surprising the expectations and surpassing the belief of the old thirteen states every year. The centre of population and of wealth and of voting and political power has long since gone over the mountains, and into the very region of which Washington spoke, and with more rapid steps is going on to a farther west. The east has always been slow to know this and own it, and make the most and the best of it. Astor seemed to see farther as a foreigner than the native born, and anticipated the movement of the nation across the Mississippi, where so much of it is to-day.

He started an overland expedition from St. Louis for the Columbia in 1810, consisting of about sixty persons. After a journey of fifteen months and much suffering, this company, reduced by death, arrived at Astoria. A company of about the same number made shorter time and arrived earlier by the way of Cape Horn. After building and properly fortifying Astoria, the vessel, the Tonquin, in which this last company came, ran up the coast on a trading cruise, where the crew were all murdered by the Indians, with the exception of one, who managed to blow up the ship, when crowded with plundering natives, and one hundred of them, with himself, perished in the act.

In anticipation of possible mishaps, Astor sent out the Beaver to follow the Tonquin, with a duplicate of her cargo and freight. She supplied the needs of the young post, after the sad fate of her associate, and then, loading with furs at Sitka, the Russian head-quarters, she put out, homeward, and for trade by the way of Canton. At this port the Beaver learned of the war between the United States and Great Britain, and, not daring to put out, lay by there till the war closed. Unfortunately Mr. Hunt, the agent of Astor, had gone in the Beaver as far as the Sandwich Islands. There he also was detained when news of the war arrived. In 1813 Astor sent forward his third vessel, the Lark, which became a total loss, by shipwreck, on the Sandwich Islands. The Lark carried instructions to Mr. Hunt to protect Astoria, and Mr. Hunt, receiving these instructions, at once sailed for that place with supplies.

Another in the series of misfortunes awaited him here, for he learned, on arrival, that a majority of the partners with Mr. Astor in this enterprise had sold out to the Northwest Fur Company of Montreal — a British concern, and one in which some of those who sold out Astoria were concerned. The sale was not free from the suspicion that it was both dishonorable and dishonest. Mr. Astor valued the property at $200,000, and received for it about $40,000. Before this sale, the Astor company, called the Pacific Fur Company, had established two other trading-posts in the interior, and had there come into competition if not conflict with the Northwest Company. These two were included in the sale.[1]

We have already noticed the plan of the Northwest Company to occupy the mouth of the Columbia, in advance of the return of Lewis and Clark, and thus to hold the whole interior drained by that river. But Laroque failed in the endeavor. In the summer of 1811, after Astoria was established, a party of the Northwest Company came down to the spot, with the hope of occupying it in advance of the Americans. They had been dispatched from Canada in the preceding year to do this. But they were delayed in finding a passage through the mountains, and being compelled to winter on their ridges they came down the Columbia to find Astoria already founded.

The leading partner in it, and the one who afterward led off in its sale, received them in a friendly and hospitable way, and not as rivals; when they returned from their vain expedition, he supplied them, not only with provisions, but with goods for trading purposes up the river, where they established trading huts among the Indians, and became rivals of the Americans. Strange to say, when the question of priority of occupation and of national sovereignty was under discussion at London, fifteen years afterward, the English put in these huts of this returning company, as proof that the English were as early as if not earlier in the Columbia than the Amer-

[1] Irving's *Astoria.*

icans. In the following year two other agents of the Northwest Company were received at Astoria in the same genial way, though the existing war was known at Astoria, and on their return they also were supplied with provisions and goods for trade by the way. Private conference between the two parties was produced afterward, as evidence of the treachery and dishonor then maturing against Mr. Astor and his company and the Americans generally.

Before the war Great Britain asked the United States to favor the Northwest Company as against Mr. Astor. This they declined to do, but immediately on the opening of the war, the English government dispatched a naval force to the Columbia with orders " to take and destroy everything American on the Northwest Coast." On arrival they were mortified and indignant that Astoria had already passed into English hands, and therefore that no plunder or prize-money awaited them. They had but the barren and ceremonial service to perform of running up the English flag, to call the post St. George, and sail for home. This was in 1813.

Therefore, to the great satisfaction of British interests in fur in North America, the American adventurers were first dishonorably bought out and crowded out on the Pacific, and then the position which they occupied was put under the British flag. By bad faith on the part of his Canadian associates, and by the chances of war, Mr. Astor was defeated in his broad plan. As a consequence grave anxieties overshadowed the American interests on that coast. We wait and watch to see how the rivals proceed, and who prospers.

CHAPTER IX.

FACE TO FACE: AMERICA AND ENGLAND.

War was declared by the United States against Great Britain, June 12, 1812, and the treaty of peace was signed at Ghent, December 14, 1814. By this treaty it was agreed that "all territory, places, and possessions whatsoever, taken by either party from the other during the war ... shall be restored without delay." This would seem to cover Astoria and call for its immediate surrender by the English authority. The next year, therefore, President Monroe informed the British *Chargé* at Washington that he should at once reoccupy Astoria. Affairs lingered till 1817, when a vessel was put in readiness for that object. Then Mr. Bagot, the English plenipotentiary at Washington, opposed the step. He made two points of objection. One was that the post of Astoria was sold by the Pacific Company to the Northwest Company before the war, and therefore had never been captured. But as such sale would convey only the use of the land with the property on it, and as a citizen cannot sell land so as to give it over to another government, he made another point, that "the territory itself was early taken possession of in his majesty's name, and had been since considered as forming part of his majesty's dominions."

Under pressure of Mr. Rush, our minister at the Court of St. James, repossession was granted, but the questions of absolute title, as to the point which government should own Oregon, the English reserved for a future settlement. So the English flag was hauled down, the Stars and Stripes went up, and the name was changed back from St. George to Astoria. This was in 1818.[1]

An incident will show with what tenacity England held to Oregon, and with what adroitness and pretense she struggled for its possession. When the question came up again, in 1826, who should own that territory, her ministry pleaded that Mr. Bagot was instructed, privately and in conversation, to allow the Americans to return to Astoria only as tenants at will, and that he must assert the absolute claim of Great Britain, and that an American settlement on the Columbia must be regarded as an encroachment and trespass. What she claimed to have then said, in private and unwritten instructions to her agent, no copy of which was made or notice served on the United States, she now made a basis of claim to sovereignty in the country, eight years afterward. To make private and unwritten instructions to an agent, held by him only in memory, a basis for a claim to territorial title, has at least the merit of freshness and novelty in the records of diplomacy.

The Honorable Rufus Choate, that rare scholar and jurist, had good reason for his words, spoken in his place in the Senate, when, years afterward, the Oregon question was a very warm one in Congress.

"Keep your eye always open, like the eye of your own eagle, upon the Oregon. Watch day and night. If any new developments of policy break forth, meet

[1] Message of President Monroe, April 17, 1822, and accompanying Documents.

them. If the times change, do you change. New things in a new world. Eternal vigilance is the condition of empire as well as of liberty."

Although Astoria was ceremonially restored, the Northwest Company of fur-traders continued to occupy it till 1845 — twenty-seven years — so finely and tediously can the threads of diplomatic delays be spun out and woven. Before it was surrendered they had made it a formidable stronghold. It was a stockade fort, one hundred and fifty by two hundred and fifty feet, with post walls twelve feet high, and two bastions on diagonal corners. It was defended by two eighteen-pounders, six six-pounders, four four-pound carronades, two six-pound cohorns and seven swivels. It was manned by twenty-three whites, sixteen half-breed Canadians, and twenty-six Sandwich Islanders.

Such a military post was a threatening declaration of intention to hold the Columbia and its basin, and it was at the same time a fair index of the manner and spirit with which the country in dispute was monopolized. Yet at the same time the English were a party to the treaty of joint occupation, in which neither should monopolize to the damage of the other, or take steps toward a permanent occupancy. Inland lines of trade, attached to small centres and knotted together in little posts and huts here and there, were embracing Oregon as with a net. Not only were the Indians won over to the English side, but they were made to feel that they had no right to trade with the Americans, and the pernicious idea was carried, wide and clear, through all the tribes, that the Americans would take their lands, while the English wished only to trade in furs.

To such an extent were the Indians thus prejudiced

and alienated, that the citizens of the United States were obliged not only to renounce all ideas of renewing their establishments in that part of America, but even to withdraw their vessels from its coasts. For more than ten years after Astoria was sold out, it would have been difficult to find an American in the country. In his "History of Oregon and California" Greenhow says that when the Hudson Bay Company was before Parliament in 1837 for the renewal of its charter, they "claimed and received the aid and consideration of government for their energy and success in expelling the Americans from the Columbia regions, and forming settlements there, by means of which they were rapidly converting Oregon into a British colony."

While the Treaty of Ghent, 1814, restored Astoria to the United States, that place was not distinctly named, but embraced in the general phrase, "all territory, place and possessions whatsoever, taken by either party." There is no allusion in the treaty to the northwest coast, or to any territory west of the Lake of the Woods. The American plenipotentiaries at Ghent were under instructions to concede no lands to Great Britain south of the forty-ninth parallel. The question of the boundary line west of the Lake of the Woods was introduced by the American commissioners, and in the same form in which it failed when the almost consummated treaty of 1807 failed. That proposition was, to extend the boundary west of the Lake on forty-nine "as far as their said respective territories extend in that quarter," and yet not far enough to bound territory claimed by either west of the mountains. Both governments agreed then to this, but the English violence to the American frigate Chesapeake stayed proceedings, and the treaty was not ratified.

When this proposition was renewed in 1814 at Ghent, the English commissioners agreed to accept it, provided it be added that the subjects of Great Britain might reach the Mississippi through American territory, and navigate it to the sea. Of course this was declined, and so the Treaty of Ghent has no reference to territory or boundary west of the Lake of the Woods.

As often as occasion warranted, the English turned with longing eyes toward that forbidden Mississippi. Its majestic current tempted them, and its long arms, thrown up into the interior of the continent and taking tribute from the Alleghanies and the Rocky Mountains, offered to carry their merchandise. When a steamer has run up from its mouths below New Orleans as far as from Liverpool to New York, it is still as far from high-water navigation, above Fort Benton, as the Azores are from New York. No wonder they coveted it, from Yorktown onward, but they were compelled to go to India and Egypt for their large rivers.

These diplomatic incidents are interesting, as showing the endeavors of the English in those early days to secure the natural sources of power on the Pacific slope. We note specially those covert efforts to regain a footing in the Great Valley, which they controlled in part for twenty years after battling with France for it for sixty years. Many questions were left undecided by the Treaty of Ghent, and in 1818 they were renewed before a joint commission at London, especially the boundary question from the Lake of the Woods west. The commission agreed to the forty-ninth parallel as the boundary from the Lake to the mountains.

But the English commissioners finally, after mutual and full discussion of prior rights on the Pacific, declared as an ultimatum that they would accede to no boundary which did not give to England the mouth of the Columbia. Then a joint occupation was agreed to in these words: —

"It is agreed that any country that may be claimed by either party on the northwestern coast of America, westward of the Stony Mountains, shall, together with its harbors, bays, and creeks, and the navigation of all rivers within the same, be free and open for the term of ten years from the date of the signature of the present convention to the vessels, citizens, and subjects of the two powers," etc.

That was a most unfortunate move for Great Britain. Ultimately it lost her the prize at stake. In that signature she signed away any chance she had to that magnificent domain. True, the compromise on joint occupation gave to the Hudson Bay Company a practical monopoly of the fur-trade. It was now in possession of this, almost to the exclusion of all other parties and interests. But the policy of this company was really hostile to English and national interests. It was to cultivate wilderness and not civilization, trading huts and not settlements, half-breeds and not English families. This was the fatal mistake of the government. Those august negotiations were inspired and consummated in the interests of beaver and not of men. They secured to one corporation the monopoly to continue to introduce, as they had for a century and a half, at York Factory, Athabasca, Fort Pelley, and Methey Portage, tea and raw spirits, trade guns, fishing and trapping gear, calico, duffle, and gewgaws. As we have shown before, the orders for goods were scarcely varied for a century. Sometimes the monotony of the clerkly work at both ends of the line was pleasantly broken by an order on the London house for a wife. This was the only resort for the bachelor, except the ordinary course of selecting from the wilderness. Interests in the great fur land would not allow an absence of from two to six years for a wife, when one could be selected to order, like raw spirits or calico, and be received and receipted for "in good condition."[1]

The Fur Company would keep back the rude implements of an opening husbandry, and the humble, virtuous beginnings of domestic life and strong citizenship. The English commissioners made a blunder when they imagined that a steel-trap would possess and hold the disputed territory better than a spade, and that a beaver dam in North America was worth more to the English crown than a factory dam. When too late, as we shall soon see, the English ministry attempted to recover from this fatal error.

[1] Robinson's *Great Fur Land*, p. 67.

CHAPTER X.

AMERICAN SPEECHES, ENGLISH STEEL-TRAPS, AND DIPLOMACY.

In the Louisiana Purchase, the southwestern line between that territory and the Spanish possessions was left not only poorly known, but quite indefinitely described. The conferences of the powers bordering on that line were protracted through years, and at times they were not pleasant. The Florida Purchase gave a good opportunity to fix that boundary, as it did, on parchment.

The parallel of forty-two on the Pacific was fixed as the dividing line running east from that Ocean to a point due north or south, as the facts might require, to the source of the Arkansas; down this river to longitude one hundred; on that parallel south till it strikes the Red River; down the Red River to longitude ninety-four; due south on it to the Sabine River; and down the Sabine to the Gulf of Mexico. This boundary affirmed the southern limits of Oregon, and so aided to give outline and definiteness to the coveted land of our narrative.

In the attempts made by the coterminous nations to survey and mark off this line with bounds, from the mouth of the Sabine to Oregon tide-water, where it washes the continent on precisely latitude forty-two, there were various delays, as there had been from 1803, in the attempt to outline the same on paper by verbal description. It was well understood that Spain was greatly dissatisfied at the transfer of the Louisiana to a republic, and was greatly displeased with France for making the transfer. Hence there was an apparent determination on her part not to agree to its southern boundary, while she waited and hoped for some contingencies that might possibly recover it from republican hands. These delays continued to the close of the Mexican war. when, in 1848, the United States became owner on the other side of the unrun line. Then, as the metes and bounds were not needed, they were never run out and set.

Congressional discussions and negotiations between the United States and Great Britain followed close and continuous on the Florida Treaty of 1818, but with little progress and less result. Only events made progress, and as these could not be brought within the compass and control of statesmen, the Oregon question moved on silently to its close.

In 1820 an inquiry was raised in the House of Representatives as to the condition of American interests on the Pacific, and the expediency of occupying, in a substantial way, the Columbia. An able report was secured, with a recommendation to establish "small trading guards" on the Missouri and Columbia, and to secure immigration to Oregon from the United States and from China. The papers went to the table for the remainder of the session; were revised in 1821, and then slept again for two years. In December, 1823, the announcement of the Monroe Doctrine tended to quicken discussion on Oregon in both Congress and Parliament, and to retard negotiations. A special committee was raised in Congress to consider the military occupation of the mouth of the Columbia. The committee recommended that two hundred men be dispatched immediately overland,

and two vessels with military supplies and stores be sent to fortify and hold that place. They also proposed that four or five military posts be established at Council Bluffs and on the Pacific.

Council Bluffs was then the most frontier military post of the United States, but is now a thriving city in the east, that is, in the eastern half of our country. Lippincott's Gazetteer of 1856 locates it "in the Indian Territory, on the west bank of Missouri River, at the highest point to which steamboats ascend." This does very well for scholarship and business that confine travel and study to Colony times and the eastern States. There are but two mistakes. Council Bluffs is put on the wrong side of the Missouri, and about twenty-eight hundred miles only short of "the highest point to which steamboats ascend."

The papers were printed, and more action seems to have been had on them abroad than at home. In the House nothing was done. The inaction left affairs to assume the best possible shape for the United States, and this came, yet not of the foresight and plans of statesmen. There appeared to be a lack of appreciation of the case, and there was a skepticism and lethargy concerning that half of the Union, which have by no means yet disappeared.

The year following, negotiations were again opened at London, and for a brief time Mr. Rush claimed for the United States from the forty-second to the fifty-first parallels, which section would embrace all the waters feeding the Columbia. This was apparently on the European theory that the discovery of the mouth of a river carries its entire basin. The English plenipotentiaries replied that their government would never yield the northern half of that basin, and they proposed the Columbia as the boundary, beginning on it where parallel forty-nine strikes it. Mr. Rush added the proposition of ten years' joint occupation, and that the Americans should found no posts north of the fifty-first parallel, or the English south of it. But there was a mutual rejection of all propositions, and so this negotiation closed. It was a gain, however, that each party had defined its claims and made offers, and so the question took on outlines, or limits, which was one good step toward a settlement.

President Monroe in his last message — 1824 — called attention to the military occupation of the country in dispute, and recommended a survey of the mouth of the Columbia, and regions adjacent, by a board of civil engineers. President Adams did the same the next year. These recommendations produced two elaborate reports, setting forth the history, geography, climate, soil, furs and other products of that region, and also the cost of the proposed military establishments and the probable expense for maintaining them. A bill favorable and corresponding was introduced, and then Oregon slept again in the halls of Congress till 1828.

Meanwhile the joint occupation for ten years was drawing to a close, and events compelled action outside. In 1821 the Hudson Bay Company and the Northwest Company had united, and by the union expensive rivalry, over-paying and under-selling, litigation, and not infrequent bloody conflicts, came to an end. The enlarged Hudson Bay Company could now cover the northern parts of North America with great power and comprehensiveness and detail. Not only through the British Provinces, but through the northern parts of the United

States their trappers and boats and agents were scattered, and their semi-military factories were near enough together to receive the furs, furnish goods in exchange and guaranty defenses.

Of course, at the end of the ten years, Oregon was mainly British in its occupants, business, and profits. Indeed, when the question of joint occupation was forced into notice by the near expiration of the first agreement, the English plenipotentiaries say, in an elaborate statement of their side of the case: " In the interior of the territory in question the subjects of Great Britain have had, for many years, numerous settlements and trading-posts — several of these posts on the tributary streams of the Columbia, several upon the Columbia itself, some to the northward, and others to the southward of that river. . . . In the whole of the territory in question the citizens of the United States have not a single settlement or trading-post. They do not use that river, either for the purpose of transmitting or receiving any produce of their own to or from other parts of the world."[1]

During this conference the old offer of each party was made over again with variations, the English tenaciously adhering to the river boundary. To aid in this they offered, additionally, a section lying on and about the Straits of Fuca, from Bullfinch's Bay to Hood's Canal. But no decision on boundaries could be reached, and the negotiations ended in extending the agreement of joint occupation indefinitely, terminable by either on notice of one year.

[1] For a full statement of the English and the American sides of the Oregon question see *President Adams' Message*, December 12, 1827, and Documents, and in Appendix to *Greenhow's History, pp.* 446-465.

This renewal of the arrangement of 1818 was confirmed by Congress, but immediately a great and protracted debate arose in that body. A bill was reported in the House authorizing the President to survey the territory west of the mountains between the parallels of forty-two, and fifty-four forty, occupy the same by military posts and garrisons, and extend the laws of the United States over it. The bill was lost, and very little interest on the subject showed itself again in Congress for many years.

CHAPTER XI.

WESTERN MEN ON THE OREGON TRAIL.

THE Oregon question failed of sympathy in the older States, and eastern interest did not keep pace with western growth. When it was a journey of three weeks from New England to any point on the Mississippi, it is not strange that the East should have but little knowledge of the immense domain beyond that river. It required the locomotive to introduce the Atlantic to the Father of Waters, and to convince the country east of the Alleghanies, that two thirds of the Republic then lay west of that stream. It is quite as difficult now to satisfy the East that only about one fifth of our domain lies between that river and the Atlantic. When "out West," meant the Genesee country in "York State," or the Western Reserve in "the Ohio," it was a hard thing to appreciate Oregon. Our first railroad to the Mississippi did not arrive till 1854, — at Rock Island. Prior to that it was a long way by saddle and wagon, and a longer and harder way still across Missouri, up the Platte, and toward the Yellowstone. Slowly and tediously, therefore, Oregon gained a hearing on the Atlantic slope, and its facts and possibilities sometimes had to crowd their way into place and power. In truth the happy and well-regulated family of states in the old half of the Union did not welcome the foundling.

In the great Congressional debate that defeated the bill last mentioned, it was urged by its opponents, that even if the United States had undisputed title, the occupation of the country would be of doubtful utility, from its barrenness, dangerous coasts, distance and inaccessibility from the States by either land or sea. If emigration should settle it, the defense of citizens there would compel a much greater outlay than any supposable income from it would warrant. This line of reasoning showed but little sympathy with a growing frontier. The logic and statesmanship were more provincial than national.

The conservative, satisfied, and untravelled East has always had a skeptical turn of mind as to the extent, growth of settlement, the political, and moral importance of the constantly receding border. Travel for pleasure has usually been directed abroad, and not inland; and the new towns and states, even as the rivers, prairies, and mountains of the west have been measured by the home standards of childhood.

When therefore a decision upon its interest took the ballot form, the frontier has too often been voted as relatively unimportant. There was a very early exhibition of the tendency to prefer old centres, and a finished state of things, when the Colonial Legislature of Massachusetts put this on her Records in 1632: "It is thought by geñal consent, that Boston is the fittest place for publique meeteings of any place in the Bay."

When we measure the worth of the Oregon of 1828, as it appears to-day for us — Oregon, Washington, and Idaho Territories — we tremble to think how near the old states were to alienating, and disowning, and losing that magnificent region.

It was left for the west — often chided, and even yet, for lack of effort to care for itself — to save the farther west, by occupying it at great peril, and so compelling attention to it. When bills in Congress for opening and possessing Oregon went to the table for a final rest, or over to the great mass of rejected papers, energetic western men went to the upper waters of the Mississippi, Missouri, Platte, and Yellowstone, in the fur-trade. Thus, by occupation and possession, they forced the discussion of this question. Having threaded the head streams of those rivers on the eastern prairies and slopes, they began to trace the gorges and cañons of the mountains. The North American and the Columbia Companies, united in 1826, did the most of this, and St. Louis became the centre of the fur trade for the United States.

From the same city, and about these times, those great caravans had begun to start off on the Santa Fé trail into New Mexico. Eminent in this foreign trade were Bent and St. Vrain, while Ashley led the way into the extreme west, and finally over the mountains into the great central basin. It was in 1823 that Ashley scattered his hardy men on the Sweet Water, a branch of the Platte, and on Green River, one of the heads of the Colorado. In the year following he planted a trading-post near Salt Lake. This was twelve hundred miles from St. Louis — the equivalent of twelve thousand now — and to it in 1826 he hauled a six-pound cannon — the first to waken those mountain-slumbers of ages. Wagons followed in 1828. That was a significant year and event, for then the Republic began to go over the mountains and at that time took one of its long and strong steps toward the Pacific. Perhaps the wagons, at sight of which the spirit of Jacob revived, were not better loaded for the human family.

When Ashley's company sent to St. Louis furs to the value of $180,000 as the product of one year, it created a profound impression, and the Rocky Mountain Company was one result, prominent in which was the early St. Louis name of Sublette. This company traversed and traded along the southern branches of the Columbia and through the most of California.

The energy, daring, and service of the western men of those times in hastening and aiding the Oregon question to settlement, are well illustrated in Mr. Pilcher. He left Council Bluffs in 1827, with forty-five men and one hundred horses; wintered in Colorado; in the summer following was on Lewis River and along the northwestern base of the mountains; in 1829 came down Clark's River to Fort Colville, a Hudson Bay post, thence by the heads of the Columbia, the Athabasca, and Red Rivers to the upper Missouri, and so returned to the States.[1]

Eminent among the western men who did so much to diffuse information and stimulate interest concerning Oregon was J. O. Pattie, of St. Louis. His adventures in the fur-trade led him through the New Mexico of those days, and Sonora and Chihuahua of old Mexico. He went up and down the Colorado and along the Gulf of California. His narrative was published in 1832, and the knowledge of those unknown regions which it revealed, the wild incidents which it detailed, and the sources which it opened to adventurers, stirred quite an excitement in the border states, and created a passion to explore the wild west and engage in the fur and Indian trades.

[1] Documents with message of President Jackson, January 23, 1829.

Captain Bonneville, of the army, may be mentioned in this connection. He led his one hundred men and more, with their wagons and goods, from the Missouri to the Colorado, and even to the Columbia. It was a two years' romance in trapping and trading and exploring. Only experience can give one a tolerable idea of the excitement and joy and intense feeling of liberty which one feels, when roaming thus at one's own wild will, beyond the borders of highways and fences, laws and cabins, locks and keys, where dinner is ordered by the rifle, tables are spread under the trees, and beds under the stars.

It was not the west alone that pressed these individual and company enterprises over the borders, and compelled Oregon to come into sight and the east to see it. Under the quiet, scholarly, and conservative elms of Old Cambridge in the extreme east, there sprang a passion for Oregon, which took shape in an emigrating company in 1832 under Nathaniel J. Wyeth. The writings of Hall J. Kelly did much to stimulate and set forward this enterprise. The company of twenty-two persons was a novel affair, and had in it more of the Yankee than was found useful out west. Near a college, and books, where men on the streets spoke a dozen languages, and in the shops were very scientific mechanics, the company got up a vehicle, half and half. Bottom up it was a wagon, the other side up it was a boat; it had oars; it had wheels. It was a mechanical hybrid, an amphibious vehicle, and took to land or water with equal delight. Indeed, the men of those classic shades called it the "Amphibium." The boys of those same shades, who have a keen perception of novelties, and who knew the oddities in the make-up of Mr. Wyeth, called it the "Natwyetheum." There were three built, and they put out from Old Cambridge for Oregon, with all their motley freight of "notions" to match.

> "O'er bog, or steep, thro' straight, rough, dense, or rare
> With head, hands, wings, or feet, pursues his way,
> And swims, or sinks, or wades, or creeps, or flies."

No wonder the company experienced some difficulties in the German neighborhoods as they passed the Alleghanies. Says the narrative: "Here we experienced a degree of inhospitality not met with among the savages. The innkeepers, when they found that we came from New England, betrayed an unwillingness to accommodate Yankees." They refused refreshment and lodgings, locked their bar-rooms, and even stood guard with rifles in hand. What else could those Dutchmen do or think, as they saw those machines climbing the mountains? No wonder the Dutchmen were afraid. Two years before the Baltimore and Ohio Railroad, over which the company had come sixty miles, so far as complete then, had been trying to run cars by sails, and now here were these three vehicles — a cross between an omnibus and a boat! Forty-nine days brought them to St. Louis and to their senses, where the wise men of the east became practical, and abandoned the "Amphibium" and the most of its knickknackery.

It is said by those who have lived on both sides of the Mississippi, that there are more Boston notions east of that river than west of it. Father Wiggin's ferry used to carry them over, in small quantities, in trunk or head, more generally than does the present magnificent St. Louis bridge.

By steamer Otter to Independence, two hundred and sixty miles, and thence out upon the prairie, they pressed on, and our Cambridge friends were well on the way for Oregon. Fortunately they then came under convoy of William Sublette and company, a Rocky Mountain trader, wise in wood-craft and aborigines. Mr. Wyeth soon found himself among the Indians, and at once saw the difference between the eastern and western Indian — the one being a book Indian, full of sentiment and high romance, and the other a live Indian, of dirt, paint, and a tomahawk. Ere long this tramping for Oregon became a plain matter of fact. The poetry was at Cambridge, and the reality on the prairies. On the Fourth of July they drank the health of the nation in water from Lewis' Fork of the Columbia. But they were a sad company, and would have preferred the frog-pond on Boston Common. The experienced Sublette and his hardy mountain boys were soon to part with them for their trading and trapping stations, and what with sickness, disappointment, criticism, and insubordination, they were nearly ready to break up and scatter.

As they went down Boston harbor to camp for ten days, on one of the islands, and learn to endure hardship, they made quite a showy and attractive appearance, in uniform suits, with a broad belt carrying a bayonet, knife, and axe. Now they were twenty-two different persons, haggard, soiled, and dejected, with many a Joseph's coat among them replacing the uniform, and not much coveted by envious brothers.

Here the company divided, and seven of them turned their backs on Oregon, among whom were Jacob and John, brothers of Captain Wyeth. The latter pushed forward and, with other mountain men who joined him, established Fort Hall on Snake River, about one hundred miles north of Salt Lake. The reader should fix this fort in his mind, for we shall have much to do with it in our narrative. The Hudson Bay Company at once established a rival post called Fort Boisé, below Fort Hall, and easily ruined the enterprise of Mr. Wyeth by a sacrificing competition.

In a memoir of Mr. Wyeth [1] to a Congressional Committee he says that "experience has satisfied me that the entire weight of this Company will be made to bear on any trader who shall attempt to prosecute his business within its reach. . . . No sooner does an American concern start in this region than one of these trading parties is put in motion. A few years will make the country west of the mountains as completely English as they can desire."

Another person long conversant with affairs in Oregon, and of the United States navy, William A. Slocum, reported to the same Committee "that no individual enterprise can compete with this immense foreign monopoly established in our waters. . . . The Indians are taught to believe that no vessels but the Company's ships are allowed to trade in the river, and most of them are afraid to sell their skins but at Vancouver or Fort George."

Hence it came about that the Americans west of the mountains at this time seldom exceeded two hundred, and they were beyond all cover of United States laws. No form of law, even the most prospective and shadowy, followed them. Their protection against man as well as brute was in their own hands. Yet around Vancouver alone the Hudson Bay Company had seven or eight hundred men. These were European, Canadian, half-breed, and Indian, but subject to the Fort. Over all the

[1] Report. House of Representatives, No. 101, February 16, 1839.

region covered by that Company, Canadian law was extended by act of Parliament. No post was beyond this code of laws, and no individual in the employ of the Company lacked it.

While, therefore, the terms of joint occupation provided for equality between the two parties, the practical working was a monopoly by one. Not only was the government of the Hudson Bay Company vital and active at every point where their employés were, but its magnitude made it formidable. Beginning at Astoria, it covered the heads of the Columbia, east to Salt Lake, north to the Athabasca and Saskatchawan, and so on to York Factory on Hudson Bay; and still later, in 1839, Mr. Wyeth says that "the United States, as a nation, are unknown west of the mountains." As early as 1834 the Hudson Bay Company had over two thousand men in the various branches of their business. The most of them had half-breed families; and over all the Company had full authority, always injurious and often disastrous to all others who attempted to trade or settle in the country. Americans were not allowed to traffic within several hundred miles of a Hudson Bay post; and Simpson, agent, and for a long time governor of the Company, said they were "resolved, even at the cost of one hundred thousand pounds sterling, to expel the Americans from traffic on that coast." At this time they had over twenty posts.

Possibly an American company, consolidated out of these we have mentioned, protected and patronized by the government, could have become a successful rival of the English one in Oregon. But it is not in the genius of our government to do such things. A gigantic monopoly comes more naturally from a monarchical government, while our democratic theory leaves privilege and success to be divided as the fruit of individual toil and competition. As will be seen, this, rather than the monopolies that are the gifts of kings, won the day.

CHAPTER XII.

THE GREAT ENGLISH MISTAKE.

The "British and Foreign Review" of 1844 made this frank and wide-reaching admission concerning the Hudson Bay Company: "The interests of the Company are of course adverse to colonization. . . . The fur-trade has been hitherto the only channel for the advantageous investments of capital in those regions." This is an exact statement, by an English authority, of the fundamental mistake of Great Britain, in her endeavors to secure Oregon. In the English view of the case, Rupert's Land, originally, and all wild land contiguous, and occupied by this Company, was reserved for fur, and the fur was reserved by charter of 1670 for the Hudson Bay Company. First and last and always, the end was the skin of a wild animal, and this Company had the delegated sovereignty of Great Britain to control the country for raising this animal, and the only and absolute right to catch and skin it. One outside the Company had no legal right to catch, buy, or sell the article. Any colony, cultivation, clearing, or residence was to be forbidden and abated as an encroachment and infringement. The nature, extent, and absolutism of this monopoly can hardly be overstated. No one unconnected with the Company could "visit, haunt, frequent, trade, traffic, or adventure" in it.

The charter covered the grand basin of Hudson Bay,

and the grant of exclusive trade finally extended from the Canadas to the Arctic, and westward to the Pacific, embracing what the Company called "Indian countries." Over so much of North America this monopoly of trade and monarchy of government extended, and everything was made subservient to the growth, capture, and sale of fur. The extent of the monopoly granted by Louis XIV. to Crozat was immense, embracing the valleys of the Ohio, Mississippi, and Missouri. But this grant of Charles II. to Prince Rupert was immensely more extensive.

It was the interest and policy of the Hudson Bay Company to hold back all this country from settlement and civilization, and continue it in wilderness as a grand and private game preserve. Down the ages it was to be kept for the raising of beaver and muskrat, mink, bear, and otter. Its primeval solitudes were not to be invaded by white men, nor its silence of thousands of years to be broken, except as licensed men should go in quietly to bring out fur. At York Factory and the Norway House, Moose Fort and Fort Simpson, Pelley, Vancouver, and Garry, a little bustle and a Canadian boat-song were tolerated once or twice a year, by batteaux brigades and dog-trains. But the coming and going of these were as if by stealth, lest they scare the game; and then silence settled down over those lone lands again, with the stillness and shadow of an eclipse. The call of herdsmen and the varied sounds of farm-work, the echo of mechanics and the sweet voices of village life, were withheld by royal charter from these regions.

A missionary at Moose Factory writes: "A plan which I had devised for educating and training to some acquaintance with agriculture native children, was disallowed. . . . A proposal made for forming a small Indian village near Moose Factory was not acceded to; and instead, permission only given to attempt the location of one or two old men, no longer fit for engaging in the chase, it being carefully and distinctly stated, by Sir George Simpson, that the Company would not give them even a spade toward commencing their new mode of life."

Care was taken by the Company that local property should not be acquired by individuals, so as to form social and village centres and thus plant the germs of civilization. Their employés were not allowed to acquire any property or income beyond their salary. As agriculture and the gain of money by any private labor were forbidden, the products of the ground were scanty, and were furnished only from the gardens and fields of the officers, and for their tables. Up to the time when American missionaries entered Oregon in 1834, there was no extra supply of potatoes. It was a luxury for head men and distinguished visitors. The Company did not encourage the cultivation.

As late as 1836, they opposed the introduction of cattle, because meat and beef tended to settlements and civilization. They had for themselves about a thousand head, but would not sell one to the Americans, of whom there were then only fifteen men in the territory. They would lend a cow, but required the calf to be returned. The next year an arrangement was made, and ten men with about sixteen hundred dollars went down to California to bring up a herd. The Hudson Bay men put all possible obstacles in the way, but the Americans brought up six hundred. On the way the Indians stole some, and suspicion was not wanting that they were procured to do it.

In some instances, and after the Americans began to introduce farming, the Company allowed a few of its broken-down men to cultivate the ground about the Wallamette, but they reserved the right to call these men back at any time to their stations. The Company under no circumstances released a man in the country, but unless he would renew his engagement they returned him from whence he came — sent him out of the country.

The plough and spade and milch cow, with a farm, under warranty deed from Great Britain, would disturb fur-bearing animals. Such a farm would soon have a neighbor, and then a neighborhood. Thus the beaver-dam might become a mill-dam, and mankind, instead of corporators and stockholders, would take possession of a country larger by one third than all Europe, and so the Hudson Bay Company be damaged.

When Dr. Whitman and his missionary party were entering Oregon in 1836, they met at Walla Walla J. K. Townsend, a naturalist, sent out by a society in Philadelphia to collect specimens of plants and birds. He said to Dr. Whitman: "The Company will be glad to have you in the country, and your influence to improve their servants and their native wives and children. As to the Indians you have come to teach, they do not want them to be any more enlightened. The Company now have absolute control over them, and that is all they require."

Christian labors among the Indians, by different sects, have been tolerated, and at times encouraged, when the purpose was to bring them up from their pagan state to a civilized condition, but they have been discouraged whenever the result tended to elevate the Indians to either principles or habits inconsistent with the labors which the Company might require. A moral tone, family ties, and local property, would damage the dividends of the Hudson Bay stock, if developed very far, and therefore Christianizing influences were not tolerated beyond certain points.

The "Colonial (English) Magazine" of 1843 puts this matter with surprising simplicity and directness: "By a strange and unpardonable oversight of the local officers of the Company, missionaries of the United States were allowed to take religious charge of the population, and these artful men lost no time," etc.

An illustration will show how necessary it was to check the development of a moral and Christian tone before it endangered the profits of the Company. Mr. Slocum of the United States navy reported to Congress on Indian slavery in Oregon: "The price of a slave varies from five to fifteen blankets. Women are valued higher than men. If a slave dies within six months of the purchase, the seller returns one-half the purchase-money. . . . Many instances have occurred where a man has sold his own child. . . . The slaves are generally employed to cut wood, hunt and fish for the families of the men employed by the Hudson Bay Company, and are ready for any extra work. Each man of the trapping parties has from two to three slaves, who assist to hunt and take care of the horses and camp. They thereby save the Company the expense of employing at least double the number of men that would otherwise be required on these excursions. . . . As long as the Hudson Bay Company permit their servants to hold slaves, the institution of slavery will be perpetuated."

The servants of the Company purchased Indian women, and half-breed families were raised. The Company found it for their profit to encourage their employés thus to marry, as it attached them to localities, and made them contented in a wilderness home, while the offspring, as the children of a slave-mother, were themselves slaves, and became both profitable and inexpensive to the Company. The mildest thing that can be said of this is that the Company were slave-propagandist by approbation and proxy. But then

> "Slaves cannot breathe in England; if their lungs
> Receive our air, that moment they are free.
> That's noble, and bespeaks a nation proud
> And jealous of the blessing."

In this struggle for Oregon the great English mistake grows more and more obvious. To understand it more plainly we must inquire as to the amount, quality, and condition of the English blood introduced. Of course foreign blood, either European or American, would finally prevail. If British North America was to become a civilized and worthy part of the British Empire, English blood must do the work. Here arises a great surprise. After an occupation of its domain by the Hudson Bay Company for nearly two centuries it was found that the number of Europeans who had devoted their lives to that country by residence in it was exceedingly small. It is doubtful whether, between the date of charter, 1670, and 1840, as many Europeans had gone in there, as have sometimes landed as immigrants, at New York, in a single twenty-four hours.

Those who go in for the Company are almost always lads or young men, and they go for life. Older persons could not enter thoroughly into the interests of the

Company, and adapt themselves fully and happily to the new and strange life. Invariably almost, they go into the service unmarried, and then halve the blood of their children with the native Indian races. Those who reach prominent positions, do so when past middle life, but find that they have no inclination to return to the European or American life, which their birth and childhood offered them. The domain of the Company has not only given them a fortune, but frontier or wilderness tastes, character, and manhood. And the fortune is ample only in the place where it has been gained. The millionaire of the forest would be a poor man at the Astor or London West End. For many reasons the retired fur men remain in the country, and become the *noblesse* of the forest — hyphens between the uncivilized and civilized world. The lowest grade imported servant has netted probably his one hundred dollars a year, the clerk his five hundred, the chief trader five times as much, and the chief factor perhaps five thousand dollars, with the incidental support of his tawny family.

While in active employment at forts, factories, and posts, these isolated communities of full and half European stock present a very peculiar class of English subjects. The description of them by Washington Irving is as good yet as it was faithful to fact a hundred years before he wrote it. "The French merchant at his trading post in those primitive days of Canada was a kind of commercial patriarch. . . . He had his clerks, canoemen, and retainers of all kinds, who lived with him on terms of perfect sociability, always calling him by his Christian name. He had his harem of Indian beauties and his troops of half-breed children; nor was there ever wanting a louting train of Indians, hanging about the establishment, eating and drinking at his expense in the intervals of their hunting expeditions."

Manitoba became a favorite residence for some of the retired servants of the company. They long cherished the desire and purpose to return to their native lands to spend their closing days. But man grows old but once, and cannot foretell his experiences and preferences. Their desires and purposes withered with the lapse of years, and the influence of family ties formed in the country, and their long indulged habits in the unrestrained life of the border, finally prevailed, and they constituted an aristocracy of the wilderness in Manitoba.

This is the famous Lord Selkirk grant, the scene of bloody strife and legal struggles between the Hudson Bay and Northwest Companies, prior to their union in 1821. Yet even there, in the only colony or settlement proper, that seemed in 1840 to show personal ownership in land, or hint toward a general colonization of the domain of the Company, there were but about six thousand persons, and the most of them were Indians and half breeds; very few of them were Europeans.

Three years before, when the Company was asking for the renewal of its charter, it admitted frankly that its efforts to settle the country embraced only a scanty supply of aged and worn-out servants. Those of European blood in the country, all told, commissioned and non-commissioned, from Hudson Bay to the Pacific, and from the United States to the Arctic, would hardly exceed three thousand. The others in the employ of the Company were about one fourth Sandwich Islanders, one fourth Orkney men, and the rest Canadian, Indian, and half-bloods — material scanty in its best quality, European, and miserable in its worst quality, for extending civilization. Yet it was as good and as abundant as the desires and plans of the Company demanded.

Suppose we make an opening here and there, and send glances in, that we may see to what extent the eighteenth and nineteenth centuries have gone up into that vast, weird land of fur animals. Two centuries, and specially the last two, are supposed to do something with a region larger than Europe. In the opening of each June the Company's ships drop down the Thames, and in August drop anchor at York Factory on Hudson Bay. Now they have two weeks, if plans work well, for each to discharge their cargoes of goods, take in furs, and leave that great inland sea before the Arctic winter closes it for another nine months. Waiting then till summer returns, the goods then hurry on to Lake Winnipeg, and down to the Arctic and over to the Yukon and Pacific. Carts and batteaux make the tedious trips with the freight, and the agent follows on the first hard winter snows, with dogs, almost as a telegram chases up an express bundle. At the end of six years the bill of goods from London is responded to by bales of furs. Over that dreary, inland line of two years from York Factory, the outside world is hauled in by dogs. Right and left from the sledge trail, as on branch roads, the life and stir of mankind are reported to lonely trading-posts — handfuls of hermits, eremites, desert-men.

At the extremity of one of these antennæ of a moving world, the chief trader, says Robinson in his "Great Fur Land," "has control of a district in many instances as large as a European kingdom. . . . He directs the course of trade, erects new establishments, orders the necessary outfits for the year, suggests needed reforms to the council, and in his capacity of chief magistrate of his principality, rules supreme." What a life those head traders must have — frontier pickets of an uncivilized commerce ! They have no companionship, and little that is congenial till they decivilize themselves, and then have no neighbors but Indians ! A dog-train leaves Fort Garry, and for one hundred and twenty days it glides over the silent plains, and for as many nights it sleeps under those northern stars — but little less unchanging than the business that runs the sledge. The trip ends at La Pierre's, on Methy Portage, three thousand miles away ! How those solitary outposts of white men on the upper Yukon must welcome the dogs and news from the living, stirring, talking world of one year more !

The home mail has been a year on the way to those most northern posts, and the file of newspapers for the year preceding the start is carefully laid away, and each number brought out and read two years from the date of its printing ! Formerly the Montreal " Gazette " was the only paper forwarded, since the copy of a second would add undue weight to the sledge. When the sledge arrives from Pembina at old Fort Good Hope, on the lower Mackenzie, the dogs have hauled it as far as from London to Quebec ; and when their howls break the stillness of twelve months, by switching off to the Rocky Mountain House, they have run about twice the distance from New York to New Orleans. How those Arctic inland St. Helenas of voluntary exiles welcome, and question, and feast, and enforce hospitality on the incoming man ! The joy is almost as if Noah should speak a second ark on the wilderness of waters.

The charter commits the government of that country to the Company with the sole condition that the government shall not be " repugnant to the laws, statutes, and customs of England." Robinson gives us an amusing illustration of one process of government: " When the Indians proved refractory around one of the Company's trading-posts, the trader in charge would wind up his music-box, get his magic lantern ready, and take out his galvanic battery. Placing the handle of the latter instrument in the grasp of some stalwart chief, he would administer a terrific shock to his person and warn him that far out upon the plains he could inflict the same medicine upon him." This process of administration is not supposed to be " repugnant " to any act of Parliament, or to any of the " customs " of the common law of Great Britain. But it shows the process of civilization in that large portion of her Majesty's dominion. It also indicates by what slips and mistakes Oregon was lost to the Crown.

One species of amusement for the middle class shows the same thing, as described by the same English author. It is a half-breed ball, when dancing, eating, drinking, sleeping, and general rough carousal run through three days and nights without intermission. " From time to time, as many as are requisite to keep up the festivities are awakened, and being forthwith revived with raw spirits, join in the dance with renewed vigor."

The hunting and trapping are done in the cold season, and annually at the close of March or in early April, when an occasional hour of softening air and snow gives hint of coming spring, the Indians leave their winter trapping-grounds, and gather about the posts to trade off their furs and obtain their scanty returns. This invasion of Indians even and their inroad on trading-house life are welcomed because they break the dull routine and solemn sameness of simply protracted existence. Through the narrow and angular passage to the grated store-room window, admitting for trade but two Indians at a time, the miserable aborigine passes in his furs. It may be his fine silver fox skins, worth two hundred dollars, for which he bargains in return the pair of three point blankets. worth fifteen dollars. Then "the high contracting parties," mutually satisfied, separate for another year.

This great trade of the Company, in all its details, has carried out of the country in two centuries, by estimation, one hundred and twenty millions of dollars in fur, reckoned on a gold basis. Yet they have so protected the wilderness against civilization, and propagated the fur-bearing animals, and apprenticed the Indian generations in their succession to trapping and hunting, that the average yearly catch has not diminished.

This is a suggestive fact. The old thirteen colonies exterminated wild animals, under bounty, that they might build up Albany and Bangor and Pittsburg, Hartford and Buffalo. They gave men, women and children preference and protection on the wild borders, over bears and silver foxes. They discarded gins, traps, and deadfalls where Manchester and Nashua and Lowell and Paterson are. They esteemed an ox above a buffalo and a sheep above a deer. Yet in the crucible of this Company in their last analysis of half a continent for highest values, population, civilization, agriculture, mining, neighborhood and city building have been thrown off as slag and dross, and only fur remains. Six generations of "Adventurers of England trading in Hudson Bay" and as many generations of trappers have been on the grand North American hunt, and the average yearly catch does not fall off.

In 1870 the posts of this Company on the Saskatchewan alone furnished thirty thousand buffalo robes, Indian-tanned. As an Indian woman can dress about ten a year, polygamy is common in that valley. A tract of country can be marked off through this valley, from the Red River to the Pacific, as good for wheat as Michigan, where a dozen starving Irelands could be located without crowding each other, and where the people could work their own land with comfort and eat their own wheat to repletion. For two hundred years Irish immigrants could not "visit, haunt, frequent, trade, traffic, or adventure" in that splendid domain of Great Britain. They would disturb the beaver.

It is due to the Hudson Bay Company that England was kept so long in ignorance of the extent and worth to her subjects of that magnificent belt westward from the Red River country. With natural advantages vastly superior to those of Canada and equal to those of the northwestern states of the United States, the Company held the region in dark reserve, and the home government was robbed of a colonial growth, while she lost her own emigrants by the hundreds of thousands when they settled in the United States.

The great English mistake, by which Oregon was lost to Great Britain, is shown at no time more clearly than in the incidents and policies of the time now under review. Let two pictures be here taken in contrast and for illustration. The great fall hunt for buffalo provided the almost entire living of many tribes for the year, and much of the income to the Company from the region west of Lake Winnipeg. Those annual hunts were probably the most magnificent and picturesque that were ever followed by any people, if we take into account the majestic prairie hunting-fields, the dignity and multitude of the game, and the numbers of men, women, and children who made up the camps. Robinson's description in his "Great Fur Land" needs no variation.

The rendezvous is usually on the borders of some large river. "From two thousand to twenty-five hundred carts line the banks; three thousand animals graze within sight upon the prairie; a thousand men, with their following of women and children, find shelter under carts and in the tents and tepees of the encampment; the smoke of the camp almost obscures the sun; and the babel of sounds arising from the laughing, neighing, barking multitude, resembles the rush of many waters."

This vast throng keep Sabbath forenoon devoutly, with priest and ceremonial, and the afternoon is given to racing, gaming, sports and plays. In due time, under trained leaders, and with the science and strategy of a battle, the hunters steal on the vast herd of lumbering buffalo and the slaughter begins. The earth trembles in the rush of the animals and their pursuers, dust and smoke cloud the air for miles, the roar of mingled sounds is heard far off at the camp of women and carts, and the bloody battle-field with struggling and dead buffalo spreads out indefinitely on the prairie and through the ravines.

After such a hunt, and mainly for robes, "the plain

for miles is covered with the carcasses of buffalo, from which nothing has been taken, save the hides and tongues, and it may be, the more savory portions of the hump."

The region of these slaughterings for robes, lying about the prairie heads of the Missouri, over to the Saskatchawan, and up its valleys, is magnificent wheat land, and was monopolized and held back from cabin and plow for this crop of buffalo.

This is one picture. At the same time American immigrants, with no monopoly, and individually carrying civilization to a farther point, were hurrying the remnants of buffalo herds over the Mississippi, and planting Indiana and Illinois and Wisconsin on the great eastern pastures of that animal. Iowa and Minnesota soon followed, and the Northern Pacific railroad now heads the march of civilization and empire to our extreme west. So up to the very boundary the United States began to raise wheat and plant cities, while over the line the Hudson Bay Company went on skinning buffalo for the London market, thirty thousand a year. The emigrant wagon, cultivation, mechanics, a various trade, and general civilization were kept on the American side of the boundary. The two policies stand out in the two pictures, and the two forces press westward. Which will win Oregon?

When this fur policy came into competition with the colonial policy of the Republic, the great English mistake became apparent. Trappers and Indian traders could outrun immigrant wagons. Yet eventually the plow would overtake them and finally obtain a warranty deed of the land. If the English government saw the mistake, it was not till it was too late. The

Company could hold its policy and monopoly till 1870. At this date the territory of the Company, or Rupert's Land, merged in the Crown. The monopoly of trade in lands outside, commonly called Indian Countries, and granted in 1821, ended in 1859.

Perhaps never in history has there been a better illustration of the danger and damage to the public of a chartered monopoly. When a corporation becomes too powerful for the government, the design or end of that government is a failure. In this case a private interest was enabled to shut off from the Crown the settlement and commerce and profits of millions of square miles. It shut off the kingdom of Great Britain from efficient growth in North America. If the possession of the Hudson Bay Company had reverted to the Crown at the end of a hundred and fifty years, it would have been returned, as received, a wilderness. To know, in comparison, what might have been, one needs only to cross the boundary line and notice the northern tier of states lying just south of that line.

The great English mistake, therefore, was double. It was a mistake in attempting to take and hold Oregon by trapping, as against colonizing: and it was a mistake to sacrifice so largely the English interests in America to a corporate monopoly.

CHAPTER XIII.

FOUR FLAT-HEAD INDIANS IN ST. LOUIS.

Four Flat-Head Indians had come in 1832 from Oregon, three thousand miles, on a special mission of their own devising. Indians were common visitors, almost common loungers in St. Louis at that time. They glided about quite frequently and freely in moccasin and blanket among the six thousand Americans, French creoles, fur men, half-breeds, boatmen, and border adventurers of that frontier town. It was common to see wigwams not far from the city, and almost the entire region above, on the west bank of the river, was Indian ground, though the river belt was shared in common by the most venturesome and irrepressible white pioneers. Even as late as 1840, I frequently met on the streets the stately, silent, louting red man, trailing his blanket and burdening his squaw, or saw him crouching over his scanty fire of kindlings and drift-wood, in the then still noted grounds of the American Fur Company. For weeks together Indians would have their squalid camps about Illinois Town, and in the bottoms toward the Big Mound and down to the romantic Cohokia Falls.

The four poor Flat-Heads, therefore, attracted no special attention. Only the expert in Indian signs and wood-craft could have marked their tribe and distant home, specially as coming over the plains the Sioux had tricked them out in gaudy and generous trappings of that tribe.

Far up Clark's River, and central in what is now Washington Territory, beyond mountain fastnesses, they had heard from an American trapper of the white man's God, and of a spirit home, better than the hunting-grounds of the blessed, and of a Book that told truly of the Great Spirit, and of that home and the trail to it. The report is that the Iroquois had given to them some of the Christian teachings which had become theirs in Colonial New York; and very likely some of the mountain trappers who left the white frontier and rude clearing, and may be the Book and family altar long years before, had done the same thing. The Indians, always religiously inclined, listened, and then inquired, and then talked it over.

It does not require much fancy to follow them in their rude processes of investigation. In those ancient groves which no axe had mutilated, God's first temples, or where solemn and sublime mountains shut them in like grand old cathedrals, we see them sitting about their dusky camp-fires. They think much and say but little of the white man's God and Book — stealthy worshippers — feeling after the true God, if haply they may find him.

Then they turn to the chase again, and feed on the red deer and big-horn; and renew their scanty wardrobe from the wolf, and the grizzly and silver-tipped bear, and pile away the beaver for the Hudson Bay man, and a new flint-lock, or three point blanket. The Rocky Mountain winter threatens them, and they follow the buffalo, whose instinct has led him north, for a warm retreat on those plains and among the vast valleys that the Pacific trade-winds keep perpetually warm and green. With the return of spring we see them coming back to the old camping-grounds of the summer, laden with furry spoils, and with a burden of thinking, too, about the white man's God and Book. They stretch their skinny hands over the light blaze and talk mysteriously, two or three of them, here and there. Now they take up the theme more freely in the tepee, and at length it comes into the high council of opinions and plans and action. They must know about this thing. Their dim hereafter needs lighting up. Perhaps it is the God and the Book of the pale-faces that make them great in their big canoes on the great waters of the setting sun. They must know more. It was gravely and anxiously settled that some of their number should go on the long trail to the rising of the sun to find the Book and bring back the light.

Two old braves were selected, one of them a sachem, for their wisdom and prudence, and well proved love for the tribe. Two young braves were added, for strength, and endurance, and daring, in any perils along the unknown path of many moons. In the silence of true heroism, that asks no trumpet at the opening, but only the crown of success at the close, the four passed off into the forest, and over the rivers, and out on the prairies. This was an improvement on the Macedonian call. They went themselves to get what they wanted.

What route did they take? Down Clark to Lewis River, and then up to Fort Hall, and so on to the Missouri? Or, avoiding the terrible Black-Feet of the Upper Plains, did they go down the Great Basin of Salt Lake, and strike the Santa Fé trail by the Gunnison region, and so to Bent's Fort on the Arkansas? No record of the route of the four Flat-Heads has found a place in literature.

We think of the hostile tribes through whose territory they went those thousand miles, traveling by night and resting by day; we note the many interviews they had with doubtful bands, and the counsel and courses they took from those whom they could trust. What little fires they kindled in secluded glens, sleeping afterward, while one kept watch as silently as the stars watched the four! Now they feasted on venison, or mountain sheep, or antelope; and now, too prudent to hunt, it was beaver or muskrat, no unsavory dish at a camp-fire, when one has for sauce a backwoods appetite.

If they were captives, and afterward escaped prisoners, no record tells of it. Perhaps, with a mystic confidence in the white man's God whom they were seeking, they avoided perils by daring them. They covered their track to foes, told their purpose to friends, made a light burden of their hardships, and kept their fears behind them, like true pilgrims of the Bunyan kind.

By whatever route of travel they journeyed, many moons came and went, we know not how many, till they arrived at St. Louis, the great tepee of white men. They wondered over the big lodges of wood, and brick, and stone; they marveled silently at the great fire-canoes, that went up and down the river without paddles; and the abundance of fine things on the streets and in the stores confused them. With very few words, and a step that no one heard, they glided up and down and in and out among streets and stores, and studied the whole. But in this world of new sights, and in a tumult of thoughts, their sacred errand was uppermost, and they must deliver it to one man.

Twenty-seven years before General William Clark had been over the mountains, and left his name on their river, and their old men had seen him or known of him. Born in Virginia, and emigrating at a tender age to Kentucky, he had much to do with Indians on "the dark and bloody ground," and just at the close of the century, while St. Louis was in Spanish dominions, he took up his abode in that city. He was associated with Captain Meriwether Lewis in the overland expedition to Oregon, and then became known, by reputation, to the Flat-Heads; the success of that daring survey was due much to his consummate knowledge of Indian character. After his return he was made brigadier-general of the Upper Louisiana, and was active and efficient in the Indian wars that harassed the western borders through the early years of the present century. He was territorial governor of Missouri till it became a state in 1821, from which time to his death, in 1838, he was Indian Superintendent with headquarters at St. Louis.

An incident will introduce the man and his times to us, and show what the early settlers in Ohio, Indiana, and Illinois had to encounter in laying the foundations of those three noble states. General Clark found himself, on one occasion, with few men and scanty supplies, in a post surrounded by warlike and haughty savages. They apparently knew his reduced condition and were disposed to cut him and his men off by a treacherous massacre. A council was called with the Indians in the fort, and, contrary to all usage and good intention, they came in fully armed, not only the leading ones, but the young and fiery braves. The General was in no condition to resent it. At the long council-table the insolent chief occupied the end opposite to Clark, and the whole air and manner of the savages made him and his few white men feel that they were doomed. The chief was silent and sullen, and at length drew from under his blanket a rattlesnake's skin stuffed with powder and ball, and threw it toward the General. It was a declaration of war, and every white man felt that he might any moment hear the war-whoop and see the brandished tomahawks. The Indians appeared to be only waiting for a signal from their chief to commence a butchery. General Clark had in his hand a kind of riding-stick with which he turned the snake's skin over and over, drawing it nearer to him. All was still as death, while they knew that their lives hung on daring. By and by he succeeded in coiling it around his whip-stick, when with a sudden motion he flirted it back to the haughty chief, and said with dignity and boldness: "If the Indians want war, they can have war."

The confidence and prompt acceptance of the challenge led the Indians to think that recruits were at hand to relieve their beleaguered victims, and they quietly withdrew from the council and from the fort. This incident was related to me three years after the General's death by the gentleman to whom he told it, and I think has never before been in print.

This was the man to whom the four Flat-Heads must open their business, as the great chief of the Missouris. Very likely the General thought they had come to talk of a war, or a treaty, or of lands, or of beaver. Their religious purpose did not much interest him, for they were only Indians, and beyond their furs and lands and wars they had never had much to win the attention of white men.

How long they were in St. Louis does not appear, only that they were there long enough for the two old men to die, and for one of the younger to contract diseases of which he died, on his return, at the mouth of the Yellowstone. They made known distinctly the fact that they had come their long journey to get the white man's Book, which would tell them of the white man's God and heaven.

In what was then a Roman Catholic city it was not easy to do this, and officers only were met. It has not been the policy or practice of that church to give the Bible to the people, whether Christian or pagan. They have not thought it wise or right. Probably no Christian enterprises in all the centuries have shown more self-sacrifice, heroism, foreseen suffering, and intense religious devotion than the laborers of that church, from 1520, to give its type of Christianity to the natives of North America. But it was oral, ceremonial, and pictorial. In the best of their judgment, and in the depths of their convictions, they did not think it best to reduce native tongues to written languages, and the Scriptures to the vernacular of any tribe. Survey three centuries, from the first Indian missions in Florida to the Gulf of St. Lawrence, around the Hudson Bay basin, and to the Pacific, and on either side of the wild mountain ranges, from the Arctic to Panama, it is doubtful whether the Romanists ever put into an Indian tongue, and through a tribe, an amount of Scripture equal to the shortest gospel.

We, of another branch of the church, honor the devotion, daring, and sacrifice, the expenditure of treasure and human life which they have lavished in their continental fields. We as deeply mourn the mistake that did not imbed Christianity in the language, and a young literature, for the poor Indians.

In that old Indian and papal city the poor Flat-Heads could not find "the Book." They were fed to feasting, they were provided with wigwam ground, they were blanketed and ornamented. They were armed and entertained cordially and abundantly. St. Louis must always have the palm for that kindness to the red men. Its traditions, earliest history, trade, growth, and some of its blood, run that way. But the heart that had come three thousand miles of toil and peril, to be filled with better ideas of God and of the long trail into the hereafter, could not be satisfied with all this.

Their mission was a failure. Sad it is that it has so commonly proved thus for the Indians where they have sought the highest good from the whites, while we have pressed the gospel successfully on pagan and even cannibal foreigners. They therefore prepared to go back to their dark mountain home, and bear to their tribe the burden of disappointment. Of course there must be a ceremonial leave-taking, and the council lodge was the house of the American Fur Company.

General Clark was then the great sachem of the whites, a true and generous friend of the Indians. He received the farewell address of the two surviving Flat-Heads. It requires no fancy of mine, but only memory, to sketch that audience room of furs and robes and the few hearers. As to the speech, it is apparently as hard for the American language as for the American people to do an Indian justice:—

"I came to you over a trail of many moons from the setting sun. You were the friend of my fathers who have all gone the long way. I came with one eye partly opened, for more light for my people, who sit in darkness. I go back with both eyes closed. How can I go back blind, to my blind people? I made my way to you with strong arms, through many enemies and strange lands, that I might carry back much to them. I go back with both arms broken and empty. The two fathers who came with us — the braves of many winters and wars — we leave asleep here by your great water and wigwam. They were tired in many moons, and their moccasins wore out. My people sent me to get the white man's Book of Heaven. You took me where you allow your women to dance, as we do not ours, and the Book was not there. You took me where they worship the Great Spirit with candles, and the Book was not there. You showed me the images of good spirits and pictures of the good land beyond, but the Book was not among them to tell us the way. I am going back the long, sad trail to my people of the dark land. You make my feet heavy with burdens of gifts, and my moccasins will grow old in carrying them, but the Book is not among them. When I tell my poor, blind people, after one more snow, in the big council, that I did not bring the Book, no word will be spoken by our old men or by our young braves. One by one they will rise up and go out in silence. My people will die in darkness, and they will go on the long path to the other hunting-grounds. No white man will go with them and no white man's Book, to make the way plain. I have no more words."

The grounds and rooms and furs of that scene are all fresh in my memory, and it does not require much of a fancy to see the group and hear the speeches and witness the sad and silent departure of the two remaining Flat-Head Indians. A steamer of the American Fur Company was just starting for the upper Missouri. This was the first "fire-canoe" that ever made the long trip of twenty-two hundred miles, past the Mandan and other tribes and villages, to the Company's post at the mouth of the Yellowstone. The two Indians took that steamer, and with them there went, also, George Catlin — the Indian historian, biographer, and painter, who in due time returned and went up to Pittsburg.

As we follow this incident history becomes romance. That speech, more impressive and sad than Logan's, because it takes hold of the world to come in its mournful refrain — "the Book was not there" — had a sympathetic hearer. A young clerk in the office witnessed the interview and noted its painful end. With some Christian sympathy for those benighted children of the mountains, he detailed an account of the affair to his friends at Pittsburg. When Catlin returned there they showed the letter to him, and proposed to publish it to the world in order to secure some missionary action in behalf of the Flat-Head tribe. Catlin replied that there must be a mistake as to the object of that Indian visit to St. Louis, and its failure, for the two Flat-Heads went up to the Yellowstone with him, and they said nothing of all this on the boat, so far as he heard. Let the publication of the letter be delayed till he could write to General Clark, and know the facts in the case. The reply from the General came at length : "It is true ; that was the only object of their visit and it failed." Then Catlin said : "Give the letter to the world."

In his "Indian Letters, Number Forty-Eight," Catlin thus speaks of this matter: "When I first heard the report of this extraordinary mission across the mountains, I could scarcely believe it ; but on consulting with General Clark I was fully convinced of the fact. . . . They had been told that our religion was better than theirs, and that they would all be lost if they did not embrace it." And afterward, in 1836, when the Rev. H. H. Spalding and wife were on their way to Oregon as missionaries, they met Mr. Catlin in Pittsburg, who detailed to them these incidents and many others. Especially he assured them that white women could not be carried over the mountains : " The hostile Indians, that hover about the convoy, would fight against any odds, to capture them."

It may here be added that Catlin enriched his Indian Gallery with the portraits of these two Indians. They are numbers two hundred and seven and two hundred and eight, in his collection. In form, features, and expression they are more attractive than most Indian portraits. They were of the Nez Percés branch of the Flat-Head tribe, but do not show the flattened head, because this band had abstained from that barbarous usage. They stand forth, in the pictures, in the rich robes and trappings which the friendly Sioux had bestowed, and they show, too, as originators in a custom of modern civilization, since their hair is so far "banged" as to cover one third of the forehead.

But though only one lived to return and he carried back a disappointment, the mission of the Four Flat-Head Indians to St. Louis was not a failure. That people, it is true, sat in the gray dawn of a possible day. But night shut in again for a time. The little captive Jewess overheard the sad story of her leprous master Naaman, and the outcome was his healing. What that clerk overheard between blanketed Indians and General Clark was a divine pivot. The poor Indians did not see it, nor the fur-trading white man, yet on it much Indian destiny and all of Oregon's turned. The result was one of the most romantic chapters in American History.

CHAPTER XIV.

"A QUART OF SEED WHEAT."

THE Americans struck Oregon just where the English failed, in the line of settlements and civilization. One carried in the single man and the other the family; one, his traps and snares, the other, his seed wheat, oats and potatoes; one counted his muskrat nests, and the other his hills of corn; one shot an Indian for killing a wild animal out of season, and the other paid bounty on the wolf and bear; one took his newspaper from the dog-mail, twenty-four or thirty-six months from date, and the other carried in the printing-press; one hunted and traded for what he could carry out of the country, the other planted and built for what he could leave in it for his children. In short, the English trader ran his birch and batteaux up the streams and around the lakes to bring out furs and peltries, while the American immigrant hauled in, with his rude wagon, the nineteenth century, and came back loaded with Oregon for the American Union.

It was the old European story over again. Spain, France, and Great Britain did not make plantations in America for the sake of America or for the colonists, but for chartered monopolies and the home governments. The colonists were as laborers on wages, or as hired agents who must make regular returns. So the *sic vos non vobis* of Virgil was the English Bucolic and Georgic of North America. By such a policy Great Britain lost her thirteen colonies, and afterward Oregon. Since the United States became a nation we have added, from what was under the Spanish flag, what would make Spain of to-day five times, and from French dominion what would equal France four and a half times. For the loss of so much realm in the New World they are indebted to their feudal system and chartered monopolies. The development of their possessions in this country was made an impossibility.

The Franco-Spanish Louisiana and the northern sections of New Spain felt the tendency imparted by the United States, and when the home governments held them back, as feudal retainers, they naturally gravitated toward the young Republic. In pursuit of the same policy England failed to take Oregon, since nothing runs the boundaries of sovereignty in a wild country like wagon wheels. The plough and fireside, hoe and bridge are more powerful than a corps of civil engineers in determining metes and bounds.

In watching the international battle, therefore, in which the prize is that magnificent Pacific section, we begin to see families and agriculture and a mixed trade taking the field, with here and there a schoolhouse and a church as permanent fortifications. It was in eastern blood from time primeval thus to push into new lands and keep at the front of a progressive race with the leading and crowning qualities of a family home.

Few men did more to shape New England than John Winthrop, the first governor of Massachusetts. While yet in England, and wishing to leave his country home for a residence in or near London, he wrote to his son, 1627, to find a house for him, saying: "I would be neere churche and some good schoole." After he arrived in America, in 1630, and till his death in 1649, he aimed thus to locate all New England families. His policy and life went to make the colonial law of Massachusetts in 1635: "It is agreed that hereafter noe dwelling howse shalbe builte above halfe a myle from the meeting-howse in any new plantacion, without leaue from the Court." The next year this law was extended to all the towns in the colony.

After serving in the old French war Rufus Putnam retired to his farm in New Braintree, in his native state, Massachusetts. After he had honorably aided his country through the perils of the Revolution, and had heard the suggestions of Washington, that the headlands of the Ohio must be guarded against the English, the Spanish, and the French, he proposed a colony for that remote region. The plan reserved thirty thousand and forty acres in each township for school and church interests. This Ohio Company early voted "that the Directors be requested to pay as early attention as possible to the education of youth, and the promotion of public worship among the first settlers." In his three months' trip out, the ox-cart and sled of Putnam carried that resolution, and other eastern notions, over the Alleghanies, and founded Marietta in 1788. The forces that have done so much to develop the magnificent delta between the Ohio and the Mississippi were in that cart. By and by, in our narrative, we shall come up with that cart again, beyond the Missouri, and on the headlands of the Columbia — another driver, but the same load. It will lead in the grand army of occupation, and the steel-trap brigades will retire.

The visit of the four Nez Percés to St. Louis was a

sharp criticism on the methods of the Romanists in planting Christianity in North America, and on the Hudson Bay Company in restraining civilization. Their failure to obtain "the Book" touched the heart of the land. The American Board of Commissioners for Foreign Missions, and the Methodist Board of Missions, at once took measures to send forward explorers and prepare the way for Christian missions in Oregon. The latter sent forward the Revs. Jason and Daniel Lee, and others. The Revs. Samuel Parker, and Marcus Whitman, M. D., under the appointment of the American Board, were to have gone at the same time, but being too late for the convoy of the American Fur Company, they went the next year. This was not only the introduction of Protestant missions into Oregon, but of civilization among the natives. Morning in the northwest dates from that time. The policy of utilizing the northern half of this continent for fur and peltry, after prevailing with marvelous exclusiveness, energy and severity for a century and a half, was finally broken.

In the seventeenth century two parallel columns of the English race began to move across the continent from east to west; one to perpetuate wilderness and propagate fur; the other to conquer the wilderness by civilization, and displace wild animals by human families. At our present time in this current record of events the invading force on the one side is about two thousand, and on the other twelve millions. The one was a close corporation, strong in the bands of a feudal monopoly; the other was one of those tidal waves of population, that, from time to time in the ages, have swept into a new country and made a nation. The one held territory — Rupert's Land — one half as large as all Europe, under warranty deed by Great Britain and in as absolute a fee simple as any one holds land in London or Boston; or, as Martin states it in his "Hudson Bay Territories," "as truly a rightful property, as is the land or houses of an Englishman's private estate." The charter of that Company had the same power, and made the same conveyance as the Massachusetts, or Connecticut, or Virginia charter. Moreover, the Company held on lease from the crown as much more territory between Rupert's Land and the Arctic and Pacific, for exclusive trade, occupation, and government.

The other advancing force, invading the wilderness, held a similar extent of territory and by similar charters, originally; and afterward in severalty in individual farms and town lots. The latter owners finally became the United States. As these two parallel columns approached Oregon, the question of prior and absolute right to go in and possess was inevitably raised. This question or issue was the right of the human race to occupation and ownership in a vacant country as against three thousand trappers and traders, for the increase of stock dividends.

Like the emigrant companies of earlier times that entered the "Holland Purchase," and "the Ohio," and the "Dark and Bloody Ground," those bands for Oregon went in with the purpose of carrying civilization and Christianity westward jointly. When the Rev. Mr. Spalding left Liberty, on the Missouri, for his long prairie and mountain trail, he took, with "the Book," "a quart of seed wheat." Our type of Christianity means farms and flour-mills, and factories and bridges, as well as school-houses and churches, and catechisms. We do not forget what hard, bloody, animal pagans our

Celtic and Anglo-Saxon ancestors were, when Christianity planted "a quart of seed wheat" in the British Islands, and Alfred gave them letters, and Bede portions of the Bible. Then began the English-speaking Christianity of to-day.

This compound of settlements and missions was a novelty in the realm of the Hudson Bay Company, as it was a surprise, and annoyance, and anxiety. Prior to this date, 1836, they had introduced some Christian ministrations, but only to a very limited extent. After American settlers and missionaries went in, the Company saw the need of doing something in the same line to hold the country. Years before, traders from the States had urged their way westward to the Salt Lake Basin, and Wyeth had founded Fort Hall on Snake or Lewis' River, and, indeed, so much trade had arisen in the mountains, that the American Rendezvous had become an annual trading-fair, on Green River, for parties both sides of the mountains. Small emigrant companies were making their way through, some to Northern California, and some to Oregon. It has always been the happy fortune of the United States to have a border population that was constantly uneasy to reach a farther front, wilder land, and harder life.

From the days of the Four Flat-Heads in St. Louis this class of population had been going west in small bodies from the Missouri, and through the mountains, prophetic of the future of Oregon, as first birds and flowers herald the spring. Many of their little companies had been turned back or scattered in the mountains or diverted to California by the men of the Hudson Bay Company, who presented all imaginable dangers, and discouragements, and impossibilities, to prevent them from opening to the States the knowledge of any pass or trail to Oregon.

Several of these companies had been thus turned back before Messrs. Whitman and Spalding appeared at Fort Hall with their wives, *en route* for Oregon. Seven emigrant trains that had reached that country were shrewdly enforced to leave it. Eleven fur companies had sought the trade of that country, but only the Hudson Bay Company survived. It had kept back and crowded out all others. Now the Methodist missionaries of the preceding year were followed by this company ; and that "quart of seed wheat," suggestive of a plough, and wife, and family, prophesied a Christian civilization for Oregon.

CHAPTER XV.

A BRIDAL TOUR OF THIRTY-FIVE HUNDRED MILES.

The exploring delegates of the American Board of Missions had designed to go over the mountains with the Lees in 1834, but they were detained till the next year. With the usual experience of dangers and rough incidents, common to the Indian country, these two men, Messrs. Whitman and Parker, arrived at the American Rendezvous on Green River, in the summer of 1835. Here they met the mountain men, and obtained interior views of the opening fields of the great and almost unknown northwest.

This meeting was of great importance to them, as they could here obtain much information from old traders and trappers concerning frontier and wild life. Here, too, they would have a broad introduction to the Indians, and could begin to study their proposed fields and people. Among these, singularly and happily, they met the Nez Percé Flat-Heads, whose Macedonian agents we have already met on the streets of St. Louis.

The two delegates, like the spies of Israel sent up from Kadesh, must have been burdened with the anxieties of their business. But being shrewd men, and practical, they soon comprehended the situation, and laid their plans. The Rev. Mr. Parker joined himself to the Nez Percés, and under their leading and protection, threaded his way to Walla Walla and Vancouver.

Studying his field for an instructive report to the Board which sent him, and enlarging his commission somewhat in the line of his tastes into scientific explorations, he remained in the valley of the Columbia till June, 1836, and then returned to the States by way of the Sandwich Islands.

The practical eye and straight sense of Dr. Whitman grasped at once his great life-work, and he returned that autumn to the States to report the field, procure his outfit, and go back to his labors. And as the delegates of Israel carried back the clusters of Eshcol, as evidences of the worth of the land they had explored, so Dr. Whitman took back with him two Nez Percé boys, as specimens of the people whom he would win to a Christian civilization.

Now there opens a chapter in American history, that for heroes and heroines, boldness of enterprise, plots, moral and physical daring, hardly has its equal in the brightest visions of fiction. The American Board saw their way clear to open a Christian mission in Oregon, but the highest prudence could not entrust this opening to less than two men, and they must take their wives with them.

At no point in this long international struggle for Oregon do the two policies, the English and the American, so radically diverge as at this point, where the successful policy takes on the honorable family type. It was traditional in the early policies of fur-trading England, and of France, and Spain, ordinarily in colonizing and civilizing the New World, to esteem lightly the institution of the family, and make but poor provisions for it.

Three persons, and no less, can carry agriculture, manufactures, trade, and civil government into a wilderness, and make it over into neighborhoods of good society; and those three are the husband, the wife, and the child. Only the honorable and honored marriage tie can hold that society from turning back into savage wilderness. Without the sacred alliance implied in those two noblest and strongest words in language, husband and wife, there is no civilization to man. These two wives whom we are about to take over the prairies and the mountains were not the first to enter Oregon, but they heralded the great coming immigration of family life, and it was a novelty on the northwest coast.

At just this point Spaniard, Frenchman, and Hudson Bay man made a vast mistake in taking possession in North America, and showed a vast weakness in holding and developing the possessions first taken. Their very idea of a colony had in it a radical and fatal defect. In the early peopling of Canada the colonists were traders, soldiers, priests, and nuns; and husbands and wives were the rare exception. To remedy this, single females were sent out afterward. Girls of the poorer classes were taken from the hospitals of Paris and Lyons. In 1665, one hundred were thus sent and married at once. Two years later one hundred and nine, mostly of a higher grade, were sent on request of officials in Canada, and a royal bonus was bestowed on officers who married them. La Motte received fifteen hundred livres for marrying in that country. The home government found it difficult to send over enough peasant girls, and many from the cities were of indifferent virtue. Yet, after full ships of them had arrived, not one would be without a husband at the end of two weeks. Some of the more notorious were reshipped to France. On arrival at Quebec and Montreal they were lodged in large houses, under matronly care, where the suitors visited and made their selections, much as servant girls are now secured.

Bounties were paid on early marriages, as for the young man under twenty and the girl under sixteen, twenty livres each, and sometimes the king's gift added a house and provisions for eight months. The father was punished who did not marry his sons and daughters at those early years, and a bachelor had little mercy shown him, for he was forbidden to hunt, fish, or trade with the Indians, or partake of Indian life. When the annual importation of girls was nearly due, government orders were issued that single men must be married within a fortnight of their arrival. "Mother Mary" informs us that "no sooner have the vessels arrived than the young men go to get wives, and, by reason of the great number, they are married off by thirties at a time."

The results were inevitable, from such an enforced condition of society. The family did not become the corner-stone of a prosperous civil state, and morals degenerated. In the absence of the real home, social vices seized the communities. Says one author: "At Three Rivers there are twenty-five houses, and liquor may be had at eighteen or twenty of them." One Jean Bourdon, a licensed innkeeper, "is required to establish himself on the great square of Quebec, close to the church, so that the parishioners may conveniently warm and refresh themselves between the services."[1]

A similar policy, with a similar and natural misfortune following, was adopted in colonizing Louisiana. In 1720, about six hundred immigrants arrived at Mobile, but many of the females were from the Hospital Géné-

[1] The *Old Régime* in Canada, Parkman, ch. 13. See, also, chs. 20, 21.

ral of Paris. This practice continued for years to the great detriment of the province. After a foolish experiment the king forbade the exportation of convicts as colonists, but continued to send girls of very mixed qualities. At the same time many poor and virtuous women were sent to Louisiana, where they founded some of the best families of the state. But this method of founding the family, under government order, without regard to affinities and choices, left that magnificent province quite in a state of nature from the days of De Soto to its annexation to the United States. Spanish and French were alike in this theory and practice of colonization, and hence failed to hold and develop their possessions in North America.

Even the English made similar mistakes and failures. When Florida belonged to Great Britain Lord Rolle, in 1764, attempted a colony on the St. John's River, "to which he transported nearly three hundred miserable females, who were picked up in the purlieus of London." Of course his Charlotia was a failure. In the Virginia colony, quite early, a wife was to be had at the cost of importation, varying from one hundred and twenty to two hundred and fifty pounds of tobacco. Yet such were maids of virtuous education and habit.

But this apparent yet not real wandering which we have indulged must be turned again to our Oregon. As I have shown all along, the Hudson Bay Company introduced into their possessions, as officers and servants, almost uniformly single men, and young men, too. It is simple history, therefore, and should be no matter of surprise, when Martin, the friendly historian of the Company, says: "A large proportion of the Company's servants, and, with very few exceptions, the officers, are united to native women." And this other statement he adds naturally, and it should come without surprise. At Vancouver, and he writes this as late as 1849, "the residents mess at several tables; one for the chief factor and his clerks; one for their wives, it being against the regulations of the Company for their officers and their wives to take their meals together." With squaw wives and half-breed children it might not be agreeable, but what is to be said of the civilization, nearly two centuries old, which interdicts the family table from Hudson Bay to the Pacific Ocean? The two brides whom we are following to the Columbia are the type of another social order and will introduce another state of society.

Now and then one ordered a wife from his native land, as already stated, and the books of the Hudson Bay Company show that the order was honored, by the receipt entered: "Received, one wife in good condition." But this was an imported luxury which few could enjoy. As a general result the increase of population was half-breed; European civilization went down towards the Indian type of life in North America, meeting half way, more or less, in the wigwam and shanty; the elevating, refining, ennobling influence of woman, which makes the larger part of the true home, was wanting, and society, in the Hudson Bay country, became a dubious hyphen between the savage and the civilized. The arrival of those missionary families, as the forerunners of the ordinary immigration from the States, foretold a new era on the north-west coast. They turned a tide that had had an Arctic course for almost two centuries.

> "Yon stream, whose courses run,
>   Turned by a pebble's edge,
> Is Athabasca, rolling toward the sun,
>   Through the cleft mountain-ledge.

> The slender rill had strayed,
> But for the slanting stone,
> To evening's ocean, with the tangled braid
> Of foam-flecked Oregon."

The betrothed of Dr. Whitman consented to the arduous mission, while more than a score of devoted men declined the howling wilderness and savage inhabitants. They preferred more inviting mission fields and easier work beyond the sea. It was a long search to find a man who was willing

> "To lose himself in the continuous woods
> Where rolls the Oregon, and hears no sound
> Save his own dashings."

Those prairie trails and mountain passes were strewn with the wrecks of emigrant trains and the bones of rival traders and trappers. Many Indians there had been so outraged by the whites that a white face was the signal for revenge. The wanton robbery or murder of unoffending natives had already cost the life of many innocent white men, and unavenged wrongs were still waiting for their chance for recompense.

Dr. Whitman deferred his marriage, and continued the search into the early spring of 1836, for an associate in his Oregon work. At length he struck the track of his man, and found himself giving chase to a hybrid vehicle, between wagon and sleigh — no uncommon carriage in the backwoods, and mechanical cousin to Wyeth's amphibium — which was cutting through the crispy and crusty snows of western New York. It carried the Rev. H. H. Spalding and his fresh bride, on their way as missionaries to the Osage Indians, then holding a reservation in that section.

The American Board had put Dr. Whitman in pursuit of this couple. He overhauled them there on the winter highway, and sent forward a hailing call that they were wanted for Oregon. Question and answer between the two carriages soon summed up the case: The journey might require the summers of two years; they could have the convoy of the American Fur Company to the "divide;" the Nez Percés, their future parishioners, would meet them as escort for the remainder of the journey; the food would be buffalo, venison, and other game meats; the conveyance would be the saddle alternating with the feet; the rivers they would swim on horseback; and their housing would be tents, blankets, and stars.

Mr. Spalding said to his wife, recently from a bed of lingering sickness, "It is not your duty to go; your health forbids, but it shall be left to you after we have prayed together." Thus talking back and forth between the sleighs, that were inverted wagons, and with each other, they entered the little backwoods village of Howard and drew rein before the small tavern. They took counsel together from on high, when the young bride was left alone for her conclusion. Ten minutes and a cheerful face brought the answer: "I have made up my mind for Oregon."

At once her husband pleaded her weak state — the fatigues and privations of so long a journey — three thousand miles at least — and two thousand of it in saddle and canoe and on foot — the Indians frantic for captives and revenge — distance from the old home and a white man's neighborhood — and all that and all that. The answer was ready; and probably man or woman never came nearer, in giving it, to the spirit of its author: "What mean ye to weep and to break mine heart? For I am ready not to be bound only but also to die on the Rocky Mountains for the name of the Lord Jesus."

When detailing these incidents thirty-four years afterward Mr. Spalding said, with charming simplicity: "Then I had to come to it. I did not know anything." We admire the heroism rather than the reasoning of the feeble woman; but ardor not unfrequently does more than logic in producing noble results.

It was all settled then at the little village of Howard. Dr. Whitman sent a messenger to his betrothed to be ready for a hasty wedding and a long bridal tour. He started off for his two Nez Percé boys. The wedding came soon; there were "no cards," and the bride would "receive" on the Columbia.

What a bridal tour for the two young wives! Travel on the frontier, or even out west, was not what it is to-day. Only six years before the Baltimore and Ohio railroad — the first for passengers in North America — had had an august opening of fifteen miles on strap-rail and with horse power. It even tried to run its cars by sail! Not twelve months before the Boston and Lowell, Boston and Worcester, and Boston and Providence railroads had opened. Only three years before the first steamer had entered Chicago, and it must be fifteen yet before the first locomotive can lead in a passenger train.

How young and small Cincinnati was when they passed it! The first white born citizen of that city, William Moody, was there to welcome them, only forty-five years of age. At Pittsburg Catlin warned the gentlemen against the presumption of attempting to take women over the plains, and through the mountains, and the tragic fate of one company was detailed, where all the men were murdered by the Indians that the one woman might be carried into a horrid and unreported captivity. Advice to turn back, warnings, prayers, and benedictions followed them from city to city, till they rounded to at the semi-American town of St. Louis, and, mid a jargon of languages, and mixture of costumes, and miscellany of merchandize on the levee, they were taken by the hand and welcomed to hospitable homes. The missionary party now consisted of five, Messrs. Spalding and Whitman, with their wives, and W. H. Gray, agent for the proposed mission.

The American Fur Company was fitting out its annual expedition up the Missouri, and to the mountains, but to admit women as parties in the expedition was a questionable novelty. However, the Doctor on his return trip the preceding year with this Company had so acted the good Samaritan when the cholera struck them, that they could not now refuse. They therefore promised to take the missionary party under convoy when they should leave Council Bluffs.

Four years before the two disheartened Nez Percés had left those same streets with heavy hearts for their dark land and benighted people, but now light and hope followed them up the river. The party pressed on in advance of the fur men, but by vexatious delays in the purchase and driving of stock a part of the way, and by the failure of the boat to take on board the Doctor and ladies at Liberty Landing, they found themselves six days behind at Council Bluffs. The convoy had so much the start out on the plains.

It was a hard chase to gain all this, and the serio-comic incidents of such a trip, in an inexperienced company, seemed inclined to concentrate on the clergyman. Inanimate nature, circumstances, "things," sometimes appear to assume a personality and take a will to make some selected one the object or butt of their rude and comic jests and practical jokes. Mr. Spalding was kicked by a mule, shaken by the ague, stripped by a tornado, not only of his tent but his blankets, and crowded off the ferryboat by an awkward, uncivilized frontier cow, to which he made a caudal attachment as a life preserver. While he had these freaks of nature played off on him, he entertained some doubts of overtaking the convoy, and had questions about a return. Between these serial mishaps and discouragements his feeble wife would bring him to himself by the remark: "I have started for the Rocky Mountains and I expect to go there."

Late in May, 1836, and at two o'clock in the morning, they came to the Loup Fork of the Platte, and were cheered to hear their signal gun answered from the opposite bank. They had almost won the chase. The convoy started off early, but left a man to show them over the river, and Mr. Spalding, lively with the memory of the incidents, says : " Late that night we missionaries filed into their camp, and took the place reserved for us, two messes *west* of the Captain's tent, and so we won by two lengths."

The caravan was now large, consisting of about two hundred persons, and six hundred animals. They marched and encamped with military carefulness. At night the stock were placed in the centre of the encampment; enclosing them were the tents and wagons ; and encircling all a close cordon of sentinels. All this was necessary because of the Indians, more or less hostile, always thieving, and seldom far from the line of march.

The fur men were exceedingly kind to the ladies. A sense of honor and a pride that they were thus entrusted with them, and withal the homage that manhood always pays to the true woman, led them to show favors and courtesies. The choice pieces of the game went to them, and their comfort and ease were a kind of pilot to the Company. No man, unless he be a sailor, carries a warmer heart and stronger arm for those who need him, and honorably trust him, than these rough mountain men.

Four of the party had it as their business to bring into camp each night four mule-loads of wild meat. Yet sometimes there was a failure, as there was of water, or sunshine. Of course the journey had its perpetual variations. There was the scenery of prairie, timber, and stream, the buffalo, antelope, and coyote, and a new style of Indian with a new trick at stealing. More ravines to be filled, a more ugly ford, and more upsets and broken wagons varied the monotony some days. Sometimes the tempest of wind and rain and thunder would come before night, which was a pleasing variation. Yet as the days wore by, measuring the distance between them and loved ones, these relieving changes dropped into the groove of sameness. Mental as well as physical weariness came over them, and they endured the passive state of being acted upon rather than acting — a painful doom to an energetic nature.

June sixth they were at Laramie, but how their nomad Arab-wandering contrasts with the activity and industries in that Platte valley to-day! On the fourth of July they entered the famous South Pass, where the Rocky and Wind-river Mountains almost come together, yet leave an opening for human tides to flow to and fro. Here, on a high plateau, the head springs of the South Platte, the Yellowstone, and the Columbia show their silver threads. This is the grand "divide" of the waters of the Continent, and here the Atlantic and Pacific keep a perpetual agency and watch that each may take its own waters in sight of the other. Sometimes it is a by-play of the jaded travelers, while resting here for a day or two, to rob each ocean by carrying a cup of the young river half a mile and pouring it into the fountain stream of the other.

It is a little amusing to trace through this pass the routes of distinguished explorers, as "Frémont, 1842," "Frémont, 1843," "Stanbury, 1849." It may give information and also divide honors with the Pathfinder to add: "Mesdames Whitman and Spalding, 1836." A United States corps of engineers discovering a pass in the Rocky Mountains six years after two women had gone through!

In the morning of that day Mrs. Spalding was quite ill, fainted, and thought she was near the end of her life journey. They lifted her tenderly from the saddle, and gave her what repose and comfort they could on robes and blankets. The long tour, with its always varying but never ceasing fatigues, had steadily increased the feebleness with which she left her New York home, and her end seemed nigh. Rallying her remaining strength, yet showing no loss of her womanly fortitude and heroism, she said: "Do not put me on that horse again. Leave me here, and save yourselves for the great work. Tell mother I am glad I came."

That column of caravan life marched on, as it does everywhere in this world, while the feeble fall out of rank and a few linger long enough to care for the dying. When, however, the company made their usual camp at evening Mrs. Spalding was brought in much revived. Was it because they gave her to drink of the brook trickling by, whose waters were to run through her great parish to the Pacific?

When they were under way again, and had advanced far enough to be on the Pacific slope of the country, twenty-five hundred miles from home, the missionary party stopped and dismounted. Then, spreading their blankets and lifting the American flag, they all kneeled around the Book, and, with prayer and praise, took possession of the western side of the continent for Christ and the Church.

There are few scenes in American records that surpass this one for historic grandeur. For a century and a half those western sections of the New World had been overrun by Europeans who left but faint traces of Christianity and civilization. The abused, plundered, and neglected natives had brought their request for light and the Book three thousand miles to the nearest Christian city, only to be disappointed. This little band proposed to give the land to a Christian civilization from sea to sea. They have now come the weary way to the western half of it. Historic figures five of them, they kneel to give half a continent to the better times of "peace on earth, and good will toward men." The two Nez Percé boys stand by, with eyes on the five, and the flag, and the Book. That act went far toward the settlement of the Oregon question, and in giving to the United States six thousand miles of Pacific coast.

We have other grand historic scenes on canvas. Balboa at Panama, taking possession of the Pacific and all its lands for the Crown of Spain; the landing of the Pilgrims; Washington assuming command of the American army; Washington surrendering that power after the Republic was established; the First Prayer in Congress, and many other noble memorials. But in compass of background and foreground; the two halves of the continent; the parting rivers for the two oceans; the moral exigency suggested by the two Indian figures; the rounding out of the Republic on the sunset side, as it came in the consequences; the kneeling men and women around the Book, with the American flag floating over them, — the scene is worthy of any panel in the Rotunda at Washington.

How well the picture harmonizes with that passage in Washington's first inaugural address: "No people can be bound to acknowledge and adore the invisible hand which conducts the affairs of men more than the people of the United States. Every step by which they have advanced to the character of an independent nation seems to have been distinguished by some token of Providential agency."

A few more stages of weary travel, and our little company, who are to do so much in adjusting the Oregon difficulties and enlarging the American Union, arrived at the great mountain rendezvous of trappers and traders, and so to the end of protection under convoy. They tarried here ten days to recruit and prepare for their separate march to the Columbia. Let us look in on the grand encampment nestled among magnificent mountains, and sketch a few scenes that disappeared with the past generation, and that in this rush of frontier life are fast receding into antiquarian background. Long since such gatherings ceased to be realities.

This annual fair of mountain men and Indians was held midway between South Pass and Fort Hall. The encampment was on the banks of Green River, a head stream of the Colorado, whose cold waters begin their long journey of twelve hundred miles by trickling down the snowy cañons of Frémont's Peak, and there rush by our motley multitude to frolic madly in the Black Cañon, five hundred miles from its mouth in the Gulf of California. Probably this is the wildest scene in the world. For twenty-five miles the river plunges down a rocky defile between precipice banks, from a thousand to fifteen hundred feet high, leaving the water unapproachable and only to be looked down upon from their giddy heights. The traders gathered here, American and English, bringing all the comforts and finery that the red man so covets, while Indian tribes, by their representatives, come in from the prairies this side the mountains, and over the rocky ranges, beyond the Great Basin, laden with the fur spoils of a year. It was their annual holiday, too, in which to break the dull sameness of their life.

The first dinner of our friends there is worthy of a record. July 20, 1836, the table is spread. It is a shaky oilcloth on the grass; the plates, tin when at Council Bluffs, now battered flakes of sheet iron; cups the same, but not so flat; knives of the butcher species; forks, sticks of local option and cut; venison, and buffalo, and mountain sheep, broiled or roasted; seasoning, some salt, some ashes, and some sand. For second course a scant service of mountain-made bread, some tea and a very little sugar. Two Indian chiefs are at the board, that is, the oilcloth, and an uncounted number of Indian waiters, — for remnants. The grounds are covered by fifteen hundred people, of mixed blood, language and costume; about one hundred of these are American traders and trappers; fifty are French of the Canadian type, and twenty citizens, including the mission party. The rest are Indians.

At the International Indian Fair at Mus-ko-gee, in

1880, I found more Indians, about two thousand, but much less Indian life, with about five hundred bronzed whites intermixed. Civil and savage life meet here to exchange goods. Similar gatherings are still observed as great holidays.

The goods of the American Fur Company are in log-pens, covered with canvas, poles, or brush, on a turf floor. The equipage of the campaign is dumped near the store-cabin, being pack-saddles and the miscellaneous whatnots of wilderness life; encircling those are the white camps, and outside of all the posted guards. Between the trading-hut and the river mules and horses are made safe against stampedes and petty thefts by a double row of tents. Adjoining on the west are the fires and screens of the trappers and hunters; and for three miles farther a miscellany of wigwams are spread along, continuous in tribal sections, hugging Horse Creek above the junction with Green River.

The red men, and the mountain men too, were not unmindful of courtesy to their white lady visitors, and so prepared an entertainment. It was an Indian tournament, quite enjoyable after it had been frightful. Six hundred Indians, mounted, plumed, painted, and decked with all the insignia of war, and with all the whooping and yelling and noise-making that they only know how to produce, with horses frantic and plunging, came rushing through the rendezvous. One needs a little Indian blood in order to be nerveless on such an occasion, even when he knows what is coming. As the parade was partly to entertain and partly to gain a view of the first two white women who had dared to enter the mountains, the line of rushing was laid by their tents. They, therefore, had all the benefit of position at the very front.

But there were others to gaze on those women. Hardy Rocky Mountain trappers, who had not seen white women for twenty-five years, were carried back by the sight to the days of a mother and sister and schoolmates, and a cottage home of childhood; and those rough yet strong-hearted men wept like children. Their manhood came back to them when they saw a gown; and all their civilization concentrated in the awkward doffing of a greasy cap, when Mrs. Whitman or Mrs. Spalding walked by. Years afterward one of these men said: " From that day when I took again the hand of a civilized woman I was a better man." It would be difficult to find a tribute to woman more hearty and noble than that. The grand element that the Hudson Bay Company had so carefully kept back, while they were preserving wilderness and propagating beaver, was on the way to add the northwest to Christendom.

The joy of the missionaries was much increased by meeting here a large delegation of the Nez Percés. When Dr. Whitman turned back from this place to the States in the preceding autumn, it was exceedingly gratifying to this tribe to be invited to meet the Doctor and his company here at this time. They were there on the arrival, and the pleasure of the meeting was mutual. The gratitude and gladness of the poor natives was quite demonstrative, and specially towards the women. They almost monopolized the ladies as the subjects of their peculiar care. Ordinary food, and such delicacies as the mountains afforded, personal services, their rude but tender and hearty kindnesses — all this was without limit.

The ten days soon ran by, letters were written for the States, goods reduced and repacked, first lessons in

Indian companionship well conned, a Hudson Bay party engaged as an escort, and finally the pioneer brigade of civilization moved on westward. They reached the English Fort Hall, run the gauntlet of its crafty impediments — of which more by and by — reduced luggage again and pressed on. In a few days they were at a log pole, and brush enclosure, called Fort Boisé. Here the Doctor was compelled by Hudson Bay Company advice, not highway difficulties, to leave his wagon.

By and by, after the incidents of ferries, and fords, mountain sides and cañons, overplus and half rations, the party descended the Blue Mountains, and looked into the valley of the long-sought Columbia. Mount Hood, the tallest sentinel of the Cascade range, stood high up, one hundred and fifty miles away, to give them welcome.

On the second of September, 1836, and four months from the Missouri, and thirty-five hundred miles of weary travel from their childhood home and marriage group, the open, cordial gates of Fort Walla Walla received them. The bridal tour was ended, and the acquisition of Oregon begun.

CHAPTER XVI.

WHITMAN'S "OLD WAGON."

The Oregon question finally turned on wheels. Even Webster and Ashburton, the high contracting parties to settle the international boundary on the north from ocean to ocean, could carry the line of division no farther west than the Rocky Mountains. Then diplomacy, civil engineering, and the two nations — all concerned — had to wait for the wagons. The taking of one through, overland, to the Columbia, by Dr. Whitman, was the most important act in all preliminaries in the settlement of the Oregon controversy.

At first only two parties took a proper view of a wagon for Oregon — Marcus Whitman and the Hudson Bay Company. In 1836, when the wagon was at Fort Hall and Fort Boisé with its two women occupants, it suggested to the Company the family and a civilized home and permanent settlement in Oregon, and a highway from the Missouri to that settlement which others could follow. The Company therefore determined to turn the wagon back, or divert it to California, or stop it absolutely. Dr. Whitman took the same view of the wagon, and therefore concluded to take it through to Oregon. But we must go back a little in the narrative.

When the fur-traders and the mission party arrived at Fort Laramie, as we have seen, it was assumed, as a matter of course, that all wagons and carts would, as usual, be abandoned, as it was thought impracticable to proceed farther with them. The Doctor had been brought up where there is much natural antagonism between wheels and mountains, and he had been educated to overcome it. He was not, therefore, disposed to give up to the Rocky Mountains. He objected to the abandonment of the wagons.

He had purchased two at Liberty, on the Missouri, and now it seemed very desirable, on account of the ladies, to take along at least one of them. There was much discussion over it between the missionaries and the traders, and finally the latter consented to make the experiment, and at the same time added one of their carts to the mission wagon. Dr. Whitman was put in charge of the carriages, and the first night out from Fort Laramie he came into camp late, warm, puffing, and cheery too, for he had had only one upset with the wagon and two with the cart. So affairs progressed, with various accidents and incidents to wagon and cart, now a capsize and now a repair, now a man and now a mule objecting and with equal Roman firmness, till they arrived at the rendezvous or great fair grounds.

When they put out from the rendezvous, all parties and persons, except the Flat-Heads, advised them to leave the wagon. However, after camp was made the Doctor came in, and to the general surprise, with his four-wheeled companion. "He was totally alone," says Gray, the historian, one of his company, "in his determination to get his old wagon through to the waters of the Columbia, and to the mission station that might be established, no one knew where."

There is no other sound like that made by a stout-loaded wagon on a rough road; and now after six thousand years or so of stillness in those wild regions, those sounds woke the echoes of the mountains. Perhaps out of respect to the pre-historic Americans we ought to double that six thousand. We can hear that Whitman wagon now, in our mental ear, and it will help the hearing if one will pronounce aloud the name that the Indians gave to the "old wagon." They put into jerky syllables the sounds it made as it rose and fell and stopped in the soft grass and among the rocks, and called it: *chick-chick-shani-le-kai-kash.*

On the caravan moved, traders and preacher, and women, and Indian, mules, pack-saddles, and ponies; the wagon far in the rear, now saying, on the grass land, *chick-chick*, and now among the rocks, *kai-kash*. Mr. Gray says, in his "History of Oregon": "It is due to Dr. Whitman to say, notwithstanding this was the most difficult route we had to travel, yet he persevered with his old wagon without any particular assistance. From Soda Springs to Fort Hall his labor was immense, yet he overcame every difficulty, and brought it safe through. I have thrice since traveled the same route, and I confess I cannot see how he did it."

Arrived at Fort Hall, about one hundred miles north of Salt Lake, all baggage and luggage were reduced as much as possible and repacked. Here all parties, mission and Hudson Bay and the Post men too, combined to say that the wagon could be hauled no farther. The terrible cañons, and bottomless creeks in the Snake Plains, made it impossible. But the iron Doctor was immovable. Then they said that he must at least take it apart and pack it, if it went on. Finally, the indomitable man made a compromise, converted the wagon into a cart, loaded in the duplicate wheels and axletree, and started again on wheels for the Columbia.

True, when they came to the Snake River, both the cart and its driver had to do some swimming, but they both came out on the west bank, and so much nearer to Oregon. So they entered Fort Boisé, two miles below the old Boisé City. This was so rude an inclosure that it would hardly pass for a cattle pen or mule corral. Here the cart took on a very serious look and so did every man when he looked at it. The expressions of opinion as to its farther advance became more decided, and some of them tersely brief, and to missionary ears more inelegant than to mountaineers. The escort of Hudson Bay men had stopped at Fort Hall, and all but the Doctor felt the need of moving on in a light and compact and very defensible order. It was again suggested to take it apart, and pack it through, if the mules carrying it would not slide from the precipices which they would have to scale and descend. Finally another compromise was effected. The wagon should be left at Fort Boisé, till some one could come back and take it on to the established mission. This was done and judgments harmonized, and soon after "the old wagon" went through, the first to pass the plains and the mountain so far towards Oregon.

Thus the irrepressible energy of this man pioneered for a carriage way to Oregon in 1836. The year before the first house had been built in San Francisco, steam cars had run out from Boston toward Lowell and Worcester and Providence, and this year twelve hundred and seventy-three miles of rail had been laid in the country, and the whistle and the rattle of locomotives were full of the prophecy of the 104,813 miles of it that we had at the close of 1881. So the *chick-chick-shani-le-kai-kash* of the Doctor was not one of the minor prophets.

This movement of the nation westward on wheels is an interesting study. One of the earliest items in it may be found in the Records of the City of Newton, Massachusetts, for the year 1687. "John Ward and Noah Wiswall were joined to our selectmen to treat with the selectmen of Cambridge to lay out a highway from our meeting-house to the Falls." I cannot trace a current tradition to any other board of highway commissioners, which says, that being instructed to lay out a highway into the wilderness, they in due time reported: "That they had laid out said highway to a bluff in the wilderness, on the Charles River, between its upper and lower Falls in Newton, and in the judgment of the commissioners that point was as far westward as any public road would ever be needed." This bluff was about ten miles "out west" from the Boston meeting-house! However, the "western fever" so prevailed that an extension of the public road more than ten miles from Boston was demanded, for in the Records of the Great and General Court of Massachusetts for 1683 we find this entry:—

"Whereas the way to Kenecticut now vsed being very hazardous to travellers by reason of one deepe riuer that is passed fower or fiue times ouer, which may be avoyded, as is conceived, by a better and nearer way, it is referred to Major Pynchon in order ye sajd way be lajd out and well marked. He having hired two Indians to guide him in the way, and contracted wth them for fiuty shillings, it is ordered that the Treasurer of the County pay the same in country pay towards the effecting the worke."

One century and one year after the Newton survey, Rufus Putnam started, and, with ox-cart and sled, in a three months' journey went farther west. Now we hear "the old wagon" of Marcus Whitman rattling along among the head streams of the Columbia. This remarkable and now historic vehicle, that had been the centre of so many doubts and hard sayings and anxieties, as a moving treasury coveted by Indians, and the subject of so many upsets and unneeded baths, and that had been developed inversely and degradingly into a cart, finally and later came out, all right, on the lower Columbia, at Fort Walla Walla. When the company arrived there in advance of "the old wagon" they had been out over four months from the Missouri at Liberty Landing, having traveled about twenty-two hundred and fifty miles. They had made an average of more than twenty-five miles a day, which was a good rate for a caravan, since the average of a Roman army was sixteen miles.

When I resided in St. Louis, the old family carriage of General Clark, the first that ever crossed the Mississippi, was turned off at auction for five dollars. Probably to-day its remains rest in some spot as obscure and covered over by drift in the stream of time as the grave of De Soto in the lower Mississippi. It would be a rare antiquity and treasure to head a procession celebrating the first or second centennial of its *L' Année du Coup*. But "the old wagon" of Dr. Whitman would now be a rarer treasure and relic. It carried more national destiny than the stately coach of the General. Very pleasant historical coincidences associate these two men and the two carriages. In 1804 the General, then Lieutenant, went over to view the newly purchased Oregon, and took the first look at the Pacific that an American citizen ever had of it from American soil. Thirty-two years afterward the Doctor followed with his wagon on the trail of the General. It would be difficult to find two single acts in the lives of two men which have so marked American history.

The work was done substantially. The wagon and the two brides, Mrs. Whitman and Mrs. Spalding, had won Oregon. The first wheels had marked the prairie, and brushed the sage, and grazed the rocks, and cut the river banks all the way from the Missouri to the Columbia. How many ten thousands have since been on that trail with their long lines of white canvas-topped teams! The first white women had crossed the continent, and not only witnessed but achieved the victory. In our great game of two nations, Oregon is already practically won. In going through, Whitman's wagon had demonstrated that women and children and household goods — the family — could be carried over the plains and mountains to Oregon. If so, the United States wanted Oregon, and afterward two hundred wagons went over and took possession of it.

CHAPTER XVII.

ANXIETY AND STRATEGY OF THE HUDSON BAY COMPANY.

In the second year following this first party a company of missionaries passed Fort Hall, with wives, nine persons in all, exclusive of the assistants. Impediments, perils, and Indians do not seem to have been put before their fancies there at that fur-traders' Gibraltar, for they had no carriages. They had acted on the already well established impressions in the east, that carriages could not travel to Oregon. In 1839 a similar company went through in the same way, without wagons, and so far as appears, without warnings and intimidations.

"In 1840 three missionary ladies from New York, Mrs. Smith, Clark, and Littlejohn, and their husbands, and the first emigrant lady, Mrs. Walker and her husband crossed the mountains and brought their wagons. But on reaching Fort Hall they were compelled to abandon their wagons by the representations of the Hudson Bay Company, who declared that wagons never had passed, and could not pass through the Snake country and the Blue Mountains to the Columbia." The Rev. Mr. Spalding, the companion of Dr. Whitman, tells us this, and adds that Mr. and Mrs. Walker left Oregon for California in 1841, and that she was the first American lady to settle in that territory.

In 1841 several emigrant families reached Fort Hall

with their teams, and, like the most of their predecessors, they were shaken from their purpose and abandoned wheels. During this period of struggle to stay the incoming tide, the Company offered to sell saddles to those who would abandon their carriages. They also were willing to furnish supplies, as flour, to General Palmer, at twenty cents a pound, but they were quite unwilling to receive, in payment, anything but money and cattle. Four cows or two yoke of oxen they considered as only a moderate price for one hundred pounds of flour.

"In 1842 considerable emigration moved forward with ox-teams and wagons, but on reaching Fort Hall the same story was told them, and the teams were sacrificed, and the emigrant families reached Dr. Whitman's station late in the fall, in very destitute circumstances."

The journal of General Palmer furnishes a good summary of the strategy of the Hudson Bay Company, and of their temporary 'success.

"While we remained at this place great efforts were made to induce the immigration to pursue the route to California. The most extravagant tales were related respecting the dangers awaiting a trip to Oregon, and the difficulties and trials to be surmounted. The perils of the way were so magnified as to make us suppose the journey to Oregon almost impossible. For instance, the two crossings of Snake River, and the crossing of the Columbia, and other smaller streams, were represented as being attended with great dangers. Also that no company heretofore attempting the passage of those streams succeeded, but with loss of men, from the violence and rapidity of the currents, as also that they had never succeeded in getting more than fifteen or twenty head of cattle into the Wallamette Valley."

"In addition to the above it was asserted that three or four tribes of Indians in the middle regions had combined for the purpose of preventing our passage through their country. In case we escaped destruction at the hands of the savages, a more fearful enemy — famine — would attend our march, as the distance was so great that winter would overtake us before reaching the Cascade Mountains. On the other hand, as an inducement to pursue the California route, we were informed of the shortness of the route, when compared with that to Oregon, as also of the many other superior advantages it possessed."

After the breach was fairly made through the mountains, and the first low waves of the coming eastern tide were heard and then felt —

> "The first low wash of waves where soon
> Shall roll a human sea " —

the Company placed men at their posts all along the Whitman trail to misrepresent facts, alarm the immigrants, delude them, turn them to California, or deprive them of their teams.

In 1842 immigrants to the number of one hundred and thirty-seven, men, women, and children, secular and missionary, had run the gauntlet of the traders, and escaped the financial steel-traps of a monarch monopoly all along the path. But they had been forced, by alarms and dangers made to order, to leave their wagons behind. This number was made up of twenty-one Protestant ministers, three Roman Catholic, fifteen church members, thirty-four white women, thirty-two white children, and thirty-five American settlers, twenty-five of whom had native wives.

Meanwhile, by the published journals of travelers in

the regions of the Company, by English Review articles, and carefully arranged newspaper editorials and correspondence in the United States, and by adroit deposit of material in the departments of State and War at Washington, the impression was made popular and deep in the American mind, that a comfortable overland transit for emigrants to Oregon was out of the question.

The managers of the Hudson Bay Company were men of rare ability, and they succeeded in putting their case *ex parte* and most successfully before the United States. What the " Edinburgh Review " said of them in 1843 was already proving to be eminently true. "They are chieflly Scotsmen, and a greater proportion of shrewdness, daring, and commercial activity is probably not to be found in the same number of heads in the world."

Earlier than most men probably they saw the weakness of the absolute claims of either government to Oregon on the ground of discovery or treaty or purchase, or of wide and early occupation. They probably foresaw, but too late, that the Oregon question would be disposed of by settlers. They began, therefore, early, and from points distant and wide asunder, to manufacture evidence and manipulate public opinion, that Oregon could not be reached by an immigrant wagon. Interested witnesses filed the evidence into fair volumes and international quarterlies, and so made up the case for the trial, which they saw was hastening. The United States were thus provided with testimony against their own interests and rights, and its power was imperceptible, and wide, and deep, to hold back immigration. Probably thousands were thus kept east of the mountains. Among those who joined the large caravan of Dr. Whitman in 1843 was a family by the name of Zachrey, from Texas, one of whom writes, twenty-five years later: "We had been told that wagons could not be taken beyond Fort Hall. But in this pamphlet the Doctor assured his countrymen that wagons could be taken through from Fort Hall to the Columbia River and to the Dalles, and from thence, by boats, to the Willamette — that himself and missionary party had taken their families through to the Columbia six years before. It was this assurance of the missionary that induced my father and several of his neighbors to sell out and start at once for this country." Mr. Zachrey speaks not only from the distant point of Texas, but probably for very many who would have been immigrants on the Oregon trail.

The Hudson Bay Company felt the emergency, and had foreseen the impending crisis, ever since the discussion and struggle over "the old wagon" at Forts Hall and Boisé, in 1836. Though laid away in quiet for a little time at the latter place, they knew that its broken bones would have a resurrection and go on the trail again, with more substance than a ghost, now muttering *chick-chick*, and now shouting *kai-kash*. Not that they could lose the absolute ownership and sovereignty of the Hudson Bay lands proper, for they held those in the honor and perpetuity of the Crown, but all else west and northwest and southwest to the Pacific they held on lease and for use only, and the Oregon portion by joint occupation with the United States. The discovery that those remote regions were worth settling, or could be settled by overland immigrants, might spoil a renewal of their lease, or terminate their joint occupation.

Moreover and specially, the Company must have known the agricultural worth of that vast region between Lake Winnipeg and the Pacific, and its natural worth to Great Britain for immigration. What is said now so abundantly and justly of that country, in the interests of the Canadian Pacific railway — a line of about seventeen hundred miles — if said in the time to which we have now brought down our narrative, might have opened that magnificent region to over-crowded Ireland and England too. It was not done, and the United States has opened her wild frontier, and diverted the swarming immigrants from the Crown to the Republic. Now since development by the United States has shown the value of what has been both carelessly and designedly called the Great American Desert, the English are looking to their part of it and to the saving of their own emigrants to their own government. The policy of exclusion and secrecy and silence maintained by the Hudson Bay Company, lest the fur-bearing animals be scared, damaged English interests quite as much as it threatened American.

It was a remarkable case of anxiety. This ablest corporation and highest monopoly in the world — the East India Company excepted — was forced to grapple with an exigency! It had had for nearly two centuries the ownership and regency of a country of fabulous extent, and when, by lease from the Crown, they added to it the "Indian countries," this domain was one third beyond all European areas. Now such a Company was driven into anxiety. It was confronted and troubled and forced into strategy by an "old wagon." Under this fear they fought all its kith and kin as they drove up to Fort Hall, and they spread the impression through the United States, from New Hampshire to Texas, that wheels could not be driven from the Snake River valley to the Columbia.

Not only did the Company hold this known pass by representing it to be impassable for carriages, but they kept the knowledge of other passes a secret. While their trappers and traders ferreted out the various paths through the mountains, the popular ignorance in this regard was surprising. When lying by at St. Vrain's Fort in 1842, and on his first expedition, Frémont could learn nothing of worth as to passes in that region for emigrants through the mountains. St. Vrain's was on the South Platte, near to the present city of Greeley and not far north of Denver. The main thing that he learned was that any possible trails would be impossible for wagons. When in that vicinity the following year he said: "I had been able to obtain no certain information in regard to the character of the passes in this portion of the Rocky Mountains, which had always been represented as impracticable for carriages."

If a carriage highway, of fair comfort for immigrants, should be discovered to Oregon, and the fact became generally known, settlements in that distant region would be hastened and multiplied. The Hudson Bay Company well knew this. From the days of the Revolution frontier life had been crowding the wilderness westward, daringly and often recklessly. If this tide should force a crevasse through the mountains it would obviously spoil the Pacific game preserve of that Company. Hence this crisis in their affairs, and great anxiety.

It is an interesting coincidence, if nothing more, that at this time, 1842-3, Sir George Simpson, for many years governor of the Company, made the tour of the continent across their possessions, spent much time with careful observations on the north-west coast, and is said to have enjoyed (about that time) protracted social relations at Washington with Daniel Webster, then Secretary of State.

From Montreal he was twelve weeks and five thousand miles distant from his starting-point in passing to Fort Vancouver, ninety miles from the sea, on the Columbia. On the way, he says, at Bear Creek " we obtained tidings of a large body of emigrants, who had left Red River for the Columbia a few days previous to our arrival from Montreal." This could have been no surprise to Sir George as governor, but it was a novelty in the policy of the Company. It was the first band of immigrants that they had ever authorized within their territory, and five years later than the Spalding and Whitman band to the same destination.

The Governor visited the headquarters of Dr. Whitman, and was led to notice and make record that " from the inhabited parts of the United States it is separated by deserts of rock and sand on either side of the dividing ridge of mountains — deserts with whose horrors every reader of Washington Irving's ' Astoria ' is familiar. Or, if the maritime route be preferred, the voyage from New York to the Columbia occupies two hundred degrees of latitude, and by the actual course, about one hundred and fifty of longitude, while the navigation of the river itself, up to the mouth of the Willamette, including the detention before crossing the bar, amounts on an average to far more than the run of a sailing packet across the Atlantic. . . . In the direction of California . . . the country, if less barren than to the eastward, is far more rugged. With respect, moreover, to the savage tribes, the former track is more dangerous than the latter."

Surely this was discouraging enough for any pioneers, who were thinking of trying a farther front in the western wilds, whether they would go by land or water. And when arrived, the colony would seem to have found only an oasis, with an unmeasured border of desert.

As to previous claims on Oregon and final possession the Governor speaks almost like an oracle: "On behalf of England, direct arguments are superfluous; for, until some other power puts a good title on paper, actual possession must be held to be conclusive in her favor." And he has passed "a large body of emigrants" coming in from the Red River, and, as we shall see, he has planned for a larger one the year following. So, those who are in possession must hold the country, and he has provided that they shall be forthcoming.

Then Sir George warms up into prophecy, and utters also challenging words: "The United States will never possess more than a nominal jurisdiction, nor long possess even that on the west side of the Rocky Mountains. And supposing the country to be divided to-morrow to the entire satisfaction of the most unscrupulous patriot in the Union, I challenge Congress to bring my prediction and its power to the test by imposing the Atlantic tariff on the ports of the Pacific." Certainly such sentences, aptly quoted from the governor of a huge monopoly into periodicals on either side of the Atlantic, would give a check to ardent emigrants from the States to Oregon. There is in this challenge the savor of long residence in a semi-civilized region, where the civil and military and financial headship have been united in one man, and made him necessarily more or less autocratic. There is, moreover, what may be called a corporation tone in the language: and it is wont to show itself, when the magnitude, and absoluteness, and perpetuity of the chartered interests, are so as to be able to keep even the creating government at a respectful distance.

In view of what took place in a few years following concerning Oregon, and California, and Alaska, these passages from the Governor are decidedly and pleasantly breezy. He proceeds : " England and Russia, whether as friends or as foes, cannot fail to control the destiny of the human race, for good or for evil, to an extent which, comparatively, confines every other nation within the scanty limits of its own proper locality." This is the language of one who has spent his life in trapping beaver, and bears, and wolves, and foxes, forgetting that men are another race of beings. Since this very English statement was made the United States have come into recognized possession of six thousand four hundred and eleven miles of Pacific coast, not reckoning the shore indentations of Alaska, while England has about four hundred and fifty, not reckoning the shore indentations of British Columbia.

It is sometimes thought that on and about the anniversary of her independence the United States indulges in an exaggerated use of the English language concerning her domain ; and then sometimes it is remembered that she inherited her mother's tongue and all its elasticity. Whether the United States has already grown to fill "the scanty limits of its own proper locality" may be a question. Another addition to her six growths would probably be one of necessity rather than of preference. She now embraces an area equal to seventy-eight Englands.

As to these vapors of Sir George Simpson concerning United States ownership and government on the Pacific coast, and growth of territory there or elsewhere, it will be kindly to remember that when he said these things he had recently emerged into this moving world from his realm, as governor; in parts of which the mail is delivered only annually, and the Canadian newspaper it brings is two years old and the European three when they read it.

Leaving Oregon he visited San Francisco, and then thought that the only way to prevent its falling into American hands was " by the previous occupation of the post by Great Britain." And he proceeds to say that England " has one road open to her by which she may bring California under her sway, without either force or fraud, without either the violence of marauders, or the effrontery of diplomacy. Mexico owes to British subjects a debt of more than fifty millions of dollars. By assuming a share of this debt on condition of being put in possession of California," etc.

The Macnamara scheme was a natural-outcome of these annexing meditations, the unsigned papers of which fell into the hands of the United States, while California, by a kind of civil gravitation, was falling the same way. So Sir George Simpson journeyed round the world. A pleasing inaptness and almost amusing awkwardness, as to these prophecies about Oregon and the United States, and policies about California, is, that after the United States had peacefully reclaimed the one, and taken possession of the other, Sir George published his narrative and opinions in 1847.

It is true the Governor had some warrant for his assumption and confident predictions. For about this time the Hudson Bay Company had twenty-three posts and five trading-stations in the northwest; it had absorbed ten rival companies, not leaving one, American or Russian, to dispute its sway; and it had turned back or broken up seven immigrant expeditions from the

States to Oregon. He had not, however, fully estimated the force, contents, and consequences of Dr. Whitman's wagon.

Meanwhile, the Doctor was receiving at his station the remnants of these broken bands, wasted and famished. They had sad stories to tell of the gauntlet they had run through the cordon of English traders, and of the high price of flour and the low price of cattle and wagons at Forts Hall and Boisé. Like certain men of old, they came to the Doctor's door with "old sacks upon their asses, and with bottles, old, and rent, and bound up, and old shoes, and clouted, upon their feet."

Immediately, those failures to get through comfortably with teams were reported back to the States, and were concentrated at Washington, and thence radiated all along the western borders. The information concerning the difficulties, and dangers, and impossibilities of passing the rivers, and mountains, and Indians, says the Rev. Mr. Spalding, "purported to come from Secretary Webster, but really from Governor Simpson, who, magnifying the statements of his chief trader, Grant, at Fort Hall, declared the Americans must be going mad, from their repeated, fruitless attempts to take wagons and teams through the impassable regions to the Columbia, and that the women and children of those wild fanatics had been saved from a terrible death only by the repeated and philanthropic labors of Mr. Grant at Fort Hall in furnishing them with horses."

These carefully prepared rumors and misrepresentations having seemed to obtain adroitly the endorsement of Mr. Webster, held back, for a time, many men, afterward eminent in the history of Oregon, till Whitman broke the spell and delusion by his immense caravan of wagons, and families, and stock, in the summer of 1843.

The story that opens here has not its superior in American history for high purpose, daring, romance, and grand result. Revere and Sheridan had their rides for the welfare of the nation. Marcus Whitman had his to provide the Republic with a Pacific side.

CHAPTER XVIII.

WHITMAN'S RIDE.

The autumn days came, and russet October, 1842, when the Oregon mission of the American Board was holding a business session at Waiilatpu. While attending to affairs, Dr. Whitman was called to visit a patient at Fort Walla Walla, the English trading-post, twenty-five miles away. The company at the Fort were in excellent spirits at the arrival of fifteen bateaux, loaded with Indian goods, and bound up stream to the Frazer River region. A score of chief factors had them in charge, and these, with the traders and clerks, made a jolly addition to the Fort's ordinary occupants. The spirits of the company unexpectedly gathering ran high, and it did seem to the Doctor as if the English already had Oregon in possession. It was a rare occasion to most on both sides, when their wilderness paths thus crossed, and they could, for an hour, break the painful monotony of their exile life, by catching a few ideas from another little wilderness world outside of their own.

Then came the dinner-table, laden with the spoils of forest and river, in the style of rude baronial halls. It would be difficult to spread a game feast where nobler dishes could be served, than that grand American preserve there offered. Post men and guests were jubilant; the officers sustained well the dignity of Old England at the head, while traders and subordinates, graded down the table, gave way to easy and rough jollity. Dr. Whitman alone represented the United States, in such a "joint occupation" of Oregon.

It has been noticed that at the close of 1841 immigrants from the United States had entered Oregon to the number of one hundred and thirty-seven, and at this time about one hundred more had been added. We have also marked the fact that in his overland trip to the Pacific, the preceding year, Sir George Simpson had passed an emigrant company, bound out from the Red River to the Columbia. The Hudson Bay Company had become well persuaded that Oregon could be taken and held only by the settlements of civilization, and their object now was to secure an advance on the Americans in this policy. They, therefore, were working, as we have seen, the double scheme of keeping Americans back, and bringing in their own people from the Red River country. The Selkirk settlement in the Red River valley was made for like purpose by this Hudson Bay Company in 1811–12, to head off and break up the rival and Canadian Northwest Company. In this they not only succeeded, but absorbed that Company in 1821. Now from the Selkirk settlement they were taking a colony to the Columbia to head off the Americans.

The first brigade from the Red River consisted of about forty families, English, Scotch, French, and half-breed, and after some dissensions under the rigid government of the Company, a part of them had made their way so far as to arrive in the upper valley of the Columbia. Their approach, already rumored, and the condition of the Americans, broken and discouraged by the opposition at Fort Hall, attracted the attention of Dr. Whitman and his associates. Still the movements of the

English did not alarm them as the year 1842 wore away, and partly because during this year their own number was nearly doubled.

While the interested dinner party were deep in their wild-wood convivialities, a messenger arrived express down the river announcing that the colony of one hundred and forty or more had succeeded in crossing the mountains, and were near to Fort Colville — three hundred and fifty miles up the Columbia. The welcome news sent a thrill of joy along the tables, and carried the excitement of the hour to a climax. The company instantly took the import of the announcement and were jubilant. Congratulations passed from man to man. A young priest, more ardent than wise, sprang to his feet, and with a twirl of his cap, and a shout, exclaimed: "Hurrah for Oregon! America is too late, and we have got the country!" The more intelligent at the table may have remembered that Mr. Canning, the English minister, had expressed his determination to maintain, as British property, any footing and position which the Company might obtain in Oregon.

As by instinct Dr. Whitman seized the fact announced, and measured its full import. He took it as an index to a policy. At once he assumed that it should be known at Washington, and a tide of immigration started for the northwest from another direction. He fixed his purpose, laid his plans, excused a hasty departure, and in two hours his Cayuse pony, white with foam, stood before the mission door at Waiilatpu. He could not wait to dismount till he had told of the English plot, the peril of Oregon, the need of making the fact known to his government, his purpose to face the winter and the mountains and plains and Indians, to carry the news, to start immediately, and to return the following season with a long train of immigrant wagons.

Of course it was with opposition, reluctance, and anxiety that his associates came slowly into the plans of the heroic man. And with reason. Few men could at once grasp the full import of that English scheme, and resolve to thwart it in person. Dr. Whitman's associates needed time to overtake his thoughts. As such national exigencies are rare, so are the men to meet them. We had another man on the Pacific coast, four years later, who was adequate to such an exigency. He took oral hints from a messenger, and the unwritten orders of circumstances, and turned pivoted California to the Union, in the face of foreign fleets and agents, who were there with well matured plans for other ends. The prompt action of Frémont and the splendid results tangled some military tape.

The winter was already on the mountains, and while a summer trip was hard enough, the cold and snows of a winter journey would reduce the chances for success and life to a minimum. He had no time for delay, for he supposed that the Ashburton-Webster Treaty, which would cover the Oregon question, was in progress, and might be hastened through before Congress should rise on the fourth of March. It was now opening October. Five months would be short time enough to allow for four thousand miles, mostly made on horseback. Allowance must be made for some terrible storms, when they would be compelled to lose days in snow-bound camps. Half frozen and winter-swollen streams were to be crossed on extemporized floats, which it would require much time to construct. Hostile Indians might make it indispensable to take detours or to hide for safety.

For some or all of these reasons, it would be the part of wisdom to avoid the direct route from Fort Hall to the Missouri, as more dangerous, both from the severity of the winter, and the hostile mood of the Blackfeet Indians. It would seem best to strike from Fort Hall southerly through the Salt Lake Basin into New Mexico, and thence to the Santa Fé trail and Bent's Fort on the Arkansas, and so to St. Louis.

A slight recollection of the terrible experiences of Frémont in those mountains, when the dangers and means of resistance and of escape were much better known, and a recollection also of the storms that have blocked railroads in the mountain passes and on the plains that lay before Dr. Whitman will prepare one to estimate the daring of the man. No wonder his weeping wife entreated and his associates almost forbade his rash enterprise. But it was in vain. All that was patriotic in the noble man added itself to the Christian in stirring a sense of duty, and he said to them that, for the emergency, he did not belong so much to the American Board, as he did to his country, and if they pressed opposition he would throw up his connection with the mission.

The issue now centred in that mission house was the possession of the present State of Oregon, and also the territories of Idaho and Washington — an area equal to thirty-two states as large as Massachusetts. After six years of residence and travel there, Dr. Whitman knew the natural magnificence and possibilities of the country, as probably no other American did. Then he realized how far off, and how little known or appreciated Oregon was in the east, and how slow the old states and settlements were to seize the grand issues involved in the new. The stoppage of immigrants at Fort Hall was fully explained, when at the dinner table the English shouted a welcome to the brigade from Red River. It was a matter of actual knowledge and certainty that Dr. Whitman could open the gates to an incoming American tide. He knew that he held the key to those gateways, and he felt a deep conviction of duty that he must use it. Then the Secretary of State must be impressed by United States evidence as well as by Hudson Bay Company's evidence, as to the accessibility of Oregon to emigrant wagons from the States. He must be enlightened enough on the general question to save the Union from an irreparable calamity.

The opposition to Dr. Whitman's purpose slowly gave way as the mission conference realized that it had before it the man who brought the wagon over the mountains six years before. At first the wife yielded, that noble woman, who had a broad American heroism. She finally gave up her husband to her country, much as she had given up herself to Christian missions among its Indians. When she assented to the daring endeavor of her husband, it could not be manly or Christian for others longer to dissent.

Now the preparations were hastened for the departure; and in twenty-four hours from the enthusiastic scenes of the dinner table at Fort Walla Walla, and the rash assertion of the ardent priest, Dr. Whitman was in the saddle, and headed for Washington. The energy and promptness of the man remind one of Xavier on a memorable occasion. He was totally surprised by his sudden appointment, by the Order of Jesuits, to the mission to Asia. When asked how soon he would be ready to depart for his continental and life work, he answered: "To-morrow."

Amos Lawrence Lovejoy, who had recently arrived from the east with the last band of immigrants, consented to accompany the Doctor on his perilous journey, so full of issues, and, as the end proved, so full of splendid ones for American history.

We may easily fancy the unsleeping mission, working through twenty-four hours to make the outfit the safest and lightest and most enduring possible; food, the inevitable axe, arms for defense and for game, medicines and whatnot for various unimaginable emergencies — all these must be anticipated, provided, and packed on horse and mule. The two horses for the gentlemen, and two or three pack-mules for a guide and supplies, were in readiness before a second sunset, and Marcus Whitman, with his companion, took the stirrup for Washington and Webster, and for a cavalcade of immigrant wagons to possess Oregon.

"Into the valley of death they rode."

If Captain Grant and the Hudson Bay Company generally made a mistake in letting Dr. Whitman through with his "old wagon" six years before, they made a greater one in letting him return on horseback to the States. But a man who carried a permit from the War Department, signed by Lewis Cass, Secretary, to travel, reside, and work for Christianity in the northwest, could not be meddled with in safety, as if he were a private trapper from the States around beaver-dams. Eleven days out and six hundred and forty miles brought him face to face with Captain Grant at Fort Hall. The party had left Waiilatpu, Oct. 3, 1842. This section of their route had been one of great peril and suffering to some emigrant and trading parties, notably that of Astor, under Wilson P. Hunt, in 1811–12. The interview between Captain Grant and his old friend the Doctor must have been an interesting one to witness, since each was conscious of a purpose to take and hold Oregon, by immigration, for the party he represented, and since both jointly knew how many companies had been broken up, or turned to California, or forwarded in saddles, after being deprived of their wagons on that familiar spot.

For reasons already given Dr. Whitman struck southerly from Fort Hall to Taos and Santa Fé. At the latter city he would come on the great Santa Fé trail of the St. Louis and New Mexican traders, and so find his way the more easily to the frontier settlements. The detour, however, in the sharp angle made at that old Spanish capital would add hundreds of miles to the journey, but it was hoped it would lessen proportionately the hardships and dangers of the terrible expedition.

No diary or narrative of the expedition was left by Dr. Whitman, but in the five years remaining of his eventful life he gave here and there, conversationally, many of the thrilling incidents of that wonderful journey, and these aid much in drawing out and connecting the thread of events. His companion as far as Bent's Fort on the Arkansas, Mr. Lovejoy, has given a graphic summary of the trip from Fort Hall to Fort Bent. Before introducing some passages from Mr. Lovejoy's account, it may be well to state that the course of the expedition was due south from Fort Hall, and mainly in the direction of the present Utah Southern railway, with Great Salt Lake and Utah Lake on the right, passing by the site, probably, of the coming Mormon city. Thence their course was south and east, across Green River, and then the heads of Grand River in southwestern Colorado, then over the upper branches of the San Juan, now so famous for its mines, and still south and east to Taos, and thence about sixty miles south to Santa Fé.

"From Fort Hall to Fort Uintah we met with terribly severe weather. The deep snows caused us to lose much time. Here we took a new guide for Fort Uncompahgre on Grand River, in Spanish country. Passing over high mountains, we encountered a terrible snow-storm, that compelled us to seek shelter in a dark defile; and although we made several attempts, we were detained some ten days, when we got upon the mountains, and wandered for days, when the guide declared he was lost, and would take us no farther. This was a terrible blow to the Doctor.

"But he determined not to give it up, and returned to the Fort for another guide, I remaining with the horses, feeding them on cotton-wood bark. The seventh day he returned. We reached, as our guide informed us, Grand River, six hundred yards wide, which was frozen on either side about one third. The guide regarded it as too dangerous, but the Doctor, nothing daunted, was the first to take to the water. He mounted his horse, and the guide and myself pushed them off the ice into the boiling, foaming stream. Away they went, completely under water, horse and all, but directly came up, and after buffeting the waves and foaming current, he made for the ice on the opposite side, a long way down the stream,— leaped upon the ice, and soon had his noble animal by his side. The guide and I forced in the pack-mules and followed the Doctor's example, and were soon drying our frozen clothes by a comfortable fire.

"We reached Taos in about thirty days. We suffered from intense cold and from want of food, compelled to use the flesh of dogs, mules, or such other animals as came in our reach. We remained about fifteen days, and left for Bent's Fort (via Santa Fé) which we reached January 3, 1843. The Doctor left here on the seventh."

At this later day, when the perils of winter travel in those mountains are better known, it seems more and more a marvel that this party was ever heard from again. When they put out from Fort Uintah for Fort Uncompahgre they were most unfortunate in their guide as well as in the weather. It was with difficulty that they could travel through the deep snows even when they knew the trail, and much time was consumed in floundering through defiles and over craggy heights. Then that terrible storm struck them there in the wild mountains, darkening the air almost to a premature night, and the ten days of enforced shelter and waiting in the gorge left the Doctor with intense anxiety about what he presumed was the progress of the treaty at Washington on the boundary question. If would not be strange if he saw, in fancy, the fatal signatures that would sacrifice Oregon. Repeated attempts were made to force the snow blockade, but in vain. One attempt, barely suggested in Mr. Lovejoy's letter, was critical, and came near being fatal to the expedition. The energy and impatience of Dr. Whitman had overruled the judgment of his guide, and the party attempted to escape their prison of mountains and snow by going over the divide. The intense cold and the mad storm made the animals quite uncontrollable, and the freezing, lonely squad of men and beasts were coming to be as immovable as a group of statuary. The guide confessed that he was lost and gave up. Then that one man, like another Napoleon struggling through Russian snows to recover from a terrible defeat, assumed the direction, and attempted to turn back for the campfire of those wasted and impatient days — a camp they had so unwisely left that morning. But the storm had done its work, and no trace of their track could be found. They wandered to and fro as men mazed or aimless. Finally man and beast became chilled, and hopeless, and stationary, and the snows were wrapping them in winding-sheets.

Then once and once only in his life, so far as appears, the Doctor yielded to the inevitable, and gave up all as lost. He dismounted and commended himself, his distant wife, his missionary companions and work, and his Oregon, to the Infinite One, and so awaited the silent, snowy burial of the party. By and by the guide, numb and stiff on his mule, thought he saw significant movements in the head and ears of the animal. That strange beast does sometimes appear to turn student and handle a problem. At least, such was the appearance in this case, as he turned his ears right and left, and then set them with a projection forward, as if he would direct attention. To his Mexican rider all this seemed to declare knowledge and convictions. To those familiar with that old Spanish country and people it will come up, on recollection, that a Mexican and a mule have a good deal in common which might be called mutual understanding. Therefore, the freezing and hopeless rider remarked: "This mule will find the camp if he can live to reach it." So saying, he dropped the bridle rein on the saddle-bow and gave the animal his full liberty.

The stupid brute, yet so full of instinct, was master of the situation. He at once left the stormy divide, turning a cañon here and a cliffy slope there, and still downward plunging through snows, and sometimes sliding over half precipices. He was neither guided nor spurred, but had his own will and gait, onward and downward, till he came to thick timber and a dark ravine. The surroundings slowly put on a familiar look to the party; then they snuffed smoke, and soon the mule stopped by the smouldering logs of the morning camp-fire, too rashly left. Here they warmed, and fed, and rested, yet other days.

But the reassured life and returning spirits of the Doctor chafed over lost time, and he was gone seven days to Fort Uintah for a new guide. If the reader will pause long enough on these pages to make that seven days' trip his own, in fancy, he will have a better measure of the peril of it, and of the man who made it. Under the new guide the party arrived at Grand River, six hundred feet of ice on each shore, with six hundred of rapid water between the two icy borders. The Doctor made the first plunge, went under, came up, steered across, and was soon as thoroughly encased in ice as ever was an old warrior in his coat of mail. His horse scrambled on the ice and to the shore like a chased deer. Soon there was the roaring camp-fire, encircled by dripping men and animals. The same man this is who made the Rocky Mountains give up to a wagon.

Again, after a hard day over a bald prairie in a wild storm, our company reached one of the branches of the Arkansas. The clean grass, without tree, shrub, or any fuel, comes down to the river brink, and to the smooth, thin ice that spreads across the stream. The opposite shore was wooded, and a fire must be had, for the wet storm had passed by, and a freezing night was to follow. The ice was a thin pretext, impassable for a horse, somewhat tempting and very doubtful for a man. Like a daring boy, when skating is not yet, and the ice will not support him on his feet, the Doctor lay flat and wriggled himself over, and then pushed back fuel and axe before him. A warm supper and a sweet sleep followed.

Alas, for the axe! The helve has been cracked and then wound with raw hide. That night a wolf, for the sake of the skin, stole it from its hiding-place under the edge of the tenting, and the company never saw it again. Nearer to Fort Hall the loss would probably have proved very serious if not fatal to the expedition. But they soon came into the vicinity of the lone cabins of daring settlers on the extreme frontier, and the wolfish act proved only an annoyance.

But we are ahead of our party on the trail. Santa Fé welcomed and refreshed them — that oldest city of European occupation on the continent. De Vaca and Coronado, perhaps Cortez, the Duke of Albuquerque, Pike, Kit Carson, and Charles Bent, its first United States governor, had been there before him, and General Kearney three years later, when he took all New Mexico for the Republic. Probably no public building in North America is so old as its adobe palace, or has witnessed so many civil and bloody changes. Its walls could tell of intrigues, plots, revolutions, and assassinations, as none other in the United States.

It was a long but easier journey to Bent's Fort on the Arkansas. This ample inclosure, somewhat fortified after the rough needs of the frontier, has made many a weary traveler glad by its hearty and abundant hospitalities. The fort was a quadrangle, one hundred feet on the sides. Its walls were of adobe, thirty feet high, and its northeast and diagonal corner supported bastions and a few cannon. The apartments were built against the walls on the inside, after the Mexican manner. In the centre stood the robe-press, where furs and peltries were deposited. Its genial founder, of Massachusetts parentage, Virginia birth, and Missouri home, pioneer in the New Mexican trade, built the post in 1829. In 1880 I found it to be a rude and wild corral, deserted and decaying.

The Republic is much indebted to Charles Bent, and his associate brothers of the border, and to St. Vrain, their partner. Charles Bent was one of the first to introduce modern times into that dwarfed offspring of Spain, of the sixteenth century. By a caravan commerce between St. Louis and the southwest, whose round trip required a full summer, he led that region up to a connection with the rest of the world. The draught-ox of the Arkansas and Rio Grande is indebted to him for its first iron shoe. A man of breadth, energy, and true love of country, he was wisely appointed by General Kearney as the first Governor of New Mexico in 1846. But he was taken off mournfully by assassination at Taos, within four months; and after a third interment his remains rest under an honorable monument and epitaph in the Masonic cemetery at Santa Fé.

Mr. Lovejoy, exhausted and broken, was left at Bent's Fort to recover himself, and in the July following he joined the Doctor and his outgoing caravan, above Laramie. The Doctor himself rested in the good cheer of the fort, and among fellow citizens, for only four days, and on the seventh of January, 1843, he pressed on for Washington and Webster.

On his arrival in St. Louis it was my good fortune that he should be quartered, as a guest, under the same roof, and at the same table with me. The announcement of the man, in the little city of twenty thousand, as it was then, came as a surprise and a novelty. In those times it was a rare possibility for one to come up in midwinter from Bent's Fort or Santa Fé; much more from Fort Hall and the Columbia. The Rocky Mountain men, trappers, and traders, the adventurers in New Mexico, and the contractors for our military posts, the Indian men laying up vast fortunes, half from the government and half from the poor Indian — gathered about Dr. Whitman for fresh news from those places of interest. Those who had friends on the plains, or in the mountains, or Spanish territory, sought opportunities to ply him with questions. For none had come over since the river closed, or crossed the frontier inward since the winter set in. What about furs and peltries? How many buffalo robes would come down by June on the spring rise of the Missouri? Were Indian goods at the posts in flush, or fair, or scant supply? What tribes were on the war-path? What were the chances of breaking Indian treaties, and for removals from old reservations? Who seemed to have the inside favor with the Indian agents? What American fur-traders had the Hudson Bay Company recently driven to the wall? What could he say of the last emigrant company for Oregon in which one Amos Lawrence Lovejoy went out? What had become of so and so, who were in previous companies that broke up at Fort Hall?

Many of their questions were as fresh and lively then as they are to-day concerning the Indian country; and as heavy fortunes lay back of them, at least it was hoped so. Our Indian field, however, has changed somewhat as to product, and now yields less fur and more greenbacks, owing to the modern use of different traps, and gins, and snares, and to a change of places in setting them — more on the Potomac and less on the Columbia waters.

But the Doctor was in great haste, and could not delay to talk of beaver, and Indian goods, and wars, and reservations, and treaties. He had questions and not answers. Was the Ashburton Treaty concluded? Did it cover the northwest? Where, and what, and whose did it leave Oregon? He was soon answered. Webster and Ashburton had signed that treaty on the ninth of August preceding, on the twenty-sixth the Senate had ratified it, and on the tenth of November, President Tyler had proclaimed it as the law of the land. While the Doctor, therefore, was floundering in the snows, or hunting a lost camp-fire, or exchanging guides, or swimming frozen rivers, somewhere on the trail of Forts Wintee and Uncompahgre, the Oregon question was settled for the present by postponement.

Then, instantly, he had other questions for his St. Louis visitors. Was the Oregon question under discussion in Congress? What opinions, projects, or bills, were being urged in Senate or House? Would anything important be settled before the approaching adjournment on the fourth of March? That might be a critical and even a closing day for great American interests on the northwest coast. Could he reach Washington before the adjournment? He must leave at once, and he went.

Marcus Whitman once seen, and in our family circle, telling of his one business — he had but one — was a man not to be forgotten by the writer. He was of medium height, more compact than spare, a stout shoulder, and large head not much above it, covered with stiff iron-gray hair, while his face carried all the moustache and whiskers that four months had been able to put on it. He carried himself awkwardly, though perhaps courteously enough for trappers, Indians, mules, and grizzlies, his principal company for six years. He seemed built as a man for whom more stock had been furnished than worked in symmetrically and gracefully. There was nothing peculiarly quick in his motion or speech, and no trace of a fanatic; but under control of a thorough knowledge of his business, and with deep, ardent convictions about it, he was a profound enthusiast. A willful resolution and a tenacious earnestness would impress you as marking the man.

His dress would now appear much more peculiar than in those days and in that city. For St. Louis was then no stranger to blanket Indians, and Yellowstone trappers, in buckskin and buffalo. The Doctor was in coarse fur garments and vesting, and buckskin breeches. He wore a buffalo coat, with a head-hood for emergencies in taking a storm, or a bivouac nap. What with heavy fur leggings and boot-moccasins, his legs filled up well his Mexican stirrups. If memory is not at fault with me, his entire dress, when on the street, did not show one square inch of woven fabric.

With all this warmth and almost burden of skin and fur clothing, he bore the marks of the irresistible cold and merciless storms of his journey. His fingers, ears, nose, and feet had been frost-bitten, and were giving him much trouble. When he came to the extreme east, to speak officially of his mission among the Indians, it is recorded that some sensitive gentlemen suggested that a certain suit of black — and a little worn — might be more becoming. That was the time when some American Geographical Society was needed to receive him with publicity and formality in his full Rocky Mountain suit, and afterward decorate him with the badges and insignia of an eminent explorer and discoverer.

Are not we Americans slow to discover historic stepping-stones till they become foot-worn?

Dr. Whitman, in St. Louis, was midway between Oregon and Washington, and he carried business of mighty import, that must not be delayed by private interests and courtesies. In the wilds and storms of the mountains he had fed on mules and dogs, yet now sumptuous and complimentary dinners had no attractions for him. He was happy to meet men of the army, of commerce, and of fur, but his urgent business was to see Daniel Webster. A few days among the elegances of cheery homes, and in the enjoyment of genial courtesies, might make him too late at the seat of government, and render worthless his four months of hardships and perils on the long Oregon trail. Four months in the saddle, and

"The fate of a nation was riding that night."

So far the horse had carried Oregon; now the Doctor must see it speedily and safely to the end of the four thousand miles. Exchanging saddle for stage — for the river was closed by ice — he pressed on, and arrived at Washington March third, just five months from the Columbia to the Potomac.

Our records are not without illustrations of heroic action of this kind. The midnight ride of Paul Revere, made classic by one of our sweetest poets, constituted an epoch in the life of the young Republic. Lieutenant Gillespie, going by Vera Cruz, the city of Mexico and California coast to Monterey, there took saddle to overhaul Lieutenant Frémont, in Oregon, with dispatches from Washington. It was quite after the old Roman order, that he look to it that the American Republic receive no damage in California. Sheridan made his marvelous ride to Winchester and turned a defeat and rout into a victory. There have been eminent express rides, full of import to families and states; these have carried messages for war and for peace, for trade and towering ambition. It would be difficult, however, to find one that for distance, time, heroic daring, peril, suffering, and magnificent consequences, could equal Whitman's Ride.

CHAPTER XIX.

OREGON NOT IN THE TREATY OF WEBSTER AND ASHBURTON.

Dr. WHITMAN arrived in Washington too late, and yet not too late. When he left the Columbia for the Potomac, his latest information from the States, brought over by his returning companion, Mr. Lovejoy, was that a treaty was under negotiation between Mr. Webster, the Secretary of State, and Lord Ashburton, English envoy, to settle the boundary question between the two nations, and it was supposed that Oregon was included. To have the northwestern boundary question covered and settled in that treaty, the Doctor was too late; for while he was yet not forty days on his national and continental journey, the treaty was proclaimed as the law of the land. Mr. Webster and Lord Ashburton had completed and signed it nearly two months before he started, and Oregon was left out. But he was not too late to furnish new and much needed information, to expose scheming, to show the accessibility of Oregon to the old east, to draw from his own residence and travel and study there, for six years, leading facts concerning its natural and national worth, and, by all this, to stay a damaging foreclosure of the question, secure final equity and save national honor — for all this he was just in time. Let us see how the case stands when this Pacific man, in fur and buckskin, weather-beaten and frost-bitten, enters the office of the Secretary of State.

The boundary between the United States and the British Possessions, described by the treaty of peace, 1783, was either unfortunately worded or most unfortunately handled. In interpreting phrases in the treaty such embarrassing questions as these were raised: Which river is the St. Croix? Where is the north-west angle of Nova Scotia? What are the highlands between this angle and the northwest head of the Connecticut River? Which stream is the northwest head of that river? May the rivers emptying into the Bay of Fundy be said to fall into the Atlantic Ocean? A joint commission of 1794 finally agreed on what is the St. Croix, and fixed a monument at its source. For forty-eight years the boundary question lingered before joint commissions, and in delays such as only diplomacy can weave, and nothing more was settled. In 1839 new impetus was given to the subject, and Mr. Webster was urged as special minister to England to hasten affairs. He drew up a memorandum of plan for settlement, which was highly approved by President Van Buren and others. But the proposed plan was not adopted, the envoy was not sent, and fruitless negotiations went on. Mr. Webster meanwhile spent a few months in a private and social way in England, and was much consulted on the boundary question.

In 1841 Mr. Webster passed from the Senate to the Cabinet of President Harrison, as Secretary of State. After the painfully early death of the President, Webster continued in the Cabinet when the Vice-President, Mr. Tyler, succeeded to the presidency. In the summer of this year 1841 Mr. Webster informed Mr. Fox, the English minister at Washington, that he was ready to attempt the settlement of the boundary question.

The antecedents of negotiation were not very encouraging, and it required some confidence in a plan, and some boldness, to renew the efforts. For it was now fifty-eight years since the treaty of peace had stipulated a boundary, and so far only the St. Croix River had been identified, and a monument set at its source. When in 1803 a joint commission was just being completed to run the line the Louisiana Purchase was made, which would carry United States territory beyond the Mississippi, up somewhere to British territory, and therefore, for prudential reasons, the United States delayed action. In 1814, by the Treaty of Ghent, another joint boundary commission was secured, but could not agree, and it settled nothing. Then the question had rest, practically, till 1827, when, through a convention, it was referred to the King of the Netherlands as arbitrator, but his decision was rejected by both parties in 1831. During his double term of office President Jackson made five separate efforts to adjust the boundary, and as many failures. His successor, Mr. Van Buren, in his first message, spoke of "abortive efforts made by the executive for a period of more than half a century," and closed his administration, leaving the question involved in greater "intricacies and complexities and perplexities," among which was the famous Aroostook war.

In view of this disheartening history of the question, Secretary Webster proposed to undertake it anew, and on the fourth of April, 1842, Lord Ashburton arrived at Washington, as envoy, with full powers to negotiate with him. Mr. Webster had not only the United States to satisfy in this delicate business, and now sensitive by the irritations of more than half a century, but Maine, Massachusetts, New Hampshire, Vermont, and New

York had state interests involved, and were alive to the integrity of their territory, and to their honor. The two ministers signed the treaty August ninth, 1842; the Senate ratified it on the twenty-sixth; Lord Ashburton sailed with the treaty for home October thirteenth; the treaty was ratified by the Queen, returned from England, and proclaimed November tenth, 1842.

The long standing of the question, the perplexities which had accumulated around it, the length of line settled, the magnitude of territory, and other issues involved, and the prompt action in four brief months, make the act a remarkable one in the history of diplomacy. When Dr. Whitman was thirty-eight days out from the Columbia, and somewhere in the snows, between Fort Hall and Taos, the treaty became the law of the land. But it contained no reference to Oregon. Neither the treaty nor the official correspondence alludes to Oregon. It determined the boundary, "beginning at the Monument at the source of the river St. Croix," and ending at the Rocky Mountains on the forty-ninth parallel.

In his annual message of December, following the proclamation of the treaty, President Tyler thus refers to the Oregon interests, and shows why they were put by for the time. "It became evident, at an early hour of the late negotiations, that any attempt for the time being satisfactorily to determine those rights would lead to a protracted discussion, which might embrace in its failure other more pressing matters; and the executive did not regard it as proper to waive all the advantages of an honorable adjustment of other difficulties of great magnitude and importance, because this, not so immediately pressing, stood in the way."

Mr. Webster regarded the negotiation of this treaty

as one of the greatest and most important acts of his eventful life. For this diplomatic success he was exposed to some criticism, grave and petty. Maine was a party to the negotiations, by her commissioners, and endorsed the result, yet some of her worthy citizens felt that her rights had not been well maintained, and that portions of her territory had been sacrificed to peace and compromise, though probably nine tenths of her people to-day approve the treaty. The total area in dispute in Maine was twelve thousand and twenty-seven acres. The west was disappointed that the Oregon question was not included and settled. A little sectional jealousy was stirred.

During the three or four following years, and till the settlement of Oregon affairs in 1846, the eastern boundary treaty was frequently a subject of adverse criticism in Congress. As Webster himself said, it was made "the subject of disparaging, disapproving, sometimes contumelious remarks." Perhaps this should not surprise us. There were men of lofty and worthy ambitions in Congress and out of it, but only one could carry off the honor of this great achievement. Then there were men who could not presume to pass around our continent, and examine with a broad and international view the boundary line at the Atlantic end and at the Pacific end. At that time, and more so now, our country was quite large for some men.

At one time the affair ran close to bloody conflict in the Aroostook war, but General Scott went down and stayed the rising passions, as afterward and for a similar purpose he visited the coasts of Oregon. Probably it was this crisis, as well as some others, that Webster covered in a remark to a leading merchant who had congratulated him on the successful work: "There have been periods when I could have kindled a war, but, sir, I remembered that I was negotiating for a Christian country with a Christian country, and that we were all living in the nineteenth century of the Christian era. My duty, sir, was clear and plain."

The mayor of Philadelphia recognized the same fact gracefully, when introducing Mr. Webster at a dinner which the city had given him: "In seasons of danger he has been to us a living comforter; and more than once has restored this nation to serenity, security, and prosperity." This was soon after the popular frenzy of "fifty-four forty, or fight," had calmed down on the parallel of forty-nine — Webster's original line. Other critical issues and irritating questions which hot blood could have turned into war came up and went into peaceable settlement, notably the Canadian burning of the Caroline, the right of search for English citizens on American vessels, and coöperation for the suppression of the slave-trade on the African coasts.

And the more is the wonder that he peacefully carried the great issue through such grave danger of war, since those were days of hot blood and foolishly high spirit. About this time, John Quincy Adams said, referring to Wise, who shot Cilley in a duel: " Four or five years ago, there came to this house a man with his hands and face dripping with the blood of murder, the blotches of which are yet hanging upon him." At the spring horse-races, in 1842, and about the days of the opening negotiations between Ashburton and Webster, the horse of Stanley of North Carolina jostled this same Wise in his saddle, and the fiery man resented the act with his cane. A duel was stayed only by the police, and the only physical harm was to the left eye of Reverdy Johnson, which a rebounding ball destroyed, while Johnson was teaching Stanley how to kill Wise. The suppression of the war spirit, in such times, was a sublime conquest.

These were the relations of Mr. Webster in the popular mind, when Doctor Whitman, rough in fur and buckskin, entered the office of the Secretary of State. Wearied as Mr. Webster may well have been in settling so much of a difficulty which many others had given half a century to, and failed; ungenerously criticised by a few, as having yielded all to England, while Lord Ashburton suffered a similar condemnation for having yielded all to the United States, we may well suppose that Dr. Whitman would not find him enthusiastic over the northwestern boundary question. Indeed, the two negotiators had paused at the Rocky Mountains, because, as the President stated, any attempts to carry the line farther would not offer hopeful results. It does not appear, moreover, that the Secretary was under any executive instructions to go into the Pacific side of the business, and certainly Lord Ashburton was not.

A great disappointment was felt in Oregon that it was not provided for in the treaty, as the people there, without full reason, had presumed it would be, and the heroic endeavor of Dr. Whitman had seemed to them to guarantee it. The mistakes appear to have originated in Oregon, where expectations were highest, and information most scanty, and disappointment was the keenest.

I have devoted so much care to the analysis and correction of this error, not only to relieve the fame of our great diplomat from an unfortunate and of course undesigned shadow, but also to set forth in its historic, and therefore noblest light, the achievement of Dr. Whitman. Oregon was on the other side of the continent, with formidable wilderness and deserts between, and information from Washington traveled slowly and scantily. The inner history of the Ashburton and Webster negotiations rested long among the semi-secrets of the Department of State. Webster himself says: "The papers accompanying the treaty were voluminous. Their publication was long delayed, waiting for the exchange of ratifications; and, when finally published, they were not distributed to any great extent, or in large numbers. The treaty, meantime, got before the public surreptitiously, and, with the documents, came out by piecemeal. We know that it is unhappily true that, away from the large commercial cities of the Atlantic coast, there are few of the public prints of the country which publish official papers on such an occasion at length."

The pressure of Oregon into the Ashburton Treaty would probably have done one of three things, prevented the treaty altogether, excluded the United States from Oregon, or produced a war. Delay and apparent defeat were the basis of our real success, and the great work of Marcus Whitman, by his timely presence at Washington, was in making that success sure.

The meeting of two such ministers of state for such high ends, and with such high resolve, is a scene good to be looked at by nations, and cabinets, and philanthropists. The scene is as much above the struggle of two armies, or navies, as reason and moral right are above muscle and steel. Some delays consumed three months among more local commissioners, and on questions of geography, compass, and chain. But, as men who are conscious of right, and of having the end in their own keeping, can afford to wait, so the high contracting parties waited, in this case, till the time was ripe, and the end came in an obvious fitness of things. The result in the Ashburton Treaty gained the general assent. Some Englishmen called the treaty the "Ashburton Capitulation," and some Americans spoke quite as narrowly of it from the United States side.

There is no evidence that Doctor Whitman was dissatisfied with the policy which resulted in the Ashburton Treaty, as evidently the best possible in the circumstances. Nor is there reliable information to warrant the assumption that he was annoyed by any opinions attributed to the Secretary that Oregon was "worthless territory," and should be traded off for cod-fisheries. All traditions to that effect have started in the assumption that on his arrival in Washington the Ashburton Treaty was still pending, whereas it had been settled for six months. But in a later chapter we will discuss this fully.

The delay, therefore, constituted Whitman's opportunity, and enabled him to turn his perilous journey into the salvation of his beloved northwest. If anyone could be intelligently thankful that the Oregon question had not been pressed into the treaty, that man must have been Marcus Whitman.

Meanwhile the bow of Ulysses was relaxed. For the very day when the Senate ratified the treaty, thirty-nine to nine, we find Webster thus writing to his Marshfield farmer: "I am against filling the floor of the barn with salt hay. It spoils the looks of things, besides being in the way. You will do better to make a third cap, large, and place it in a convenient spot near the piggery, as I am not at all certain but what you and I shall make a barn the last two weeks in September and the first two in October."

If Dr. Whitman could have created all the circumstances and ordained his own time, his arrival in Washington could not have been more apt for seizing the condition of things and saving Oregon. Its destiny he had brought over on his own saddle, and now held it in his solitary hand. His knowledge of the case was original, personal, and experimental, and at Washington he made it declarative. With his understanding of the whole affair, and with his practical sense and energy, he was anxious to venture the issue for Oregon on an experiment, and the Cabinet were willing he should do it. Frémont was promised as an escort for the returning caravan that was to constitute the experiment. The settlement, therefore, of the Oregon question, and the crowning of that wonderful ride, waited on that emigrant cavalcade that was about to move off into the wild west from Westport, Missouri.

CHAPTER XX.

IS OREGON WORTH SAVING?

WHEN Dr. Whitman arrived in Washington it was a common question there, and so poorly understood as to be variously answered, whether Oregon were worth saving. It was several months distant from our national capital, and had been but little examined and reported by Americans, and occupied by settlers only about twelve months. The information obtained from explorers, traders, and trappers from the United States had been slight, mostly indefinite, and not very tempting to emigration. The popular and prevailing impression was that Oregon was wild, rough, and inhospitable, and not inviting to immigrants and specially to family life. It was thought to be no place for white women and their children, nor even for business men in the ordinary pursuits of agriculture, mechanics, trade, and commerce. Even if these things were otherwise, and the whole region were tempting to American life, it was not accessible by land; and to double Cape Horn in a voyage of weary months was out of the question. Prior to the arrival of the Doctor this ignorance made it impossible to settle the question in dispute. The emigrant scheme contained the solution of doubts.

Was Oregon worth having by the United States? Doubtful, as the case then stood in evidence. The northwest was opened and made known to the United

States by the Hudson Bay Company, as it became in the course of their progressive trade the natural extension of their magnificent game preserve. Their policy, as a grand mercantile monopoly, was to keep it in their own hands. As already stated, that broad Scotchman and fur-trader, Alexander Mackenzie, had gone across — first of white men — to the northwest Pacific, and painted his mark there upon rock. Thus his discoveries by land closed in with those of Captain Cook by sea, made fifteen years before, and the English arm was stretched across from sea to sea. A little later, 1806, Simon Frazer made a settlement on a river there, with his name. "The first made on the west of the Rocky Mountains by civilized man."[1]

The publication of Cook's voyages, 1784-5, introduced many rival and adventurous traders into those northwestern seas, and from that time the Hudson Bay Company urged, energetically, their monopoly there, as we have before seen. The American purchase and the exploration by Lewis and Clark were not followed by colonies from the States for many years. The first independent emigrating party of men, women, and children — one hundred and twenty — to that country was led over in 1842 by Elijah White, Indian agent for the government in the northwest. This was the company that informed Dr. Whitman of the negotiations for the Ashburton Treaty, and hastened him on his ride.[2] Prior to this a few missionary bands had gone over, but their information was mostly concerning their work. The va-

---

[1] *The Oregon Question Examined.* By Travers Twiss, Professor of Political Economy, Oxford, 1846, p. 13.
[2] *A Concise View of Oregon Territory.* By Elijah White, Indian Agent for Oregon Territory, Washington, 1846, pp. 1, 65.

rious American trading parties had gained much knowledge of that country in the line of their business, but they were not accessible as an organized fraternity, and so could not impart much valuable information. No doubt a watchful reporter, hanging about St. Louis from the return of Lewis and Clark in 1806, to Whitman's arrival there in 1843, could have picked up many valuable facts concerning that vast northwest. Old traders and trappers, and Mississippi boatmen of the Mike Fink stamp, a species long extinct, must have made many a saloon, and verandah, and shanty on Water Street and the Levee fascinating with their stories. The quarters of the American Fur Company must have been full of profitable information, but little literary ambition was there, and only financial facts went into their huge folios. We would sacrifice a portly alcove to-day for a few hours with such pioneer traders as the Sublettes, and Davenport, and Campbell, and the Bents, and Choteau, and St. Vrain, and others. One may be pardoned for coveting what those men carried with them to the grave. An incident, with headline only, may hint at our loss. About Christmas, 1830, William Sublette had *cached* his furs on the Bighorn River, and having joined the camp of his brother Milton, crossed over into the valley of Wind River to winter. When he had well quartered his men, he put out for St. Louis, with Black Harris, traveling on snow-shoes, with a train of pack dogs. What a story to be lost!

At the time of the interview between Whitman and Webster the most of the information received in the States from the northwest had of necessity, therefore, come in through English channels, and was moulded to Hudson Bay interests. While that country lay as an obscure right between the two nations, and the Company saw an advance opening for their trade, it was quite natural that they should diminish temptations to visit it, and weave obstacles between it and a rival on the border. This they did to a successful extent up to the time when Whitman arrived on the Potomac. They had made it quite obvious to the uninformed, says Gray, "that the whole country was of little value to any one. It would scarcely support the few Indians, much less a large population of settlers."

English volumes of travel and scholarly Review articles were teaching the same delusion abroad. So the "Edinburgh Review" said: "Only a very small proportion of the land is capable of cultivation." "West of the Rocky Mountains the desert extends from the Mexican (Californian) border to the Columbia," and it endeavored to show that the country east of the mountains was "incapable, probably forever, of fixed settlements," where now are Kansas, Nebraska, and Dakota. The "British and Foreign Review" preached to the same application and conclusion: "Upon the whole, therefore, the Oregon territory holds out no great promise as an agricultural field." The "London Examiner" was quite pronounced, if not petulant, that the ignorant Americans did not give up a country equal in area to England eight times: "The whole territory in dispute is not worth twenty thousand pounds to either power."[1]

This worthless region, as they wished to show it, they nevertheless occupied eastward from the Pacific to the heads of the Missouri and Mississippi. When Lieutenant

---

[1] Vol. lxxxii. p. 240. Also July, 1843, p. 184. *British and Foreign Review*, January, 1844, p. 21. *London Examiner*, quoted in Webster's Works, i.: Introd. cxlix.

Pike, in his expedition of 1805, found the Hudson Bay Company flying the English flag within our territory, and required it to be hauled down, he wrote to Captain McGillis: "I find your establishments at every suitable place along the whole extent of the south side of Lake Superior, to its head, from thence to the sources of the Mississippi, down Red River, and even extending to the centre of our newly acquired territory of Louisiana."

Their trappers and traders, in a gossipy way, were undervaluing Oregon, as the stately quarterlies were doing in a more dignified manner. This depreciating view of that country came to possess our own literature and popular speech. Captain William Sturgis, who had trafficked on the northwest coast and at the English posts there, uses this language in a lecture before the Mercantile Library Association of Boston, two years even after the arrival of Whitman: "Rather than have new states formed beyond the Rocky Mountains, to be added to our present Union, it would be a lesser evil, as far as that Union is concerned, if the unoccupied portion of the Oregon territory should sink into Symme's Hole, leaving the western base of those mountains and the borders of the Pacific Ocean one and the same."[1]

A similar view of Oregon's value probably led Benton to make that remarkable utterance, in 1825: "The ridge of the Rocky Mountains may be named without offence as presenting a convenient natural and everlasting boundary. Along the back of this ridge the western limits of this Republic should be drawn, and the statue of the fabled god Terminus should be raised upon its highest peak, never to be thrown down." As late as 1844 Mr. Winthrop, calling attention in the Senate to this sentiment, remarked: "It was well said."

[1] Boston, 1845, p. 24.

The same article from which we have quoted in the "Edinburgh Review" thinks that the American colonists in Oregon have been "misled by the representations of the climate and soil of Oregon, which for party purposes have been spread through the United States." Then the "Review" becomes prophetic: "It seems probable that, in a few years, all that formerly gave life to the country, both the hunter and his prey, will become extinct, and that their place will be supplied by a thin white and half-breed population, scattered along the few fertile valleys, supported by pasture instead of the chase, and gradually degenerating into barbarism, far more offensive than the backwoodsman." This defamation of Oregon is naturally followed by the English writer with the declaration that "No nation now possesses any title, perfect or imperfect, by discovery, by settlement, by treaty, or by prescription."

The Ashburton Treaty had been then ratified, Oregon was omitted, and the next step must be anticipated. Evidently the "Review" was making and exporting opinions for American use, and forty years ago it was no inferior power in determining the affairs of this country. It is right to add, however, that twenty-four years afterward, the "Westminster Review" had the candor to confess: "In spite of the disparaging estimates of Mr. Edward Ellice and Sir George Simpson, and the unfavorable impression of the territory, which has been so industriously propagated by the Hudson Bay Company, we are compelled to believe, on overwhelming testimony, that the Fur Company possess, or claim to possess, a grand estate, larger than most kingdoms, and a great portion of it of unequalled natural resources."

Mr. McDuffie, in a speech in the Senate, reflected,

roughly and crudely, the English and Hudson Bay Company's teachings on the subject: —

"What is the character of this country? Why, as I understand it, that seven hundred miles this side of the Rocky Mountains is uninhabitable, where rain scarcely ever falls — a barren and sandy soil . . . mountains totally impassable, except in certain parts, where there were gaps or depressions, to be reached only by going some hundreds of miles out of the direct course. Well, now, what are we going to do in such a case as this? How are you going to apply steam? Have you made anything like an estimate of the cost of a railroad running from here to the mouth of the Columbia? Why the wealth of the Indies would be insufficient. You would have to tunnel through mountains five or six hundred miles in extent. . . . Of what use will this be for agricultural purposes? I would not, for that purpose, give a pinch of snuff for the whole territory. . . . I wish it was an impassable barrier to secure us against the intrusion of others. . . . If there was an embankment of even five feet to be removed, I would not consent to expend five dollars to remove that embankment, to enable our population to go there. . . . I thank God for his mercy in placing the Rocky Mountains there."

This speech in the Senate was delivered on the 25th of January, 1843. An interesting coincidence comes in here. On the 7th of this month Whitman had left Bent's Fort for St. Louis and Washington; on the 13th had encountered that terrible and memorable "cold wave" of the interior, and in his lonely saddle was pressing on to the States, with a bundle of facts that would reduce so many speeches, like that of McDuffie, and so many English Review articles, to deceptive rhetoric.

Indeed, it was unfortunate for the American interests, that outside, foreign, and rival parties furnished the basis and tone of public opinion on the question. The Great American Desert was made a standing intimidation to the emigrant. "From the valley of the Mississippi to the Rocky Mountains, the United States territory," says the "Westminster Review," "consists of an arid tract extending south nearly to Texas, which has been called the Great American Desert." "The caravan of emigrants who undertake the passage," says Mr. Edward J. Wallace, "take provisions for six months, and many of them die of starvation on the way."[1]

That "Desert" still forms quite an African feature in the visions of some eastern people, who have read only "Pike's Expedition," and Long's, and Wilson P. Hunt's, and who remember faithfully Morse's and Cumming's geographies of their childhood. What a dreary Arabian centre that Great American Desert gave then to the map of the United States! Missouri, and Kansas, and Nebraska, and Colorado, and Dakota, and other splendid farming regions are now good substitutes for that Zahara.

But unfavorable impressions of the west, this side and beyond the mountains, were not due to the English alone. The east was jealous of the west, and consequently negligent of it. A question in McDuffie's speech is a hint of this. "Do you think your honest farmers in Pennsylvania, New York, or even Ohio or Missouri, would abandon their farms to go upon any such enterprise as this?" And Mr. Winthrop is appalled by the same desert. "Whether that spirit [of emigration], indomitable as it is in an ordinary encounter, would not

---

[1] Edward J. Wallace, Barrister-at-Law. *The Oregon Question Examined*, London, 1846, p. 29.

be found stumbling upon the dark mountains, or fainting in the dreary valleys, or quenched beneath the perpetual snows, which nature has opposed to the passage to this disputed territory, remains to be seen." In 1846 this veteran statesman is still speaking of "a wagon-road eighteen hundred miles in length through an arid and mountainous region" to the shores of the Pacific.

The fact is constantly meeting us, in this historical inquiry concerning the origin, growth, and acquisition of our Oregon, that the vastness of our territory, the great distance of fascinating portions of it from the old east, and the long trails of our daring emigrants, made it exceedingly difficult for the government to appreciate it and provide for it.

The time is not far past when a tour to Illinois was more tedious and even dangerous than one to-day to China. Lieutenant Pike was not the only one who feared the ruin of the Republic by the thin diffusion of its population by emigration.[1] Similar lack of foresight and knowledge, and practical, though unconscious indifference to our magnificent western growth, was shown when efforts were made to withhold all public lands from sale and settlement after the Louisiana purchase, beyond the Mississippi, till wild lands east of that river were taken up. And it is not to be concealed that the east bore it ill that the old centres of wealth and voting and general control were going "out west."

It is still difficult to persuade benevolent capitalists and benevolent organizations that their most hopeful fields are frontier fields. The handful of grain, whose

[1] Explorations on the Sources of the Mississippi, Missouri, Platte and Arkansas, 1806, Appendix II.

fruit is to shake like Lebanon, is prairie corn, and Pacific wheat. The old fields east of the Ohio, and specially east of the Hudson, have done raising these large crops of prophecy. The benevolence is reverent and filial and lovely that still decorates the old altars of religion, and wreathes the monuments of the fathers, and adds new turrets and alcoves and elms to the classic shades and walks of our younger feet. But if, by and by, we would rest in shrines, to which the godly and the scholarly will make pilgrimage, and as reverently, and filially, and lovingly as we do now to those of the fathers, we must put our legacies, and sympathies, and labors, as they did, into a growing frontier, and make the wilderness bud and blossom.

Prior to 1843 discussions on Oregon were not infrequent in Congress, but no legislation was had anticipating its settlement and protection. The first movement of this nature was in a resolution introduced into the House, in 1820, by Mr. Floyd of Virginia, but only debate followed. In 1843 a bill by Mr. Lewis of Missouri passed the Senate, making some legal provisions for Oregon, but it was lost in the House under an adverse report made by Mr. John Quincy Adams. In those times western enterprise, in the form of Fur Companies, did the most to compel attention to that neglected portion of our domain, notably, Ashley's, 1823, Jackson and Sublette's, 1827, Pattie's, 1830, Bonneville's, 1832, and some few others.

But the Hudson Bay Company did all they could to bring failure upon these, and they were generally successful. Governor Pelley of that Company well says in 1838: " We have compelled the American adventurers to withdraw from the contest, and are now pressing the

Russian Fur Company so closely, that we hope, at no very distant period, to confine them to the trade of their own proper territory." The Hudson Bay Company finally leased from the Russians that long, narrow strip of Alaska between British Columbia and the ocean, in no place more than thirty miles wide. The rental paid was two thousand land otter skins a year. The American adventurers generally returned to the States dissatisfied, and they charged much to climate, long journeys, and desert regions, which was really due to the harsh monopoly of English rivals.

All this tended to defame and depreciate Oregon in the popular mind, and congressional delays and inefficient action were the natural consequence. Feeble and not very successful missionary efforts in 1834 and the years following kept a kind of life in the Oregon question, and, uniting with the trading interest, brought it down to the times of the Ashburton Treaty. To one who has traced these facts, it will not seem strange that it did not gain recognition in that treaty. It had not definiteness or vitality enough in the American mind, which lay in ignorance of its true merits, and it could not have been handled as a whole and with international equity.

Indeed, when Dr. Whitman arrived many still held to the idea expressed, in his early career, by General Jackson to President Monroe: " Concentrate our population, confine our frontier to proper limits, until our country, in those limits, is filled with a dense population. It is the denseness of our population that gives strength and security to our frontier."

We have noticed Mr. Benton's rhetorical erection of the god Terminus on the Rocky Mountains. In a speech made two years even after the arrival and the alarming information of Dr. Whitman, Mr. Winthrop said: "Are our western brethren straightened for elbow-room, or likely to be for a thousand years? Have they not too much land for their own advantage already? . . . I doubt whether the west has a particle of real interest in the possession of Oregon. . . . The west has no interest, the country has no interest, in extending our territorial possessions." Mr. Webster renews the declaration of General Jackson and Mr. Winthrop, when opposing, in 1845, the admission of Texas: "The government is very likely to be endangered, in my opinion, by a further enlargement of the territorial surface, already so vast, over which it is extended."

Another question, traditional from colonial times, was floating about Washington and affected the other, whether Oregon was worth having, when Dr. Whitman appeared. It was whether smaller domains and several independent governments were not preferable to one total and inclusive Union. When the colonies were feeling their way toward independence, newspapers, pamphlets, and conventions handled this question, and among other plans a northern and middle and southern confederation or separate government was proposed. Sectional feeling and separation were high. After independence and the Union were made sure, Washington discovered strong tendencies to a separate government in the southwest: "The western states hang upon a pivot. The touch of a feather would turn them any way." Jefferson carried along toward Whitman's day the colonial notion of separate governments for the Americans, and was therefore disappointed by the failure of the Astor colony and plan. "I considered as a great public acquisition," he wrote to Mr.

Astor after the failure, "the commencement of a settlement on that point of the western coast of America, and looked forward with gratification to the time when its descendants should have spread themselves through the whole length of that coast, covering it with free and independent Americans, unconnected with us but by the ties of blood and interest, and enjoying, like us, the right of self-government." . . . "The germ of a great, free, and independent empire on that side of our continent."

In 1829 an organization was formed in Boston to promote the American occupation of Oregon, and it asked of Congress a colonial government, or an independent one, as that body might advise.

The venerable Gallatin, in his very able letters on the Oregon question, remarks: "The inhabitants of the country, from whatever quarter they may have come, will be, of right, as well as in fact, the sole legitimate owners of Oregon. Whenever sufficiently numerous they will decide whether it suits them best to be an independent nation, or an integral part of our great Republic. . . . Viewed as an abstract proposition, Mr. Jefferson's opinion appears correct, that it will be best for both the Atlantic and the Pacific American nations, whilst entertaining the most friendly relations, to remain independent, rather than to be united under the same government."[1]

Such were the antecedents and surroundings of the Oregon question when Dr. Whitman arrived in Washington, and neither Oregon, nor Webster, nor Whitman can be made to stand in a true light if placed outside this historical framework. Without making an extensive study of the case, the special friends of Oregon have felt

[1] Letter V.

that it was at that time neglected, and some of the friends of Dr. Whitman have felt that his perilous mission did not gain a just attention in the office of the Secretary of State. The facts in the case, so far as discovered, do not show disappointment by the one or neglect by the other. The Doctor seems to have gained all he asked, and the Secretary to have kept at the very front of circumstances; and the result, which is the logical conclusion of events, was the acquisition of Oregon to the full extent of any government claim by the United States.

It is reported as a coincidence of weight that Sir George Simpson, Governor of the Hudson Bay Company, visited Washington during the critical days we are now considering. Sir George had been the head of the Company in America for many years, and had been resident in the country much longer. Probably no living man could bring to the investigation of the question so much knowledge of the natural resources of Oregon and its value for some national domain. Certainly no one had a better understanding of the interests, plans, and secret policies of the Hudson Bay Company concerning that region. It was a coincidence, therefore, that Governor Simpson should start on an inland tour from Montreal to the heads and valley and mouth of the Columbia, make a double excursion up and down the Pacific coast, and survey carefully the Russian, English, American, and Mexican possessions there, while the Oregon interest was coming to the front. Without commission on the business, yet full of information, as no other man was, and then as fond of frontier life and forest sports as Webster himself, he could meet the Secretary of State informally and socially and frequently as a kind of untitled *tête-à-tête* plenipotentiary. For practical results, though uncommissioned, it was as when one is omitted or absent at the court dinner, but lunches privately with the king. No doubt each used the opportunity informally, for his government, but for the English side it was like putting forward the best Hudson Bay expert, while the most of the evidence on the American side came by way of Great Britain. But with no correspondence between the two gentlemen extant, and no records of visits preserved, so far as appears, it would be quite unwise to base any assertions of things done or proposed, on conjectures, inferences, traditions, and unadmitted reporters.

Very likely the Governor, at those splendid dinners, said some things to the Secretary which he afterward published in his "Narrative of a Journey Round the World." In passing the bar at the mouth of the Columbia he nervously describes the "spot already preeminent, among congenial terrors of much older fame, for destruction of property and loss of life." How could the United States wish to own that dangerous piece of property? But the English were willing to take it! He is confident "the United States will never possess more than a nominal jurisdiction, nor long possess even that, on the west side of the Rocky Mountains." He even challenges Congress to impose the Atlantic tariffs on the ports of the Pacific. And, giving full scope to England and Russia to control the destinies and dimensions of other peoples, he assumes to "confine every other nation within the scanty limits of its proper locality." Haughtily said by one who headed a land monopoly one third larger than all Europe. But it does not read so frightful and dwarfing to us now, when the

United States have land enough on which to set down all England seventy-eight times, with clippings that would comfortably seat Scotland, while we own six thousand miles of Pacific coast against the English four hundred and fifty.

The Governor grows bold in his book prophecies: "San Francisco will, to a moral certainty, sooner or later fall into the possession of the Americans — the only possible mode of preventing such a result being the previous occupation of the post on the part of Great Britain.... The only doubt is whether California is to fall to the British or to the Americans." In 1839, Captain Sir Edward Belcher had surveyed the California coasts to San Francisco and below, and the English government was informed, as if in anticipation, of the value and desirableness of that then almost Mexican waif.

So the Governor is chatty, and prophetic, and diplomatic, in his narrative of two volumes.[1] Whether he said these things, more or less, to Mr. Webster, in some most genial interviews, does not appear. But, indeed, it was a singular coincidence if Sir George Simpson, Governor of the Hudson Bay Company, was visiting in Washington just at that time. And it was another as singular coincidence, that at the same time Dr. Marcus Whitman should enter the office of the Secretary of State, and with wonderful intelligence be able to speak to the question: Is Oregon worth saving?

---

[1] *Narrative of a Journey Round the World.* By Sir George Simpson, Governor-in-Chief of the Hudson Bay Company in North America. In 1841-1842. London, 1847.

CHAPTER XXI.

TITLES TO OREGON.

The question of threescore years begins to show an end. The discussion, at home and abroad, is narrowing to an examination of titles, of discoveries, and settlements. At this later stage, therefore, in our study of the Oregon question, a statement of the respective claims of the two parties will not only be necessary, but it can now be made more briefly and intelligibly than it could have been at an earlier period.

The extent of the original Oregon of controversy is worthy of careful thought. By common consent the forty-second degree of latitude was the boundary between Oregon and California. The Pacific coast of Oregon ran from the forty-second degree to fifty-four forty, north. From that northern point on the coast it ran due east to the heights of the Rocky Mountains, and followed that divide down to the forty-second degree again. The territory so inclosed was the original, not the final, Oregon, extending about seven hundred and sixty miles north and south, by about six hundred and fifty east and west. This area is equal to Massachusetts sixty-three times, and to Great Britain and Ireland four times.

In 1790, Spain claimed for herself, both from discovery and settlement, even farther north than this, and denied the right of any other nation to make establishments there. In this year Great Britain made issue with Spain on these assumptions, the result of which was the Nootka Convention, so called. It is not expedient to go here into details as to the claims of the two nations in that quarter of the world. They are absurd enough on either side, and after an illustration for each party, we will skip two hundred years and more, and come to results.

When Balboa discovered the Pacific Ocean, at the Isthmus, in 1513, he took possession of it for his king as a private sea; and its navigation, trade, fisheries, and adjoining country, he vowed to defend for the king and crown of Spain. A half century or so later, 1579, Sir Francis Drake, buccaneer, filibuster, and marauder-general — honorable and honored in the times and court of Elizabeth — accepted for his queen, and from the natives of that northwest coast, coronation, sceptre, and sovereignty. The poor creatures, scantily clothed in a few skins besides their own, went through the ceremonial farce; and the pillar that the admiral erected in commemoration of this transfer of dominion to his queen was a monument of folly. The two absurdities are well matched together by the Spaniard and the Englishman.

On occasional visits by vessels, temporary trade with the natives, some fishing, and a few shanties, the two rival nations built claims to sovereignty. The English claimed "an indisputable right to the enjoyment of a free and uninterrupted navigation, commerce, and fishing, and to the possession of such establishments as they should form, with the consent of the natives of the country, not previously occupied by any of the European nations." While doing this, the English vessels and property were seized and confiscated by the Spanish.

Hence negotiations opened that resulted in the Nootka Convention of 1790.

By this convention or treaty Great Britain gained the right to navigate, trade, and fish, on the northwest coast, and make temporary settlements for these purposes. Spain conceded only this, and retained her sovereignty or right of eminent domain over the coasts, islands, and land inward. The times in Europe were then anxious; revolutions threatened, and the era of Napoleon was just opening; the ministry of Pitt eased off from its hard demands on Spain, and the secret and adroit management of Mirabeau made the negotiations almost or quite barren for the old rival of France. The convention does not show that Spain conceded any of the sovereignty which she claimed over the land. The conference and the treaty were commercial and not territorial. England sought a division of the territory, but it was not gained. While the English could not "navigate or carry on their fishing in the said seas within the space of ten leagues from any part of the coast occupied by Spain," the settlements where the English could trade were made common to Spain also. Indeed when the convention was discussed in Parliament it was asserted that England had lost more than she had gained, while Spain was left unrestricted and unmolested in her old assumptions and assertions of sovereignty. I dwell the more minutely on this treaty, because afterward the United States became full owner, by purchase, of all that Spain owned, and had left to herself, by the Nootka arrangement, of the country north of the forty-second degree.

It should here be added that the war between England and Spain in 1796 abrogated this treaty, according to the common theory, as stated by Lord Bathurst, "that all treaties are put an end to by a subsequent war between the same parties." This would carry back the extent of the gain of the United States by the Louisiana purchase to all that Spain owned north of forty-two prior to the Nootka Convention.

Spain and Great Britain entered into a new commercial treaty in 1814, in which the Nootka Treaty was reaffirmed. This was a practical concession by England to Spain of all the territorial sovereignty which Spain had claimed on the northwest coast, north of the parallel of forty-two. In order to understand with definiteness the American claim to Oregon by the Louisiana Purchase, several particulars should be here carefully noted. Prior to the Nootka Convention Spain claimed the sovereignty of the Oregon coasts. As the Nootka Convention makes no reference to this claim, it is silently conceded to Spain. In 1796 that convention is abrogated by war between the two parties, and Spain is reinstated in all her ancient claims, commercial and territorial. In this condition of things Spain reconveys to France the ancient Louisiana, which was assumed to embrace the Oregon territory, and soon after France conveyed it to the United States by the same limits by which she had received it from Spain. In 1814, Great Britain reaffirms the Nootka Treaty, and so renews the concession to Spain of her territorial claims on that coast. It would appear, therefore, that the United States derived from Spain through France a title to Oregon which, as late as 1814, Great Britain had conceded. When we come to examine the Florida Treaty we shall see how this Spanish title is confirmed and supplemented for the United States,

Some good authorities, even Bancroft, have expressed doubts whether the northern boundary of the ancient Louisiana was fixed west of the Lake of the Woods and on the forty-ninth parallel, and if not, whether any territory west of the mountains was conveyed back and forth as we have stated. The Treaty of Utrecht, 1713, provided for determining " the limits which are to be fixed between the said Bay of Hudson and the places appertaining to the French."[1] Mr. Madison says: "There is reason to believe that the boundary between Louisiana and the British territories north of it was actually fixed by commissioners appointed under the Treaty of Utrecht, and that the boundary was to run from the Lake of the Woods westwardly on latitude forty-nine;" and he says the boundary was run " along that line indefinitely." Mr. Monroe, United States minister to England, writes, 1804, to Lord Harrowby, the British Secretary of Foreign Affairs: "Commissioners were appointed by each power, who executed the stipulations of the treaty in establishing the boundary proposed by it. They fixed the northern boundary of Canada and Louisiana," etc.[2] Mr. Greenhow in his "History of Oregon," expresses doubts of this, however, and sets them forth in an elaborate note.

The obscurity of this fact would be unfortunate, since the territory so defined on its north and west was ceded by France to Spain in 1762, and by Spain to France in 1800, and by France to the United States in 1803. But a late and highest authority, the honorable Caleb Cushing, in "The Treaty of Washington," says: "The paral-

[1] Treaty of Utrecht, art. 10.
[2] American State Papers, Foreign Affairs, vol. iii. p. 90. See, also, Message of President Jefferson, with documents, March 30, 1808.

lel of forty-nine degrees was established between France and Great Britain by the Treaty of Utrecht."[1]

The conclusion seems warranted, therefore, that when France, in 1762, conveyed secretly to Spain all her possessions west of the Mississippi, she conveyed up north and out west on this line between her and Great Britain, according to the Treaty of Utrecht, — the 49th parallel. On this same northern and westward line Spain reconveyed this identical territory to France in 1800, and in 1803 France sold the same in both area and boundaries to the United States.

The hasty reader would think that he here finds an original and continued title to the Oregon, vested in Spain. While there are negotiations about the territory, they pertain to tenancy and not to ownership. Touching the latter Spain is constantly sensitive, prior to the Nootka Convention, and down to her final transfer of the region to France, keeping the ownership in her own hands by the assertion of her claim. She lingered over that ownership with a wonderful tenacity. For after she had reconveyed the territory to France in 1800, she was indignant that France sold it to the United States, and delayed to pass the papers of sale, and entered protest against it, in informal ways.

Both France and the United States grew anxious over the delay, and the latter was quieted by the assurance of Napoleon that he guaranteed the cession. But the conveyance was made embarrassing, and the formal transfer of territory and sovereignty at New Orleans, by France, to the United States, December 20, 1803, was not free from anxiety. The Spanish had formally transferred the territory to France only twenty days

[1] *The Treaty of Washington.* By Caleb Cushing, 1873, p. 208.

before, and the officials on both sides had fears that the old Spanish populace, with the French more or less consenting, would make a popular demonstration. However, the august occasion passed in quiet.

The national spirit, more than the letter of any treaties with England, showed that Spain constantly affirmed her title on the northwest up to 54° 40′. Up to the forty-ninth she conveyed the same back to France, and so France to the United States. If she had any remnant there after this, it was conveyed to the United States by the Florida Treaty of 1819, which conveyed all hers, north of forty-two, to the United States.

CHAPTER XXII.

THE CLAIMS OF THE UNITED STATES TO OREGON.

The claims of the United States to Oregon, as the question drew its slow length along through threescore years, became a tedious, and perplexing, and annoying topic. In few cases has diplomacy showed better its ability not to do a thing, than in the settlement of the Oregon question. Yet, now that it is settled, the salient points stand out with singular simplicity and strength. It is not surprising that the extent of domain and the vast natural values in the territory in dispute should stimulate great national desire, and draw into the case all the misty indefiniteness of the laws of nations, so called, and all the finesse of astute negotiation. It must be confessed, too, that the affair had some inherent difficulties. Few men of state in the generation of noble ones then on the stage were better fitted to handle this question and speak of it than Albert Gallatin, and in one of his most helpful letters on it he says: "It is morally impossible for the bulk of the people of any country thoroughly to investigate a subject so complex as that of the respective claims of the Oregon territory."

A tract of country four times as large as Great Britain and Ireland, already half in the grasp and within the possible monopoly of a government whose realm lies scattered around the world, could not but interest intensely that government. A territory that would make sixty-three states as large as Massachusetts, and naturally quite as inviting to human homes as that ancient domain was in its primitive state, could not be abandoned by the United States in the face of four separate and independent titles to it, till each had been shown to be worthless. Of course it was or should be a question of right and not of power, though several times it came near to a vindication of the right by artillery and bayonet.[1]

A few passages will serve to state the substance of the grounds on which the United States claimed Oregon.

1. By prior discovery. As the new world was a novelty to the old, so sectional discoveries in it by different nations introduced into the law of nations novel rights and laws concerning newly discovered lands. By general consent the discovery of the St. Lawrence gave the basin of that river to the French, and that of the Hudson to the Dutch, and of the Potomac to the English, while the coasts and basins of New Spain fell in the same way to Old Spain. On the same general principles and usages the United States claimed the country drained by the Columbia, since that river had been discovered and explored by Captain Robert Gray, of the ship Columbia, of Boston, in 1792.

Suspicions of such a river had been abroad, and the Spanish and English had carefully examined the coast for the mouths of large streams, and some had come nigh to making the discovery, as Meares and Vancouver. The former was led on by old Spanish charts which laid down such a river under the name of the St. Roque. Meares failed to find the mouth of the supposed river, where he was led to explore for it in the Straits of Fuca, and made

---

[1] The territory finally conceded was equal to thirty-two states like Massachusetts.

permanent record of his failure in the two titles he left there — Cape Disappointment and Deception Bay. In a similar search Vancouver passed the mouth of the Columbia, and noticed "river-colored water — the probable consequence of some streams falling into the bay. . . . Not considering their opening worthy of more attention, I continued our pursuit to the northwest," being satisfied that "the several large rivers and capacious inlets that have been described as discharging their contents into the Pacific, between the fortieth and forty-eighth degrees of latitude, were reduced to brooks insufficient for our vessels to navigate, or to bays inaccessible as harbors for refitting."

Vancouver scrutinized that coast for about two hundred and fifty miles, and so minutely, he says, "that the surf has been constantly seen from the masthead to break on its shores." Thus he failed to discover the mouth of the Columbia, mistaking the breakers on its fearful bars for coast surf. This entry was made in his journal April 29, 1792.

It is a striking coincidence that in the afternoon of the same day Captain Gray of the Columbia fell in with Vancouver, in the Strait of Fuca, north of the river in question, and informed him that he had very recently been off the mouth of a river in latitude forty-six ten, "where the outset or reflux was so strong as to prevent his entering for nine days." "This was probably the opening," continues Vancouver, "passed by us on the forenoon of the 27th, and was apparently inaccessible, not from the current, but from the breakers that extended across it." The two captains parted — the Englishman going north and the American south, on their discoveries.

Thirteen days afterward, May 11th, Gray rediscovered the mouth of the river, and ran in under full sail between the breakers — Vancouver's "surf." He anchored ten miles up from the mouth, spent three days in trade and in filling the water casks, and then ran up fifteen miles farther and anchored. After spending nine days in the river, he left it, giving to it the name of his ship.

The British statement of the Oregon case, filed in for the sixth Conference, in 1826–27, admits that Gray discovered the Columbia. "It must, indeed, be admitted that Mr. Gray, finding himself in the bay formed by the discharge of the waters of the Columbia into the Pacific, was the first to ascertain that this bay formed the outlet of a great river." Yet, singularly, they call this a "single step in the progress of discovery," and would compel the American captain to share the honors with his English successors, who afterward went farther up the river England is brought in for a large share of honors and claims, because Vancouver went up afterward a hundred miles farther than Gray went at first. And he did this only after Gray met him the second time and informed him of his discovery of the Columbia, and where he would find it. Without this information Vancouver would not have renewed his search ; and as it was, he simply sent his lieutenant to take soundings and bearings farther up stream, under the information of the captain of the Columbia. This is the English "discovery" of the Columbia River !

Thus the discovery of a river is made a progressive work by English claimants, as if one could discover the Mississippi at New Orleans, and another at Memphis, another at Cairo, another at the mouth of the Missouri, and so on to the Falls of St. Anthony. As if the discovery of a lost cable were progressive, as the separate links in the chain are hauled on board. If this had not been said by "plenipotentiaries" we should call it puerile. Yet even Professor Twiss of Oxford, in an elaborate discussion of the Oregon question, says: "Captain Gray's claim is limited to the mouth of the Columbia." A few years afterward Lewis and Clark struck its head waters in the Rocky Mountains and followed them to the mouth, and so its discovery, outlet and sources, were American. By the usage of those times, which was the law of nations, so called, that discovery of a large river on an unexplored coast by an American citizen gave its basin to the United States.

2. By the Louisiana Purchase. This constituted an important point in the claims of the United States to Oregon. We have already noticed that in 1762 France ceded to Spain all her territory west of the Mississippi, that Spain returned it in 1800, and that France sold the same to the United States in 1803, " with all its rights and appurtenances," says the treaty, "as fully, and in the same manner, as they have been acquired by the French Republic." We have also seen that the northern boundary of this Louisiana province was the forty-ninth parallel, running westwardly "along that line indefinitely." As this northern boundary is not said, in any specific words of the negotiations or treaty of sale and purchase, to be extended to the Pacific, but only in that direction "indefinitely," there is room for a doubt how far west the Louisiana extended on that parallel.

If, however, the claims of France failed to reach the Pacific on that line, it must have been because they encountered the old claims of Spain, that preceded the

Nootka Treaty, and were tacitly conceded at that time and in it by England. Between the French claims on the south of that line prior to the transfer of 1762, and the Spanish claims prior to the Nootka Treaty, and the re-transfer to France in 1800, there was no unclaimed territory on which England could base a claim. If the United States did not acquire through to the Pacific on the south of that parallel of forty-nine by the Louisiana Purchase, it was because Spain was owner there prior to the first and second and third Louisiana transfers. The English were not there by discovery to encounter a United States extension, by the purchase, to the Pacific, for the United States had preceded the English in discovery; they were not there by concession from the Spanish, for the Spanish refused the claim and England did not reaffirm it, either in 1790 or 1814; they were not there by occupation, for they had no settlements.

If, therefore, the United States failed to gain the Pacific coast in that purchase it was because Spain had not relinquished her rights there. This point will receive a separate consideration at the close of this chapter on the United States claims to Oregon.

3. By prior explorations. The purchase of the Louisiana by the United States was known at once among the nations. Immediately, and openly, under their full view, and as if with full right to go and examine a piece of newly purchased property, the United States sent Lewis and Clark to explore this grand addition to the Union. The expedition consisted of the joint commanders, nine young Kentuckians, fourteen United States soldiers, two Canadian *royageurs*, and one negro, the body servant of Captain Clark, — twenty-eight persons. It spent the winter of 1803-4 in camp on the Mississippi,

at the mouth of Wood River, just below Alton, and opposite the mouths of the Missouri. They broke camp May 14, 1804, and made the round trip to the Pacific and back in two years, four months, and nine days — saluting St. Louis, and receiving a most hearty and noisy welcome from that polyglot village, September 23, 1806, at noon.

This was no private enterprise, as of scientific men or Indian traders. Hearne had explored his way to the Arctic, and Mackenzie to the Pacific, in the interests of a corporation, the Hudson Bay Company, for commercial gain; but this was a government enterprise, and confessedly for government ends. The official exploration of the property, recently and notably purchased, was not followed by any objection or warning from any party once or still in interest on the northwest coast, as the Russians, Spanish, French, or English. This is the more noteworthy, since there were national ambitions and sensitiveness over the ownership of those vast regions presumed to be embraced in the Louisiana.

The Spanish tone of that day is illustrative. Lewis and Clark had proposed to run up the Missouri to La Charrette, a frontier settlement, and spend their first winter there; but the governor of this upper province of Louisiana forbade their entering the territory, since he had received no official notice of its transfer. When sixteen days up the Missouri the following spring they learned that the letter, announcing there the sale of the territory, was burned publicly in indignation.

England was never behind Spain in her ambition and technical pleas for territory, as India, and China, and the Belize, and Afghanistan, the Zululand, and the Transvaal, and Egypt, will show. Yet the assumption by the United States in this expedition that Oregon had been purchased by her was not questioned by Great Britain.

Resting on the exploration, the government, from time to time, farther assumed the ownership by Congressional bills and discussions and enactments; and the people followed this up with private companies, organized for trade within the territory. So it came to pass that the entire region from the head waters of the Columbia and its affluents, and, to an extent, those of the Sacramento and Fraser's rivers, was explored by enterprising Americans, as on their own soil. What Pike and Long did in the eastern sections of the purchase, Lewis and Clark, and Frémont and Whitman and Parker accomplished in and beyond the mountains.

4. By prior settlements. We distinguish here between the occupation and the settlement of a country. Hudson Bay traders and trappers occupied Oregon for peltry and furs, and thereby gained the rights of hunters. Such pursuits and rights are the same as those of the native Indians. It is claimed that the interests of civilization cannot leave vast tracts of wild country to the Indians, for a game life. But this English company used and were usurping the country in question for no broader purpose, only that they procured a surplus of hunter spoils, and put it on the market of the world. They did not increase the natural productions of the country, they did not propose settlements that imply a family and a plow and water-wheel.

The first corporation and colony to contemplate settlements was Astor's. His project, as his correspondence with government through Jefferson shows, anticipated civil society, and government favored his plans, as comprehending civilization on the northwest coast, and binding over the territory to the Union by settlements. That Astor took possession of American domain, and had possessions in the land that were national, is evident from the fact that after the war of 1812 and the English capture of Astoria, it was restored to the United States, by treaty, which stipulated the restoration of "all territory, places, and possessions whatever, taken by either party from the other during the war." In the restoration the English official calls it "the settlement." This was the first made by white men in the valley of the Columbia, and establishes the claim of the United States there by prior settlement.

Following the restoration of Astoria in 1818, which was the first germ of civilization planted on that coast in 1811, there came at length the family and the white man's frame house, the plow and seed wheat and the garden, the saw and grain mill and printing-press. These were the first ripples of that coming human tide of civilized life that now flows and ebbs so splendidly on those far-off shores. Domestic animals crowded off the wild ones, and the pursuits of the chase gave place to the industries that have there made a noble people.

In almost every instance where the labors and arts of society broke up the wild life of the trapper and trader and factor, the innovation and elevation came from the United States. It is not necessary to itemize, for all histories, sketches, and travels touching primitive times and the dawn of civilization in that country, came in the line of its discovery and purchase and exploration by the United States.

Concerning the claims of Spain on the northwest coast, and the effect of the Nootka Treaty of 1790 on them, an additional remark should here be made. That treaty made stipulations concerning navigation and commerce, and left a right common to Great Britain and Spain to occupy the country temporarily for trade. But rights of sovereignty and jurisdiction were not conveyed by the latter to the former. The question of sovereignty was expressly kept in abeyance. However arrogant, therefore, the claims of Spain were to sovereignty over the territory of Oregon before the Nootka Convention, they were not yielded or abridged by it, and it was admitted in Parliament that England lost rather than gained by the new arrangement.

The whole treaty was abrogated by the war which soon followed between the parties; and afterward, 1814, only the commercial articles in it were renewed. The territorial claims of the parties to Oregon were, therefore, never adjusted between them, and the ancient assumptions of Spain were still in force when the United States purchased Louisiana in 1803, and made the Florida Treaty with Spain in 1819. In this Florida Treaty is a clause very significant to the interests of the United States. By the Treaty of Utrecht, 1713, between the English and the French, Mr. Madison says: "There is reason to believe that the boundary between Louisiana and the British territories north of it was actually fixed by commissioners appointed under the treaty, and that the boundary was to run from the Lake of the Woods westwardly on latitude forty-nine," and he says it was run "along that line indefinitely."

When France conveyed the Louisiana to Spain in 1762 she conveyed up to and along this line westward. It is a common historical conviction that she conveyed westward to the Pacific on that parallel of forty-nine. If she did not, it must have been because, over the mountains, she encountered the more ancient Spanish claims. Be it either way, after the conveyance, Spain owned westward from the Mississippi along the parallel of forty-nine and south of it to the Pacific.

When Spain reconveyed the same to France it was, in the language of the third article of the treaty, " the colony or provinces of Louisiana, with the same extent which it now has in the hands of Spain, and which it had when France possessed it, and such as it should be, according to the treaties subsequently made between Spain and other states." Now as Spain, in the Nootka Treaty, had not alienated any of this territory, and as she had made in the interval no other treaty by which she could, she retroceded to France all which she had received from her. That was westward to the Pacific, or to her possessions on the Pacific, be the fact of possession as it may. If, therefore, after the United States had made the Louisiana Purchase, she did not own through on the forty-ninth parallel to the Pacific, it must have been because Spain owned the Oregon prior to the Treaty of Utrecht, 1713, did not acquire it from France in 1762, and could not retrocede it to France, so as to become a part of the Louisiana Purchase by the United States. It is, therefore, pertinent to remark that when Lewis and Clark explored Oregon, they explored either United States or Spanish territory.

From that date till 1819 Spain made no changes of ownership, sovereignty, and jurisdiction touching Oregon. And now come the important concessions by Spain to the United States in the Florida Treaty of 1819.

After marking the boundary line between the two countries west of the Mississippi, beginning at the mouth of the Sabine in the Gulf of Mexico, and running variously north and west till it reaches the Pacific on latitude forty-two, the third article in the treaty says: "His Catholic majesty cedes to the United States all his rights, claims, and pretensions to any territories east and north of the said line; and for himself, his heirs and successors, renounces all claims to the said territories forever." This made the United States the owner, in the place of Spain, of all the territorial right of the latter in the northwest, north of the present southern boundary of Oregon. The value of that concession, by the law of nations, must be estimated by the facts now given.

The validity and strength of the claims of the United States to the Oregon, as discoverer, purchaser, explorer, settler, and as successor to Spain, were realized, and to an extent conceded, by Great Britain. During negotiations in 1826–27 her plenipotentiaries said formally what England usually said from first to last: "Great Britain claims no exclusive sovereignty over any portion of that territory. Her present claim, not in respect to any part, but to the whole, is limited to a right of joint occupancy, in common with other states, leaving the right of exclusive dominion in abeyance." In view of the facts given, this confession approximates a quit-claim.

Therefore, in the matter of the American claim to Oregon below forty-nine, two things may be said in concluding the investigation of titles to it. First, that the United States obtained it in the Louisiana Purchase. Second, if any portion of it was not thus conveyed, being retained in the rights of Spain, then Spain conveyed it in 1819 in the words of the Florida Treaty: "His Catholic majesty cedes to the United States all his rights, claims, and pretensions to any territories east and north of the said line,"—the forty-second parallel of latitude on the Oregon coasts.

CHAPTER XXIII.

HISTORY VINDICATED.

There has been an impression that Mr. Webster failed to grasp the Oregon case, slighted the American interest, and would have compromised our rights, if President Tyler had not interposed to delay negotiations. There is no doubt that Mr. Webster viewed the case much through the English medium. No doubt the Hudson Bay Company had been long and carefully preparing testimony in public opinion to carry the settlement in their favor. It would not be strange if Webster shared the views and feelings of the statesmen and other public men of the day on the general question. The East has always been conservative and sometimes unfortunately and painfully laggard concerning the extent and growth and worth and hastening power of the West. In matters of education and religion in the West, as affecting vitally the future of the Republic, shortsightedness is yet far from being cured. Yet the partisans of Oregon must not think that the great statesman held the Pacific coast of no account because he would not adopt the motto: "Fifty-four Forty, or Fight." In 1845, and before the Oregon struggle was ended, he wrote to his son Fletcher: "You know my opinion to have been, and it now is, that the port of San Francisco would be twenty times as valuable to us as all Texas." The Secretary entertained no extreme views either way concerning the titles and final possession of Oregon, nor does it appear that there was ever any radical change in his views. The settlement was finally made on the boundary and terms which he proposed, after his interviews with Whitman, and the country was satisfied with the result. Indeed, in 1839, four years before, when some spoke of Mr. Webster as special envoy to England to settle the northeastern boundary, he drew up a memorandum of plan for settlement for the use of Mr. Van Buren's cabinet. In his life of Webster Mr. Curtis says: "The germs of the negotiation, which afterward led to the Treaty of Washington [Ashburton's] were contained in this memorandum." Through that ardent Oregon era he showed the interest of a patriot and the wisdom of a statesman. His state of mind, always predisposed that way, needed both the information and the plan which Whitman took to his office, and his course afterward showed that he used the one and adopted the other. In a letter the next year to Mr. Everett, our minister to England, Mr. Webster, says: "The ownership of the whole country is very likely to follow the greater settlement, and larger amount of population " — the great idea which Whitman brought to him over the mountains.

He gave full credit to Dr. Whitman for all this, in a remark to a legal gentleman and personal friend: "It is safe to assert that our country owes it to Dr. Whitman and his associate missionaries that all the territory west of the Rocky Mountains and south as far as the Columbia River, is not now owned by England and held by the Hudson Bay Company."

When President Tyler communicated the Ashburton Treaty to the Senate, in August, 1843, he said that they found, early in the general negotiations, that there was little probability of agreeing then on the Oregon part of the boundary, and it therefore seemed best to omit it from the treaty. In his annual message in December following, he again says that a failure to agree on the Oregon question would have probably carried with it a failure of the entire treaty, and so Oregon was left out. He then adds: " I shall not delay to urge on Great Britain the importance of its early settlement." And closely following the proclamation of the Ashburton Treaty Mr. Webster wrote to our minister at St. James to urge the settlement. What he said afterward, with emphasis, and for both nations to hear, he was ready to say, early as well as late, in this long discussion : " The government of the United States has never offered any line south of forty-nine, and it never will. It behooves all concerned to regard this as a settled point. . . . England must not expect anything south of the forty-ninth degree."

No doubt Dr. Whitman, on his arrival in Washington, received and appreciated all these facts. Oregon had not been included in the Ashburton Treaty, because the times were not ripe for it, and he was wanted to furnish the needed information, and open an easy trail to the Pacific. In judging whether Mr. Webster was peculiarly lacking in interest for Oregon at that interview, the tone of the times should be considered. When the Doctor arrived the omissions of the Ashburton Treaty had been under elaborate discussion in Congress. Linn's resolution, calling for information on the omission of Oregon had prolonged the debates, and then a bill for the occupation and settlement of Oregon, had been rejected in the House only fifteen days before his arrival. The times, not the Secretary, deferred action, and Oregon was waiting for Whitman at Washington, instead of being delayed and half declined by the indifference of Webster.

Some remarks made in the Senate in August, 1842, by Mr. Calhoun, in this discussion on the omissions of the Ashburton Treaty, are pertinent in this place: " Would it be wise to reject the treaty because all has not been done that could be desired? He placed a high value on our territory on the west of those mountains, and held our title to be clear, but he would regard it as an act of consummate folly to stake our claim on a trial of strength at this time. . . . Our population is steadily, he might say rapidly advancing across the continent to the borders of the Pacific Ocean. Judging from past experience the tide of population will sweep across the Rocky Mountains with resistless force at no distant period, when what we claim will quietly fall into our hands without expense or bloodshed. Time is acting for us. Wait patiently and all we claim will be ours; but if we attempt to seize it by force, it will be sure to elude our grasp."

Probably Whitman was more glad than any one that negotiation had not again been forced, since failure would have been inevitable. The wisdom of the President and Secretary must have satisfied this eminently sensible man. He found his information as welcome as it was needed, and his plan to save Oregon cordially adopted. As yet Oregon was safe against any diplomatic committal, and he had the assurance of the government that it would wait on his plan. Practically the destiny of Oregon lay in his hand, for a reasonable time, by the consent of the government. Dr. Whitman could ask no more, nor do any writings or data of that time show that he left Washington disappointed. Specially he was relieved of the great burden of anxiety that he brought over the mountains, lest the interests of Oregon should be sacrificed or put in more imminent peril by the Ashburton Treaty. That grave fear was quieted when we welcomed him in St. Louis from the Santa Fé trail, in February, 1843, and informed him that the Ashburton Treaty had been concluded six months before, and in no way referred to the Oregon question.

The Doctor had arrived in Washington just in time to make such a visit of the greatest service in weakening the English and strengthening the American claims; and to him above any other man, and beyond comparison, must be given the credit of saving Oregon. He does not appear to have left any memoranda, written or printed, of his interviews with the President, Secretary of State, or members of Congress; nor is there found, as yet, any record by himself of his views and feelings as to his reception at Washington. He gained his point, made a hurried visit to Boston on missionary business, met his appointment with the emigrant bands on the Missouri borders, led them to Oregon, and thus practically closed the Oregon controversy. Words and views, therefore, reproduced from memory, many years afterward, and attributed to Dr. Whitman, must be adjusted to the official documents and printed data, speeches in Congress, and correspondence of those days. An impression that Mr. Webster failed in hearty interest for Oregon has gained some circulation, though, as is well known, he gave the great weight of his influence and labors to bring about the result so generally acceptable. This wrong impression is traceable, substantially, to three sources, recently assuming printed form after having been traditional for twenty years or so.

In 1870 the Rev. H. H. Spalding, the honored and venerable missionary, and early associate of Dr. Whitman, had these passages in a lecture which he gave here and there in the East: "The Doctor pushed on to Washington and immediately sought an interview with Secretary Webster, . . . stated to him the object of his crossing the mountains, and laid before him the great importance of Oregon to the United States. But Mr. Webster lay too near to Cape Cod to see things in the same light with his fellow statesman, who had transferred his worldly interests to the Pacific coast. He awarded sincerity to the missionary, but could not admit for a moment that the short residence of six years could give the Doctor the knowledge of the country possessed by Governor Simpson, who had almost grown up in the country, and had traveled every part of it, and represents it as one unbroken waste of sand deserts, and impassable mountains, fit only for the beaver, the gray bear, and the savage. Besides, he had about traded it off with Governor Simpson to go into the Ashburton Treaty, for a cod-fishery on Newfoundland."

He then had an interview with President Tyler, " who at once appreciated his solicitude and his timely representations of Oregon, and especially his disinterested though hazardous undertaking to cross the Rocky Mountains in the winter, to take back a caravan of wagons. He said that although the Doctor's representations of the character of the country, and the possibility of reaching it by wagon route, were in direct contradiction to those of Governor Simpson, his frozen limbs were sufficient proof of his sincerity, and his missionary character was sufficient guarantee for his honesty; and he would, therefore, as President, rest upon them and act accordingly, would detail Frémont with a military force to escort the Doctor's caravan through the mountains, and no more action should be had toward trading off Oregon till he could hear the result of the expedition, . . . the swapping of Oregon with England for a cod-fishery should stop for the present."

The substance of this, from the same author, Mr. Gray found in a California paper, and copied into his "History of Oregon," published in 1870.

The Rev. Mr. Hines, also the author of a history of that territory, as quoted by Gray, says: "On the arrival of Dr. Whitman in Washington he found he had not started one day too soon to save the northwest coast to the United States. The Webster-Ashburton Treaty, by which the United States were to relinquish to England the title to that part of Oregon north of the Columbia, was about to be executed. On his representations of the value of the country, and of the practicability of a wagon road across the continent to the Columbia, the President hesitated. But when these representations were enforced by the fact that the Doctor's own wife, accompanied by only one white lady companion, had already crossed the continent, and were now in the valley of the Walla Walla, lone representatives of Christianity and American civilization, he hesitated no longer, but adopted the course of action which resulted in securing to the United States the title to Oregon up to the forty-ninth degree."

The "Missionary Herald" for 1869 represents Mr. Webster as saying to Dr. Whitman: "Wagons cannot cross the mountains. Sir George Simpson, who is here, affirms that, and so do all his correspondents in this region. Moreover, I am about trading Oregon for Newfoundland and the English cod-fisheries." The same article makes President Tyler say: "Dr. Whitman, since you are a missionary I will believe you, and if you will take the proposed emigration to Oregon the bargain shall not be made" (pp. 76–80).

The "Atlantic Monthly" has this paragraph: "Mr. Webster was at one time disposed to cede the valley of the Columbia River for the free right to fish on the colonial coast of the North Atlantic; Governor Simpson of the Hudson Bay Company having represented Oregon as worthless for agricultural purposes, and only valuable for its furs. Just then Dr. Whitman arrived at Washington, dressed in the Mackinaw blanket coat and buckskin leggins in which he had crossed the Rocky Mountains, to plead for the retention of Oregon. 'But you are too late, Doctor,' said Mr. Webster, 'for we are about to trade off Oregon for the cod-fisheries.'"[1] Another authority states it thus: the treaty "was nearly ready to be signed, but Dr. Whitman made such representations respecting the value of the country and its accessibility that Mr. Webster promised the treaty should be suppressed if the Doctor would conduct a caravan through to Oregon, which he engaged to do."

In 1881 the American Board published a book called the "Ely Volume," designed to show the incidental contributions of its foreign missions to civilization, science, and the growth of nations. In it Webster is reported as saying to Dr. Whitman: "'I am about trading that worthless territory for some valuable claims in relation to the Newfoundland cod-fisheries.' He [Dr. Whitman] then went to President Tyler and said the same things [that he had said to Mr. Webster]. The

[1] *Atlantic Monthly*, October, 1880, p. 534.

President replied, 'Dr. Whitman, since you are a missionary I will believe you, and if you take your emigrants over there, the treaty will not be ratified.'"[1]

To the same purport the "Missionary Herald" says in 1882, that Dr. Whitman "barely succeeded in preventing the exchange of that whole region west of the mountains for some additional privileges in the Newfoundland fishery."[2]

The three passages, however, from Mr. Spalding, Mr. Hines and Mr. Gray, appear to be the original triplet that have produced the impressions referred to, that Mr. Webster did not well meet and handle the Oregon case. Like the three grains of wheat of which Humboldt speaks, which the negro slave of the great Cortez found in the imported rice, and sowed in New Spain, so that the New World became a wheatfield, these three statements have multiplied exceedingly. Within a few years they have reappeared in the newspapers, secular and religious, and in the classic monthly and portly volume.

What is the historical ground for the rumor that Webster slighted Oregon? These statements are produced from memory twenty-five years, at least, after Dr. Whitman submitted the Oregon case to the Secretary of State. They assume that the Doctor was barely in time to keep the loss of Oregon out of the Ashburton Treaty; as Webster "had about traded it off with Governor Simpson [of the Hudson Bay Company] for a cod-fishery on Newfoundland." This representation is singular in four particulars:

First, Oregon was not a matter of negotiation between Ashburton and Webster. In preliminary and informal

[1] *Ely Volume*, p. 14.   [2] October, 1882, p. 375.

conversation, when they first met, they saw that they could not agree on this part of the boundary question, and so agreed to omit it. Indeed, Lord Ashburton was not prepared, by his papers of instruction, to take up the question, and was not authorized to do it, and it nowhere appears, as yet, in the papers of the department of state at Washington, or in the Congressional discussion over the Ashburton and Oregon treaties, that the Secretary expected, or was expected by the government, to include the Oregon question in the Ashburton Treaty. There is, therefore, no reference to it in the treaty, or in the documents accompanying the treaty.

Second, the charge against Webster is that he was about to exchange Oregon for certain English fishing interests on our northeast coasts, and that the timely arrival of Whitman at Washington prevented the Secretary of State from executing the exchange in the Ashburton Treaty. The Ashburton Treaty was concluded six months before Whitman arrived at Washington. The two negotiators signed it August 9, 1842; on the eleventh of that month it was submitted to the Senate; on the twenty-sixth it was approved, and Lord Ashburton started with it the same day for England; and, having been ratified and returned to the United States, it was proclaimed on the tenth of November. Dr. Whitman arrived in March following.

Third, Governor Simpson was not an agent of Great Britain, and had no authority to trade off cod-fisheries for Oregon. If Sir George Simpson even visited Washington at that time the evidence is yet wanting, except in rumors. His "Narrative of a Journey Round the World" in 1841–1842, in which he crossed the continent direct and with expedition from Boston, *viâ* Montreal to the Columbia, makes no mention of a visit to Washington, and seems to allow no time for it. If Webster made the reference attributed to him, it must have been playfully, as when he wrote his daughter, Mrs. Paige, a few days after signing the treaty: "The only question of magnitude about which I did not negotiate with Lord Ashburton is the question respecting the fisheries. That question I propose to take up with Mr. Seth Peterson [Mr. Webster's Marshfield farmer] on Tuesday, the 6th day of September next, at 6 o'clock, A. M. In the mean time I may find a leisure hour to drop a line on the same subject at Nahant."

Fourth, I find nothing in Mr. Webster's speeches, correspondence, official papers, or life, going to suggest that it was ever a plan with him to exchange American interests in Oregon for English interests in the fisheries.

The statements of the authors quoted are, therefore, totally at variance with known facts. Memory may have failed the three original or first writers in the long lapse of years, or traditions and rumors may have come to seem like historic truths. In those earlier days Oregon, where these three writers lived, was a whole summer from Washington, and information was fragmentary, and not always reliable. There were strong probabilities in the case that the Secretary did not and could not make such plans and offers. The United States had never offered to yield any territory there south of the forty-ninth degree. The commissioners for the Treaty of Ghent, 1814, were instructed to this effect: Monroe offered forty-nine in 1818 and 1824; Adams in 1826, and Tyler in the year of Dr. Whitman's visit. The nation was committed against the offer attributed to Mr. Webster, and his remark, already quoted, was but the voice of the government; that "the United States had never offered any line south of forty-nine, and it never will."

It is easy to see why those rumors arose and were repeated. Certain parties and persons were disappointed in the Ashburton Treaty — in the East for what it contained, and in the West for what it did not contain. The West was the more dissatisfied, because the northwestern boundary was not touched, and it could not appreciate the reasons for failing to do it.

It might have been quieting to consider what President Van Buren said five years before: "It is with unfeigned regret that the people of the United States must look back upon the abortive efforts made by the executive for a period of more than half a century, to determine, what no nation should suffer long to remain in dispute, the true line which divides its possessions from those of other powers. . . . We are apparently as far from its adjustment as we were at the time of signing the treaty of peace in 1783." And the question came into the hands of Mr. Webster with increased "intricacies and complexities and perplexities."

Local ambitions on the two extremes of the Union were wounded because each section did not gain all it had claimed or coveted. A recent writer in the "Collections of the Maine Historical Society," gives expression to the dissatisfaction of the Eastern extremists: "Never was there such a history of errors, mistakes, blunders, concessions, explanations, apologies, losses, and mortifications."

When Mr. Webster undertook the settlement of the northeastern boundary question it had been in hand between the two governments about sixty years. Geographers, civil engineers and diplomatists, had sought

the lines of the treaty and of equity, and failed. No
new light could be reasonably looked for in the direction of the three-score years past. Mr. Webster struck
out on a new and confessed line of compromise as the
only hopeful and at the same time peaceful line. He
had not only the thinly settled inland borders of New
England, but the whole United States, as his client. He
had not only three hundred miles of boundary to run
for New England, but three thousand for the Union.
Should not the national scope of the question insure its
broad historical treatment in our day.

It annoyed the Western extremists that only the eastern portion of the boundary was covered, and it was
said, with some feeling: "The East can gain its ends
at Washington, but the West must apply at London."
With more patriotic ardor than practical sense some
would have taken all the territory in dispute, which
included the present British Columbia, up to Alaska,
under the watchword: "Fifty-four Forty, or Fight."
To all such Mr. Webster could give no aid or sympathy.
In an article on Dr. Whitman, written in 1880, this rallying cry is attributed to his visit to Washington, and to
his success in taking back such a band of emigrants.
The writer repeats the statements which we have criticised, and reproaches the Secretary for damaging Oregon. Of course Mr. Webster must disappoint such a
man till war should become an inevitable and last resort; and meanwhile a damaging rumor or tradition that
he was indifferent to Oregon might gain the position
and dignity of a historical item.

When a national election had been carried under this
war-cry, and before its administration was well under
way, Mr. Webster spoke on the Oregon question in

Faneuil Hall, Boston, and he set these sentiments in some of his noblest forms of English speech. Only a passage need be given : " No, gentlemen! the man who shall incautiously, or led on by false ambition or party pride, kindle those fires of war over the globe on this question, must look out for it — must expect himself to be consumed in a burning conflagration of general reproach." This great peace speech was reproduced in nearly every language on the continent of Europe.

To any and all who purposed to possess all of the ancient Oregon, up to fifty-four forty, the present northern limit of British Columbia, even at the sacrifices and issues of war, Mr. Webster was an intentional, operative, and formidable obstacle. Herein, no doubt, he offended some who may have represented his policy for peace as neglect of Oregon.

Dr. Whitman's information supplemented that of the President, Secretary, and Congress, generally ; it rectified the wrong impressions and unjust bias which English statements had made, and it exposed the bold scheme of the Hudson Bay Company to capture the territory by stealthy colonization. Full time was promised him to show to the government that a carriage-route to Oregon was feasible.

"There is no doubt," said the Honorable Elwood Evans, "that the arrival of Dr. Whitman was opportune. The President was satisfied that the territory was worth the effort to save it. The delay incident to a transfer of negotiations to London was fortunate ; for there is reason to believe that if formal negotiations had been renewed in Washington, and that for the sake of settlement of the protracted controversy, and the only remaining unadjudicated cause of difference between the two governments, had the offer been renewed of the forty-ninth parallel to the Columbia, and thence down that river to the Pacific Ocean, it would have been accepted. The visit of Whitman committed the President against any such settlement at that time." [1]

This was progress for Dr. Whitman, and in the direct line of his wonderful ride, and he crowned his plan in the success of his cavalcade of immigrants. After his arrival with these, time was necessary to bring back the fact of success, diffuse through the country the information of which he had such a wealth, and so lead up to legislative and diplomatic action. Three years were not an unduly long time to bring the desired and acceptable end in the Oregon Treaty of 1846. For the peaceable, honorable, and satisfactory character of that end the United States and Great Britain are preëminently indebted to Marcus Whitman and Daniel Webster.

[1] Senate Document 31, of 41st Congress, 3rd Session, Feb. 9, 1871, p. 23.

CHAPTER XXIV.

TWO HUNDRED WAGONS FOR OREGON.

Doctor Whitman was the envoy extraordinary of circumstances to Washington, to quiet the two governments. When he came up the Santa Fé trail on that wonderful journey through southern Colorado and central Kansas and struck the lone cabins on the Missouri borders, he started rumors of a great emigrant caravan to Oregon in the spring. He assured the scattered settlers of a wagon road to the Columbia. This, he said, was his fourth trip to and from those waters,—including his first round trip of exploration to the rendezvous. He had taken his wife over, and she, with other white women, were there among friendly Indians, awaiting his return with a great immigration, the approaching autumn. The fears and difficulties and dangers were manufactured, he assured them, at Fort Hall, and for a purpose. Emigrants had only to pass by, attending to their own business. An escort of friendly Cayuses would meet them beyond Fort Hall. He would meet the company at Westport in June. Would they be ready?

The Doctor both uttered and printed his plans, and his words went up and down that border-land like bugle notes when hunters and hounds open the chase, or as the fiery cross traversed the Scottish highlands, when the clans were to be suddenly gathered. For a citizen of the old East to understand the temper of the region to which he spoke one needs to read the life of Boone and Crockett, or walk along behind the ox-cart of Putnam those months when it was hauling the family and civilization from the Connecticut to the Ohio, or stand in 1796 and see " the nearly one thousand flat-boats, or ' broadhorns,' as they were called, pass Marietta, laden with emigrants on their way to the more attractive regions of southwestern Ohio." [1]

That families comfortably settled should break up, load a few camp-articles into a stout wagon, leave all cabin smoke behind, and plunge into unknown wilds a thousand or two thousand miles, is a large fact in our history and a question in social philosophy.

A letter written in 1868, by one Zachrey, a Texan, who went with Whitman to Oregon, will serve to illustrate how widely that border-call went up and down the great valley. One of Whitman's circulars found its way to the Zachrey home in Texas, while others went up the Ohio and Mississippi, and wherever steamers were then running on the fourteen thousand miles of navigable rivers between the Alleghanies and the Rocky Mountains.

"Early in June you will meet me," this was the flying notice as Dr. Whitman came up the Santa Fé trail, those January and February days, into St. Louis. I shall never forget the appearance and ardor of the man as our interview, enjoyed under the same roof for twenty-four hours in St. Louis, then impressed me. Only the enthusiasm and indomitable will of Columbus, as he went from court to court, fired with the passion of his one purpose, can serve me as a good illustration.

Having posted the government to the latest date on

[1] *Walker's History of Athens Co., Ohio*, p. 111, Cincinnati, 1869.

Oregon affairs, and having obtained assurance that new negotiations should not commit the United States on the question till he could take over his caravan of emigrants and report, Dr. Whitman felt that he had gained the end of his mission and made sure of Oregon.

Before turning his face westward again he made a flying call at the missionary rooms in Boston, where he had been commissioned seven years before. The officers, so the histories of Oregon say, did not measure the scope of his national ride, and the interview was much as when Eliab questioned another man who was too far ahead of the times to be understood: "Why camest thou down hither? and with whom hast thou left those few sheep in the wilderness?" David and the Doctor answered in due time, and quite to the satisfaction of the people.

"Instead of being received and treated as his labors justly entitled him to be," says Mr. Gray, "he met the cold, calculating rebuke for unreasonable expenses, and for dangers incurred, without orders or instructions or permission from the mission to come to the States. . . . For economical and prudential reasons, the Board received him coldly and rebuked him for his presence before them, causing a chill in his warm and generous heart, and a sense of unmerited rebuke from those who should have been most willing to listen to all his statements, and most cordial and ready to sustain him in his herculean labors."

It will be remembered that Mr. Gray went out with Dr. Whitman in 1836, and was his associate in the Oregon mission, as the secular agent of the Board. He therefore knew this matter personally from the Doctor, who had assumed to take a commission from circumstances and providences to do this grand work.

It should be said in apology for both parties at this late day, that, at that time, the Oregon mission and its managing Board were wide asunder geographically, and as widely separated in knowledge of the condition of affairs. Dr. Whitman seems to have presumed that his seven years' residence on the northwest coast would gain him a trustful hearing. But his knowledge gave him the disadvantage of a position and plans too advanced — not an uncommon mishap to eminent leaders. Coleridge says of Milton: "He strode so far before his contemporaries as to dwarf himself by the distance."

Years afterward, when tardy times and men at the rear caught up with men on the ground, their mistake was discovered, as one of the officers writes: "It was not simply an American question, however; it was at the same time a Protestant question." Quite recently justice has been rendered to Dr. Whitman in "The Ely Volume." In providing by will for the expenses of this work the honorable donor expressed the wish that it detail some of the "instances where the direct influence of missionaries has controlled and hopefully shaped the destinies of communities and states." The compiler says: "Perhaps no event in the history of missions will better illustrate this than the way in which Oregon and our whole northern Pacific coast was saved to the United States." This was the very idea and work of Dr. Whitman, yet quite in contrast with some of his experiences when he was achieving the grand enterprise. The credit is due, not to missions so much as to the total and sensible independence of the Doctor. But the misfortune of foresight befell him, and he worked and waited.

With some qualifications the aphorism of Ralph Waldo Emerson must be accepted: "To be great is to be misunderstood." So men pay the penalty of true nobility of plan and action, do their work, and wait for the acknowledgments of following generations.

The company of emigrants seeking Oregon under Dr. Whitman was gathered at Westport on the Missouri. This had long been the point of last departure from the settlements, as adventurous companies set forth on the Santa Fé, or California, or Oregon trail. Kansas City and its radiating network of railways, so like a huge spider's web hanging in the dew, has quite obscured that hopeful little town near by, and the locomotives have moved the point of departure for prairie wagons a thousand miles, more or less, to the front.

In the early part of that leafy, blushing June, 1843, the rattling, clustering wagons, with their dingy white tops, and the muscular, bronzed, and wideawake families that hung fast and loose about them, made a perfect gala-day at Westport. Some of them may have had as many new homes and plans of life as the Cherokees, who are now living under their sixteenth treaty with government beyond the great river. How strange that the Indians do not settle down and make good citizens! Texas was there with Whitman three years before it was in the Union, and no doubt other southwestern states, as well as Illinois, Indiana, and the farther east. I remember how, in those years, caravans crossed at St. Louis, and struck for the interior, their long line of canoe wagons, with high bow and stern, creeping to the ferry through Illinois Town, and passing over, and winding up the streets.

Those were red-letter days for ferryman Wiggins and that unconscious play of his thumb and finger on picayunes and levees. One of the wagons would be a curiosity to-day, with the heads of women and children at every loop and rent of the canvas, and kettles, cows, dogs, and sundries made fast behind. Father and sons, lank and swaying, stroll awkwardly on either side, each carrying the inevitable rifle. This phase of life has never been seen except in the United States. There were several in the company at Westport, noble and conspicuous afterward in Oregon, who had purposed to go before, and some had even started, whom the fears and adroit impossibilities manufactured at Fort Hall had turned back.

When the Doctor started out from the Missouri, two hundred wagons fell into line. Many of the men had property, yet it often happens that such wanderers have little with them, while they have left nothing behind. They are wealthy only in children, and are easy and affluent, financially, only in expectations. The weather, roads, fare, mishaps — it is all well — nothing disturbs the even tenor of their prairie ways, for they are " going West." Rent, taxes and laws, markets, store bills, and the fashions, Wall Street prices and Washington news, — of all these annoyances of the higher civilization they are in blissful ignorance. At the same time there are, inside and outside of those wagons, the noble germs and best elements of American life. It was the same when the pioneers took the Ohio, and cut up the northwest territory into magnificent states, and added Kentucky and Missouri and Iowa and others to the Union.

For fourscore years such families and wagons have been carrying our frontier forward sixteen miles a year annually, along its entire line from the English boundary to the Mexican, a movement which has made the annual area of new settlements equal to two and a half states as large as Massachusetts. Just at this time, 1843, one section of the long frontier wave was combing into a breaker, and throwing its spray against and over the Rocky Mountains. In the growth and spread of a people, and in the occupation of wild land by tilled fields and neighborhoods and highways, the world never saw so sublime a sight. The table lands of Asia have in prehistoric times tilted toward Europe, and thrown forward human masses, but not a civilization; and great armies have cut their way through frontiers with scythe chariots; but the American scythe chariots are the reapers, and they win battles for progress and humanity on our vast wheatfields. Gladstone well says: "While we [Great Britain] have been advancing with portentous celerity, America is passing us by in the canter."

It was some days after leaving Westport before they fell into good marching order, with guides, and a highway construction gang; the women and children and supplies were placed midway, and scouts and hunters ranged wildly loose. The long undulating line drew its slow length over the Kansas prairies, and the evening camp-fires were a wonder to Indians and buffalo and yelping coyotes.

When well under way Dr. Whitman was all along the line, like a commanding general. "Through that great emigration," says Mr. Spalding, "during that whole summer, the Doctor was their everywhere present angel of mercy, ministering to the sick, helping the weary, encouraging the wavering, cheering the mothers, mending wagons, setting broken bones, hunting stray oxen, climbing precipices, now in the rear, now in the centre, now at the front, in the rivers looking out fords through the quicksands, in the desert looking out water, in the dark mountains looking out passes at noontide or midnight, as though those were his own children, and those wagons and those flocks were his own property."[1]

There lie before me many letters from men in that company, kindly furnished by Mr. Gray, the historian of Oregon, to whom I am otherwise greatly indebted in preparing this volume. They are from the Honorable Jesse Applegate, Robert Newell, and J. W. Nesmith. A few passages quoted here and there will give us a good idea of the journey. The night encampment had much to do with the safety of the expedition. The Doctor usually selected the spot in advance, and laid out the ground in a circle, and as the train came up he located the first wagon on the circle. "Each wagon follows in its track, the rear closing on the front, until its tongue and ox-chains will perfectly reach from one to the other, and the hindermost wagon of the train always precisely closes the gateway." Thus a fortification was made of the wagons, and the animals were turned loose to feed.

"His great experience and indomitable energy were of priceless value to the migrating column. His constant advice, which we knew was based upon a knowledge of the road before us, was, 'travel, travel, travel; nothing else will take you to the end of your journey; nothing is wise that does not help you along; nothing is good for you that causes a moment's delay.'

"All able to bear arms in the party have been formed into three companies, and each of these into four watches." Each company took the watch every third night. After the evening meal there was a social

[1] Senate Document 37, of 41st Congress, 3d Session, February 9, 1841, p. 22.

time within the circle, and all were merry. The children frolicked, the young people enjoyed the violin and flute and dance and song, while the older recounted incidents of the twenty miles' travel, and forecast the morrow and anticipated Oregon. The Doctor and the main guide sit aloof in grave consultation till they have "finished their confidential interview, and have separated for the night." Slowly the prattle and dance and violin become quiet; lovers there in the wilderness say their good-night; the guard cries, "Ten o'clock, and all is well;" the smoldering camp-fires fall asleep as do their late attendants, and the stars come out and watch the silent camp, even as they watched the tents of Abraham when emigrating to his Oregon.

No very serious obstacles were encountered till the party arrived at Fort Hall, 1,323 miles from Westport. Here the Hudson Bay men declared further progress with the wagons to be impossible, and, to convince us, says Mr. Nesmith, Captain Grant of the Fort " showed us the wagons that the immigrants of the preceding years had abandoned." With these were the agricultural tools and other bulky appliances for civilizing the new country.

Serious troubles confronted the Doctor. He could feed a thousand people on the plains, ford the rivers, and force the mountains, but to run the gauntlet of the Hudson Bay post, whose interests were so deeply involved in stopping him, was another labor. While he was here and there, up and down the long line, in a varied superintendence, the head of the column reached Fort Hall. The numbers in this caravan were formidable, and the more so, that they were made up of families who were evidently anticipating homes and civilization on the Pacific slope. This would damage a fur-bearing country and strengthen American ambitions and claims for the territory. A desperate effort must be made to scatter, or divert, or turn back the company.

When Dr. Whitman came up to the head of the column he found that the old arts had been applied, and with no little success. It would be Indians, if they went on with that valuable retinue, and captive women and children; and it would be sickness and abandoned wagons and goods, and then starvation, and all that. But when he spoke to them of his own experiences on that route through several trips, and then of the interest the fur-men had to keep them back, and then appealed to their generous and honorable feelings to trust him till he had at least once failed them, they rallied with enthusiasm and moved on. So far as appears he did not lose a man or a wagon at the Fort. What aided much to this result was the presence of a large body of Cayuse Indians, who had taken this journey of hundreds of miles to meet their old teacher and lead him back safely to their mountain homes.

As this expedition turned the balance for Oregon, so Fort Hall was the pivotal point. This Fort Hall, on Lewis, or Snake River, about one hundred miles north of Salt Lake City, was originally an American trading-post, built by N. J. Wyeth, but the Hudson Bay Company crowded him off by the many monopolizing and outraging means which a wilderness life made possible. Many of his traders and trappers were scattered wide; some of them were killed, and his business generally was ruined. At this point many immigrant companies had been intimidated and broken up, and so Fort Hall served as a cover to Oregon, just as a battery at the mouth of a river protects the inland city on its banks.

Here the post men had made the fatal mistake of allowing the "old wagon" of the Doctor to go through, seven years before. Now two hundred followed it. In later days, when the spirit was aroused for "the whole of Oregon or war," the question was raised whether it was to be taken under the walls of Quebec or on the Columbia. Neither was the place. Oregon was taken at Fort Hall. For it will be seen that from this time the grand result in the Oregon case was no longer an open and doubtful issue; only details and minor adjustments required attention.

It is reported that President Tyler promised an escort under Frémont to Dr. Whitman, in leading out his emigrant company. This may have been so, but more or less traditional matter clusters about that noted interview, and at this late day finds its way into print. Nothing of the kind, however, was done; Frémont followed Whitman. In the preceding year Frémont had led an exploring and scientific expedition from Kansas City to the South Pass, 250 miles east of Fort Hall. The last few hundred miles of this, from Fort Laramie, was over the old trail of Whitman and Spalding in 1836. But the two expeditions of Whitman and Frémont in 1843 were not in company. They both left the same point on the Missouri about the same time, but by different routes. Frémont kept to the south of the Kansas, bore away almost due west along the Smoky Hills, Republican and Solomon rivers to St. Vrain's Fort on the South Platte, with the snowy heights of the mountains before him, and possibly Pike's Peak in the dim southwest. Thence he made a detour of nineteen days to Bent's Fort and Pueblo on the Arkansas, and back by Colorado Springs, and near to the coming Denver, to St. Vrain's.

Thence he went over the mountains for Fort Hall by the Cache à la Poudre River, and early in August he struck the Sweet Water, and his route of the preceding year, which was the ordinary Oregon trail. Some scientific delays, and a visit to Salt Lake, delayed the Lieutenant, so that he did not arrive at Fort Hall till September 19th.

Dr. Whitman had passed this point of intrigue and peril, and the grand depot of wagons and farming tools, and was at his old home on the Columbia, in October, — not many days after Frémont reached the Fort. The very day that the head of the Doctor's army corps came upon his old home on the Columbia, Frémont was emerging from the cañons that concentrate around Salt Lake, and was hauling his rubber boat through ooze and slime to navigate, first of white men, that American Dead Sea. When, therefore, Doctor Whitman was on the Columbia his promised "escort" was on Salt Lake, and Lieutenant Frémont arrived at Whitman's Station October 23d — forty-nine days behind. Frémont has been justly and honorably called The Pathfinder, but in this instance he followed a trail, in its most difficult sections, which Whitman had beaten out by several trips, and that had been threaded and dared by American women seven years before.

I have spoken of those calls of the Doctor for emigrants, as he came up the Kansas and Missouri borders in his marvelous ride, and we have traced the eight hundred and seventy-five on their way with him thus far toward Oregon. But his rallying words went farther, and started more for the Pacific than have been yet indicated. We shall better see the power of that man, and his grand and saving plan for Oregon, if we fall in with Frémont, and travel and camp with him, while he finds his way, at the same time, into that farther west. For the truth is, Whitman stirred all the wild border, and the states inside of it, with a fascination for that romantic, half mythical Oregon.

Whitman and Frémont took different directions when they left Westport, at about the same time. On the third evening out Lieutenant Frémont encamped among emigrant wagons freighted with families, goods, and farming utensils for Upper California. "For four days," says Frémont, "trains of wagons were almost constantly in sight, giving to the road a populous and animated appearance." This was on the trail yet common to California and Oregon. When Frémont struck southerly on the California branch he saw no more of this till he returned to the Oregon trail on the Sweet Water. Now he finds "the broad smooth highways where the numerous heavy wagons of the emigrants had entirely beaten and crushed the artemisia" or sage bush. They notice graves where two or three pilgrims for a better land had passed on to a country that has no lands beyond. By and by they find a cow and calf, the estrays of some emigrant wagon, and they enjoy again the coffee of civilization.

And again, "Our animals fared badly, the stock of the emigrants having razed the grass as completely as if we were again in the midst of the buffalo." The next night he "encamped with a family of emigrants, two men, women, and several children, and six or eight yoke of cattle. It was strange to see one family traveling along through such a country, so remote from civilization." Some time afterward "the edge of the wood for several miles along the river was dotted with the white covers of emigrant wagons, collected in groups, at different camps, where the smoke was rising lazily from the fires around which the women were occupied in preparing the evening meal, and the children playing in the grass, and herds of cattle grazing about in the bottom. . . . The road in the morning presented an animated appearance. We found that we had encamped near a large party of emigrants, and a few miles below another party was already in motion."

The ordinary supply of fresh meat by the chase had failed Frémont's mountaineers, following thus in the footsteps of the emigrant bands. "There had been very little game left on the trail of the populous emigration." This was several weeks after Doctor Whitman had passed along. Midway in the long and charming Indian summer of that region the Lieutenant arrived at the station of Dr. Whitman, finding here and there clearings, and corn and potato fields and rude houses, finished and unfinished, and other evidences of settlement and civilization.

The most, if not all the emigrants thus overtaken and passed by Frémont were probably stirred to the expedition by the tocsin and rally of that man of purpose and furs and frosted fingers. Too late for the company who were hurried off from the Missouri under the motto, " travel, travel, travel," they followed as best they might. Others may have come, as the Texan Zachrey, from very remote points, and made their twenty miles a day, like Whitman, and still failed of his company, though volunteers for that army of occupation, because of his grand border-call to save Oregon. Some of them went over the Cascade Mountains late, in sleet and ice and threatening winter, famished and jaded, but they found open doors and warm fires and hearty tables at Waiilatpu on the Walla Walla, as only a frontier housewife can spread them.

In these details of a most romantic history lying among the germs of the Republic on the Pacific side an amusing coincidence occasionally appears. In the "Edinburgh Review" for July, 1843, there is this statement: "One thing strikes us forcibly. However the political question between England and America, as to the ownership of Oregon, may be decided, Oregon will never be colonized overland from the Eastern States. . . . With those natural obstacles between, we cannot but imagine that the world must assume a new face before the American wagons make plain the road to the Columbia as they have to the Ohio." While this portly and scholarly quarterly was following the English language over the world, and its fresh-cut leaves were revealing these magisterial dicta in libraries and private circles, in those identical July days the two hundred wagons of Marcus Whitman were doing this impossible thing, and the fourteen of Lieutenant Frémont were closely following.

Doctor Whitman set foot in stirrup at his door for Washington, October 3, 1842, and dismounted there again early in October, 1843. Eleven months that heroic wife and the mission band waited for the first word or rumor while he twice crossed the continent. They heard the clatter of his horse's feet die away, as he rode off up the Walla Walla, and knew afterwards only that the mountains received him and their winter awaited him. What months of waiting for them, and of working for him! Again the clatter of a horse's feet is heard on the Walla Walla, and the rider leaves stirrup for the threshold of his cabin door. There followed him down the Cascade Mountains and into that splendid valley, in little companies, and in long, weary file, jaded and battered, and mended after mountain style, two hundred emigrant wagons. They emptied their families here and there, the women and children; and scattered all about were cattle and dogs; while lank backwoodsmen, with the inevitable rifle, lounged and strolled. And they continued to arrive even after the light snows of the country have come. It was the army of occupation for Oregon.

CHAPTER XXV.

THE PEOPLE DISCUSS THE OREGON QUESTION.

In old colony times few questions of public concern were settled without a town meeting, and that meeting was formidable. In revolutionary days the Royalists could take Bunker Hill and other noted fields of rebellion, but they could not conquer Faneuil Hall and the Old South meeting-house. The orderly gatherings and free discussion of important interests by the people were too much for Great Britain. When the people took up the Oregon question, gathered in the facts and talked them over together, it was soon settled.

In the United States general legislation follows the people, and their will, previously ascertained, takes the form of law. So in this matter of Oregon, the people led off and Congress followed. Prior to the negotiation of the Ashburton Treaty Congress was almost totally inactive as to the use and occupation of that territory. It was tardy in beginning, dilatory in progress, and negative in producing results. It contented itself with the policy of joint occupation, inaugurated in 1818. The efforts of Mr. Linn to close this policy in 1839 and 1841 were a failure, and while the treaty was pending soon after, it was of course only courteous in Congress to be quiet on any boundary question.

It was a disappointment to many that the treaty made no reference to the northwest, but the people acquiesced when they understood the policy which had been adopted and the necessity for the omission. Able and protracted debates in Congress followed the submission of the document to them, and the discussion was reported, and then renewed by the people. In this way much information concerning Oregon was scattered abroad, when it was much needed. Thus both knowledge and interest were developed, which must take place before the rights of the United States in Oregon could be fully and safely asserted.

In his message of December, 1842, President Tyler remarked, that "the tide of population which has reclaimed what was so lately an unbroken wilderness in more contiguous regions, is preparing to flow over those vast districts which stretch from the Rocky Mountains to the Pacific Ocean. In advance of the acquirement of individual rights to those lands sound policy dictates that every effort should be resorted to by the two governments to settle their respective claims."

In his message covering the Ashburton Treaty the President had already said that it was impracticable to extend the negotiations involved in the treaty so as to include the northwest. Therefore Oregon still represented a great and growing international interest, and Mr. Linn of the Senate, early after the December message of 1842, introduced a call for information why Oregon was not included in the treaty, and also a bill for the occupation and settlement of the territory. A popular outside pressure carried discussions on these propositions to an engrossing extent for weeks. The bill was barely carried in the upper and then lost in the lower house. This was only fifteen days before the arrival of Dr. Whitman with his important information. It will be seen how timely his advent was, and of how much worth his facts and plans and assurance, while an uninformed Congress stood so evenly balanced on the Oregon issue. The call of Mr. Linn for information was answered from an unexpected quarter, and more amply than was possible from the portfolio of the Secretary of State. It is very rare that coincidences have so combined, and adaptations conspired in matters of moment to the state.

Congress closed on the day following his arrival, and official public action rested till another December. But the people took up the question. The growth of knowledge and of opinion which he had started went on. The Cabinet knew his purposes and plans and his rigid confidence in their success, and so they shaped delays and waited to hear again from Marcus Whitman. During the interval of warm months and quite as warm popular discussion, the public became sensitive under the rumor that if the bill for occupation, lost in the House, had become a law, England would have regarded it as equivalent to a declaration of war.

Congress convened in December, 1843, stimulated by the people to action. On the 8th of January news came from Oregon that Dr. Whitman had made a complete success of his emigration scheme. The same day a resolution in the Senate called for the instructions to our minister to England, and all correspondence on the subject. The resolution did not pass, but a similar one in the House did pass two days later. So these stirring incidents made those times lively.

A prevalent opinion, and one thoroughly confirmed by the Doctor, increased the popular ardor. The people had the conviction that the English were reaping all the advantages of the "joint occupation" by pressing an unscrupulous monopoly, and excluding all American traders and trappers as far east as Fort Hall. Parties like Wyeth's had been broken up, and the scattered numbers were telling their griefs through the states. The news from Dr. Whitman spread wildly, and hundreds were roused to take the trail of his emigrant caravan and make homes and fortunes on the Pacific.

It was, therefore, quite a matter of course, as popular impulses go, when they seek the form of law by Congress, that action should be taken there to terminate the joint occupation by giving the required notice of twelve months. Mr. Buchanan urged this with extreme earnestness, and was among the first to put into prominence the claim for all of the primitive Oregon up to 54° 40'. Others made speeches similar in tone and extent of demand. The spirit of those urging the notice was daring and at times belligerent, and produced the ordinary effects on the populace of such appeals. Unkindly feelings were kindled against Great Britain by limited statesmen and demagogues; and the Stamp Act, and tea tax, and Yorktown, and Lundy's Lane were paraded in and out of the halls of national deliberation. The people were put on their guard lest they be despoiled of valuable domain in the northwest, as it was said they had been in the northeast. For they would not understand that some partisan Englishmen felt that England had been outdone and despoiled in the Ashburton Treaty quite as much as some Americans felt the reverse. Indeed, in Parliament the treaty was assailed as violently as in Congress.

The feeling mounted high as to the extent of the American claims compared with the English rights.

Even the cool and conservative Winthrop was willing to say : " For myself, certainly, I believe that we have as good a title to the whole twelve degrees of latitude," *i. e.*, up to 54° 40′. Mr. Benton, in presenting some petitions for the settlement of the question, was for taking Oregon at once, and letting consequences follow as they would. " Let the emigrants go on and carry their rifles. We want thirty thousand rifles in the valley of the Oregon; they will make all quiet there, in the event of a war with Great Britain for the dominion of that country. The war, if it come, will not be topical; it will not be confined to Oregon, but will embrace the possessions of the two powers throughout the globe. Thirty thousand rifles on the Oregon will annihilate the Hudson Bay Company and drive them off our continent and quiet the Indians."

To all this tone of feeling and tide of words, favored by many, which might have cost the nation much treasure and blood, but a poor show of honor or acres in return, Mr. Choate well expressed the sentiments of the party for delay and peace.

" In my judgment this notion of a national enmity of feeling towards Great Britain belongs to a past age of our history. My younger countrymen are not unconscious of it. That generation in whose opinions and feelings the actions and the destinies of the next age are enfolded, as the tree in the germ, do not at all comprehend your meaning, nor your fears, nor your regrets. We are born to happier feelings. We look on England as we do on France. We look on them from our new world, not unrenowned, yet a new world still, and the blood mounts to our cheeks; our eyes swim; our voices are stilled with emulousness of so much glory; their trophies will not let us sleep. But there is no hatred at all, no hatred; all for honor, nothing for hate. We have, we can have, no barbarian memory of wrongs for which brave men have made the last expiation to the brave. . . . Do not say that theirs is an unfortunate, morbid, unpracticable, popular temper on the subject, which you desire to resist, but are afraid you shall not be able to resist. If you will answer for the politicians, I think I will venture to answer for the people."

This speech for peace, as the clarion of a herald between two hostile armies, was well followed by the practical suggestions of others. It was urged that negotiations for a friendly solution of difficulties were about to open; that immigration was rapidly strengthening our prospects; that delay was gain; that to precipitate a war on such an issue, with its costs of treasure and horrors, would be unpardonable in the authors, if they had not first exhausted all reasonable endeavors in the line of peace.

In his annual message in December, 1844, President Tyler announced that since the close of the last session negotiations had been formally opened for the settlement of the Oregon question, and it was understood that a special envoy was awaited from Great Britain. Pakenham arrived at Washington in February, 1845. Still the war spirit did not suddenly abate, and even the message renewed the old and rejected proposals for a chain of military posts from the Missouri to the mouth of the Columbia, and for the extension of United States laws over American citizens in Oregon. But neither was done, and a grave silence, full of promises of good, prevailed at Washington for a twelvemonth following, down to the first annual message of President Polk, December, 1845. Much indeed was done then, but little of the work appeared to the public, except as the subject was touched now and then incidentally in Congress. Meanwhile the politicians were not inactive with the voting people. The press, the caucus, and the convention fed the American appetite on Oregon. It was too good a plank for the makers of platforms to overlook in the exciting canvass for a new chief magistrate.

Let us here pause and see to what dates and stages of growth our Oregon question has come. Through January, 1843, Congress was mainly discussing the policy of occupying that territory with our citizens and laws. The debate opened the whole question of title, treaty, and joint occupation, American traders and English monopoly. The strong men of the land, Linn, Calhoun, Benton, Choate, Woodbury, McDuffie, Berrien and Rives, naturally came to the front when the Pacific was put in danger. The milder plans were adopted, and affairs were left to run on languidly with Great Britain.

During that same January Whitman was struggling over the mountains and across the plains to execute his plan for saving Oregon. During the first quarter of 1844 a similar struggle with similar results was waged on the floor of Congress. Meanwhile the Hon. Mr. Pakenham arrived as minister plenipotentiary to negotiate the affair, and Mr. Buchanan is associated with him for the United States. In December Mr. Tyler presented his last annual message. In this he revived the military schemes and also recommended the extension of United States laws over the territory. But the subject had a quiet sleep in Washington till Mr. Polk's administration opened it in March, 1845. Up to this date three points had been gained: the people had been drawn into a discussion of the subject, and with much intelligence; emigration in large numbers was following Whitman's "old wagon;" and plenipotentiaries for the two governments were in Washington discussing the question for a settlement.

The English were not claiming exclusive sovereignty over this territory, equal in area to Great Britain and Ireland five and a half times, but only the rights of joint occupation. The United States claimed to 51° as covering all land drained by the Columbia and belonging to the United States by discovery. Also, as successor to Spain on that coast, the United States held that their title as high as 60° was superior to that of England or of any other power. This claim was advanced early in the controversy, 1824. Mr. Rush, who entered the claim, afterward proposed 49°, and the English Commissioners proposed from the mountains to the Columbia, and thence down it to the sea. Both failed in 1824. Two years later the two parties renewed these proposals, but only to be mutually rejected. Mr. Gallatin, however, gave notice that his government would not hereafter feel bound to any line previously offered, "but would consider itself at liberty to contend for the full extent of the claims of the United States." Such was the condition of the case even down to the first annual message of President Polk, December, 1845.

CHAPTER XXVI.

IMMIGRANTS SETTLE THE OREGON QUESTION.

"When the 4th of September, 1843, saw the rear of the Doctor's caravan of nearly two hundred wagons emerge from the western shades of the Blue Mountains upon the plains of the Columbia, the greatest work was finished ever accomplished by one man for Oregon on this coast." This testimony of Mr. Spalding is true concerning his old companion in travel. It was necessary now only to report this success of the expedition along the frontier and among the friends of the party of nearly nine hundred, to stir the border heart for wilder fields. The news soon spread, and the passion to follow became infectious. In the saddle, by the camp-fires and cabin hearths, and around the stores and gossipy corners, the expedition was discussed, and a western fever set in that took off great numbers the next year. Greenhow estimates the American population of Oregon at the close of 1844 at more than 3,000. Mr. White, the Indian agent for government, sets it at about 4,000, while Hines says: "In 1845 it increased to nearly 3,000 souls, with some 2,000 or 3,000 head of cattle." Through the whole west there was a warmth of anticipation and a growing zeal for the settlement and possession of Oregon.

Perhaps no one expressed better these feelings than Mr. Owen, in the House of Representatives from Indiana:

"Oregon is our land of promise. Oregon is our land of destination. 'The finger of nature'— such were once the words of the gentleman from Massachusetts [J. Q. Adams] in regard to this country,—'points that way,' 2,000 Americans are already indwellers of her valleys, 5,000 more . . . will have crossed the mountains before another year rolls round." Mr. Semple, senator from Illinois, thought that 10,000 would go over the next year.

These speeches were made in January, 1844; and they were not very visionary, since in 1846 the white population of Oregon was about 12,000. Probably all of these, except 1,000, were American immigrants. All this must have been exceedingly interesting to Dr. Whitman, as he saw the long lines of white wagons and the thousands of cattle come down the Cascade Mountains, crowning the heroism of his ride, and also of his "old wagon." Like many a radical that wagon was ahead of the times and dishonored, but finally honor overtook it.

For the sake of any Eastern reader who is burdened with a provincial skepticism about this marvelous emigration over our border, a few data of crossings of the Missouri may be reported for 1846. At St. Joseph's, Elizabethtown, Iowa Point, Council Bluffs, and the Nishwabatona, 271 wagons passed over for Oregon and California. Allowing five persons to a wagon there were about 1,350, and their live stock may be estimated at 5.000 head. At Independence 187 wagons crossed. Here are nearly 2,000 persons at these six crossings headed for the Pacific that season. Yet the oracular "Edinburgh Review," deep in the interests of the Hudson Bay Company, is confident that " Oregon never will be colonized overland from the Eastern states." "Whoever is to be the future owner of Oregon, its people will come from Europe."

The mistake is not, perhaps, strange, since the narrow compass of England can but poorly appreciate or allow for long journeys and vast rivers and mountain ranges, with which the American is necessarily familiar, and takes to easily. When all the twenty realms of Europe can be laid down in the United States, and broad margins be left here for sections of Asia, we must not expect an insular English quarterly to define our capacities for emigrating travel. Some twenty years later, when emigration to Oregon and California was at high tide, one of our college presidents, coming in over the border, met in one day, he informed me, eight hundred and nineteen yoke of emigrant oxen, hauling their wagons and carts "out west."

As already stated, while Doctor Whitman was in the East the first steps for a civil government by Americans in Oregon were taken at the "wolf meeting." An article in the first section of the original code for that territory is an index to the tone and purpose of the people: "Religion, morality, and knowledge being necessary to good government and the happiness of mankind, schools and the means of education shall forever be encouraged." A state house was built, and so like the foundation of things, as that it might well satisfy the most economical. "Posts set upright, one end in the ground, grooved on two sides, and filled in with poles and split timber, such as would be suitable for fence rails, with plates and poles across the top. Rafters and horizontal poles held the cedar bark, which was used instead of shingles for covering. It was twenty by forty feet. At one end some puncheons were put up for a platform for the president; some poles and slabs were placed around for seats; three planks one foot wide and about twelve leet long, placed upon a sort of stake platform for a table, for the use of the legislative committee and the clerks." The Pilgrim or Jamestown Fathers could not have been more primitive in their first halls of justice. But equity between man and man is not necessarily a matter of architecture, upholstery and the woolsack.

This government was set up while Whitman was at the head of his two hundred wagons, and it set aside, so far as the Americans were concerned, the royal one transferred from Canada. Soon after it was inaugurated, it was strengthened by the arrival of the Doctor and his great immigration. This foreclosed the Oregon question, leaving for the future only the dry and tedious details of diplomacy and Congress.

When the Hudson Bay Company saw an American government over their game preserve, and the invasion of it by that long cavalcade, and heard that Oregon was not touched in the late treaty, they changed their tactics, and renewed their struggles to save their monopoly on the Pacific. All Americans who proposed to settle in the territory were denied employment or supplies by them. All who could be persuaded to remove to California — as yet a Mexican province — were provided with a generous outfit, and also with notes payable in California, which, it was understood, were never to be collected of those who took them under pledge to leave Oregon. And this policy to deplete Oregon of Americans was pursued till the final adjustment of the question by the two governments. Yet, strange to say, the Company were at the same time following up most stringent measures to keep back immigration to their own side. When, in 1857, the time drew near for the Company to renew its lease of the Indian territories — wilderness on the west of Rupert's Land — the subject came before a select committee of Parliament, and the "Westminster Review" of July, 1867, thus reports the testimony of one Isbister, a native and employee of the Company:

"He confirms the statement that all further settlement was opposed by the government, all trade practically stopped, since those who held land were prohibited from importing goods from any port but London, from any part of the port of London except the warehouses of the Hudson Bay Company, by any ships except their vessels, or into any port in Rupert's Land except York Factory in Hudson Bay, where they were charged a duty of five per cent. . . . In 1845 the same body passed a resolution imposing twelve and a half per cent. on all the goods landed at York Factory for the Red River Colony. . . . A very decided amendment proposed by Mr. Gladstone, recommending that the country capable of colonization should be forthwith withdrawn from the jurisdiction of the Company, was negatived by the casting vote of the chairman."

If the Hudson Bay Company wished to retain Oregon for England, their policy was spoiled by more than a fallacy; it had in it a fatuity. The Company was thus working, also, in violent conflict with the interests of the government that incorporated it. The case is an emphatic illustration of a corporate monopoly that can outgrow and override the government that incorporated it. It is a case worthy of study by American legislators.

In this connection it should be stated that five years

before, the intention of the Company had been declared to intrust the Indians to the Jesuits for opposition to the Americans, and to arm their eight hundred half-breeds and employees against any military force from the States. They had stationed a ship of war at Vancouver, and after the provisional government had been inaugurated they strengthened that fort with bastions, and furnished the Indians with military supplies. Meantime the scattering of immigrants at Fort Hall, the charges to them there for flour at forty dollars the barrel, and other supplies in proportion, and the introduction of colonists from the Red River, must not be forgotten.

The outlines of American government gradually took on form and expansion and strength, and, though they had no criminals to imprison, the legislative committee of 1844 recommended the building of a jail, with the remark: "We are assured that it is better policy to have the building standing without a tenant, than a tenant without the building." The committee also suggested provision for the insane. Quite after the spirit of the colonial legislatures of early times, they expressed the hope "that Oregon, by the special aid of Divine Providence, may set an unprecedented example to the world of industry morality, and virtue," and by "a diligent attention to agriculture, arts, and literature, attain an elevation as conspicuous as any state or power on the continent."

While the government was making this general progress the Indian agent reported the suppression of the liquor trade among them, their fine crops, the export of wheat, beaver, salmon and lumber, and the import from the Sandwich Islands of sugar, molasses, tea, and coffee, orderly and decorous proceedings in the courts, hopeful Indian farming, small Catholic schools, and a Methodist institution, where much proficiency had been shown in the primary branches. In the year following, 1845, the agent says: "Moral and religious influence, I regret to say, is waning, yet it is gratifying to observe an increasing interest upon the subject of schools and education, and I am happy to say we have now eleven schools this side the mountains, most of them small, to be sure, but they are exerting a salutary and beneficial influence."

The intelligent American will see here those germs of a territorial organization, and the foreshadowing of a state, such as have enriched and enlarged our borders from colonial times. The interest shown in education, morals, and religion are quite a repetition of the territorial history of "the Ohio."

The American principle of rule by the people and by majority vote had come into Oregon, and the minority paid it deference. The boast of Mr. Dunn is seen to be baseless: "The Americans, with the exception of a few missionary and agricultural establishments, have scarcely any possession or hold on the country. . . . They have not an inch of land from California to the Pole, from the Rocky Mountains to the Pacific, to which they have undisputed right, and not one single trading-post or station."

As the whole of Oregon was in question between the two governments no one had "undisputed right" to a cabin lot even, and if the Americans had no trading-posts they had family homes of unmixed blood, and schools and court room and ballot-boxes.

The theory of both nations, title by colonial and domestic occupation, had been put into practice. Few men appreciated this theory better, or more aptly urged its practice, than the Honorable Rufus Choate. Against vindictive feelings toward Great Britain, or schemes of demagogues, or sectional ambitions, or the indiscreet ardor and impulses of real patriotism which would have precipitated war, he urged immigration from the states as the wisest and most speedy means to gain the title. With his own inimitable grace of thought and language he spoke in the Senate in 1844 against the resolution to close the arrangement for joint occupation: —

"Oregon, which a noiseless and growing current of agricultural immigration was filling with hands and hearts the fittest to defend it — the noiseless, innumerous movement of our nation westward. . . . We have spread to the Alleghanies, we have topped them, we have diffused ourselves over the imperial valley beyond; we have crossed the Father of Rivers; the granite and ponderous gates of the Rocky Mountains have opened, and we stand in sight of the great sea. . . . Go on with your negotiation and emigration. Are not the rifles and the wheat growing together, side by side? Will it not be easy, when the inevitable hour comes, to beat back plowshares and pruning-hooks into their original forms of instruments of death? Alas, that that trade is so easy to learn and so hard to forget!" Quite in contrast with the war spirit and speech of Colonel Benton: "We want thirty thousand rifles in the valley of the Oregon."[1]

So the point was carried by immigrants rather than soldiers. The United States found to be true what the world knows, that plows hold a country better than steel-traps; and Great Britain learned that the law of nations in assigning a new country is apt to follow the track of

[1] *Debates in Congress*, vol. xv. 142, and preceding.

immigrant wagons. Stopping them at Fort Hall was but a temporary expedient, and when two hundred passed by, as cars pass a station, and went over peacefully into the valley of the Columbia, the end of controversy was brought very near; the army of occupation had moved into Oregon, and it remained only to talk over the conclusion, to draw up and sign the papers.

CHAPTER XXVII.

"FIFTY-FOUR FORTY, OR FIGHT."

PRESIDENT POLK devotes one fifth of his long message of December 2, 1845, to the Oregon question. In it he rehearses the attempts at settlement, states the offers on both sides and their mutual rejection, and declares that there has been not only a total failure as to settlement, but no progress toward it. He informs Congress that "the proposition of compromise, which had been made and rejected, was, by my direction, subsequently withdrawn, and our title to the whole Oregon territory [from 42° to 54° 40′] asserted, and as it is believed, maintained by irrefragable facts and arguments."

Mr. Polk recommended that the joint occupation be terminated by the stipulated notice, that the civil and criminal jurisdiction of the United States be extended over the whole of Oregon, and that a line of stockades and military posts be established along the route from the states to the Pacific, together with an adequate force of mounted rifles, for the encouragement and protection of immigration. As early as 1824 Mr. Monroe had recommended the establishment of one post at the mouth of the Columbia. Should the notice be given, he thought the government should put itself in a position to maintain firmly its rights in that territory at the expiration of the year of notice. Hence the partisan watchword; "Fifty-four Forty, or Fight."

A very grave issue was thus put before the American people; indeed, few had equaled it. For more than six months it engrossed Congress, and the whole country was agitated by it. Had the hopeful condition of things in Oregon been better understood, so much excitement would have been impossible. But then that country was farther from Washington fourfold than China to-day, and the germs of a new state for the Union were not obvious even to observers. The ardor spread into all parts of the land and pervaded all departments of American life. What Spalding's half pint of seed wheat had become to the broad fields of the Columbia, the purpose and plan of Whitman had become in the States. Only war was no part of his plan and was in no proper way necessary to its success. That was the tares that would possibly work in among the wheat. War with England would probably have stayed the Mexican war, then imminent, or given different issues to it.

England had her MacNamara scheme to plant an Irish colony in California, bring about the revolt of that province from Mexico, and put it under an English protectorate. Peace with England and war with Mexico enabled the United States to spoil that plot and take California herself. Frémont, with more energy than red tape, wrought great things in California for North America. Quite naturally Alaska followed California to the United States, and now our domain on the Pacific coast runs 6,411 miles to England's 450. Fighting for 54° 40' would, perhaps, have lost us the whole.

It was a wonderful battle of fact, argument, and patriotism in Congress, and the men were worthy of the struggle, now grandly historic. When we name a few on both sides, the whole are suggested — Crittenden, Benton, McDuffie, Webster, and Calhoun, Adams, Cass, Choate, and Winthrop. The grandeur and gravity of that high debate were enhanced by the facts, above hinted, that during those same months Texas came into the Union and the Mexican war with it.

Following close on the message of the President, and quite naturally, there arose a long discussion on the national defenses, since, as Mr. Crittenden announced, "war might now be looked upon as almost inevitable." Resolutions were offered affirming Oregon to be part and parcel of the territory of the United States from 42° to 54° 40', and that notice should be given at once to terminate the joint occupation of it. A key to the tone and ardor of the House may be found in a single remark there: "No doubts now remain in the minds of American statesmen, that the government of the United States holds a clear and unquestionable title to the whole of the Oregon territory." There were not wanting Hotspurs to echo this sentiment.

McDuffie would " rather make that territory the grave of his fellow-citizens, and color the soil with their blood, than to surrender one inch." At this time the Hudson Bay Company had about thirty trading posts in the territory, which were really forts and defensible in frontier war. The United States had about 7,000 citizens in the same country. Mr. Yancey considered the question of notice a very grave one. "This notice, if given, would be a war move. It is argued as such. Mr. Polk deems it as such. In itself it is such a move. What, then, is the object? I am told, to obtain all of Oregon. I, too, go for all of Oregon. I go for it up to 54° 40'." But at the close of a war he thought "Oregon would be found in the hands of England, and Canada would be in our possession. . . . We are on the point of purchasing the magnificent territory of California, which, with Oregon, would give us a breadth of Pacific coast suited to the grandeur and commercial importance of our Republic. All this would be blighted by a war. California would be lost to us. A debt of five hundred millions would be imposed upon the country."

Yet Douglas of Illinois denied this, and argued that the notice would not lead to war; while Jefferson Davis urged peace measures as the surest way to secure all our rights. As the great debate progressed in the high councils of the nation, strong hostility to Great Britain was developed, and one senator, Westcott, went so far as to say: "I have no feelings of friendliness for Great Britain, none whatever. . . . I saw the torch which wrapped the Capitol in flames applied by the hand of the incendiary. . . . If war should once be declared, my whole soul and my whole strength will be exerted on the side of my country."

The question of notice was discussed with increasing ardor in the House, with necessary intermissions, for more than forty days, and then it was carried by the decided vote of 163 to 54. The depth of honest conviction, and at the same time opposition of view may be seen in the fact that John Quincy Adams voted in the affirmative, and Robert C. Winthrop in the negative, both from the same state, and of high international renown.

In the Senate the struggle was much longer. There it was asserted that England would not dare to carry the controversy to the extreme, since, "the first act of our government in case of war would be to expel the British power from all her possessions on this continent." If the view of Senator Clayton may be admitted, the certainty of war and its fearful devastations were already assumed facts, for he said: "The apprehension of war has decreased and almost paralyzed the business of the country. Already the capital of traders is withdrawing itself into chests and drawers and old stockings." Insurance increased on commerce, and returning vessels remained inactive at the wharves.

Mr. Benton affirmed that negotiations had made no progress toward settlement since the Treaty of Ghent, and he agreed with the President in the measures proposed. He had been clear against joint occupation for twenty-eight years, as "a treaty of unmixed mischief to the United States." Joint occupation he regarded as an anarchy, an impossibility, and an absurdity, and that to terminate it by notice would be a peace measure, and he would adopt it, "regardless of consequences."

The discussion became not only engrossing, but almost monopolizing, for threescore bills and resolutions were kept waiting on the calendar for their time. Crittenden moved into the debate at a late hour, seeing no need of haste, and still maintaining that the difficulties should be kept open to negotiations. It was a quieting announcement of personal opinion, when he said: "A majority is decidedly in favor of preserving the peace of the country honorably, and of settling this question peaceably and honorably, by compromise, negotiation, arbitration, or by some other mode, known and recognized among nations, as a suitable and proper and honorable mode of settling national questions."

Mr. Webster, fresh from the Ashburton Treaty, long held himself aloof from the great debate, while yet a watchful listener. When he broke his silence he did it briefly, excusing his fewness of words on the ground that the matter was in negotiation, and if it would not be indecorous for Congress to discuss it during negotiations, it might embarrass the administration in coming to the best results. But he early foretold the way in which the difficulty would be settled, — by compromise, — and on what line, — the forty-ninth.

This could readily be foretold by him, for in his preparations to meet Lord Ashburton, and in the profound historical discussions resulting in the draft of that treaty, he traversed the ground of discoverers and explorers and fur traders and settlers, as well as all conventions and treaties of the United States, and of other nations, pertinent to the settlement of the northwestern boundary. All this information he had made available at the time only for the postponement of the Oregon question. Now, in full possession of the facts of right in the case, and knowing the American lack of absolute title up to these high pretensions, he enjoyed a dignified silence in seeing partisan debaters strike right and left blindly with their "impregnable facts and arguments" to show "that our title to the whole of Oregon is clear and unquestionable." Some of the speeches do not show knowledge enough of the case to embarrass the purpose or the eloquence of the speakers.

Knowing that historical data and treaties were wanting to settle the dispute as one of pure rights, and knowing, too, that on all exciting and popular topics a certain amount of speech-making is irrepressible, and therefore indispensable, he waited patiently and silently for the wagons of Whitman, and the compromising pens of negotiators. In one compact sentence Webster put himself on the record of those days: "I say, for one, that, in my opinion, it is not the judgment of this country — it is not the judgment of the Senate — that the government of the United States should run the hazard of a war for Oregon by renouncing, as no longer fit for consideration, the proposition of adjustment made by this government thirty years ago, and repeated in the face of the world."

While the debate was in progress, and in one of its suspensions, Mr. Webster did one thing, indirectly, to dignify the discussion, and lift it from the partisan and provincial into the national and international; he imparted the needed thoughtfulness and emotion to bring the conviction that a question of territorial rights on a treaty line of a thousand miles, and of war between two great nations, was a question of great gravity. The Ashburton Treaty had been made a target, in and out of Congress, for barbed arrows aimed somewhat at it, and somewhat at its American author. For two or three years the position of Mr. Webster, in the Cabinet or in private life, had made it unfitting for him to notice these attacks publicly. Now in the Senate, when the same great question of boundary was before that body and the country, he deemed it both useful and fitting to make a defense of the Ashburton Treaty. The speech of two days was a noble apologetic in the best sense of that old word, and while it set forth the treaty in its most important relations to two great nations, its indirect and powerful influence was to add weighty anxiety to the discussion then progressing on the northwestern boundary.

More and more daily, as the weeks of this great debate went by, the claims and the hopes of peaceable conclusions gained ground. Calhoun rose to the dignity of the occasion and to the solemnity of the issue, while he urged delay and peaceful steps, saying: " A question of greater moment never has been presented to Congress from the days of the Revolution to the present."

Mr. Dayton followed in the line of thought that finally prevailed: " I would insist that things remain exactly as they are. I would meet Great Britain by a practical adoption of her doctrine, that title to this country can be acquired only by occupancy. . . . The very question to be settled is, What is our own? After twenty-seven years of debate we are no nearer a conclusion than we were at first." He, too, saw the end only in the plan of Dr. Whitman, which was so silently and energetically taking possession of the valley of the Columbia.

When the debate had well progressed, Mr. Evans boldly foreshadowed a limitation of the claims of the extremists, and so narrowed the discussion and drew it toward the close : " I will not sit here and be told, over and over again, that our title to 54° 40' is so clear, so beyond all possibility of doubt or hesitation that he who falters in maintaining it at once by the sword is recreant to the love of his country."

The United States had offered 49° from the mountains to the sea, and Great Britain had offered 49° from the mountains to the Columbia, and by it to the sea. Hence these incisive words of Mr. Evans cut off much verbiage and moved the controversy far along from rhetorical and political harangue toward an intelligent and equitable conclusion. " What, then, is the actual matter in dispute? It is only that strip of land lying between the Columbia River and the latitude of forty-nine, being a triangle, extending along the Pacific two hundred miles and from the river to the ocean three hundred and fifty, containing in all, according to my computation, about 58,000 square miles."

Mr. Calhoun braced these views and hastened the conclusion by compromise in one of his best speeches, and Mr. Webster added impetus again in the same direction: "One who has observed attentively," he said, "what has transpired here and in England within the last three months, must, I think, perceive that public opinion, in both countries, is coming to a conclusion that this controversy ought to be settled, and is not very diverse, in the one country or the other, as to the general basis of such settlement. That basis is the offer made by the United States to England in 1826."

To this complexion the Oregon question had come in the Senate at the close of March, 1846, and the end seemed near. However, Mr. Cass renewed the struggle, asserting that the just claim of the United States "extended from California to the Russian boundary," and he was disposed to press that claim, at the peril of war, which, he thought, had been too gloomily represented. But this created only another verbal eddy in the majestic current of thought and speech that was flowing on toward the peaceful sea. As the debate went on over the resolution of notice to quit joint occupation, the tendency to compromise on 49° grew more and more evident, and finally this appeared inevitable. It remained only a question of time based on the calculation how much would be needed to deliver prepared speeches and work party tactics and advance personal interests.

The resolution of notice had passed the House February ninth, and came at once to the Senate. So fully had the expectation of a compromise line and peace possessed the Senate, while it was known that favorable negotiations were going on, that it became a matter unimportant whether the vote for notice passed or not. But it was passed April 23, 1846, by a vote of forty-two to ten, with two important amendments: a strong suggestion to both governments that the differences between them be adjusted amicably and speedily, and that the President take his own time to serve the notice, and give it "at his discretion."

The notice was thus relieved of its war features, and Congress and the people of anxiety about war. For men, prominent in both houses, had asserted that both nations would favor a compromise, and so an amicable adjustment. In the confident expectation of a treaty on this basis, anxiety abated, and commerce, trade, and the general pursuits of peace began to resume their old currents.

For four months and twenty-one days after its introduction by the message of President Polk this subject had engrossed Congress and the country. The lack of knowledge concerning it made the progress of discussion tardy and warm. For it was a tedious and trying process, in a deliberative body, to separate the traditions, assertions, impressions, and patriotic passions from the real facts and rights in the case. But the great debate over "Fifty-four Forty, or Fight" ended in a peaceful and mutually satisfactory manner.

CHAPTER XXVIII.

AT LAST A TREATY.

The first article in this treaty reads as follows: " From the point on the forty-ninth parallel of north latitude where the boundary laid down in existing treaties and conventions between the United States and Great Britain terminates, the line of boundary between the territories of the United States and those of her Britannic Majesty shall be continued westward along the said forty-ninth parallel of north latitude to the middle of the channel which separates the continent from Vancouver's Island, and thence southerly through the middle of the said channel, and of Fuca's Straits to the Pacific Ocean: Provided, however, that the navigation of the whole of the said channel and straits, south of the forty-ninth parallel of north latitude, remain free and open to both parties."

For the United States and Great Britain to write and sign that article required fifty-four years, two months, and six days. On the 11th of May, 1792, Captain Robert Gray, of Boston, discovered the Columbia River, and so established a United States title to the country that it drains. On the 17th of July, 1846, this article having been previously ratified by each government, was exchanged at London between the two governments, and so the title was confirmed to the United States.

When the two governments were in negotiation as to

the northern boundary of the Louisiana Purchase in 1807, Mr. Jefferson wished the forty-ninth parallel to be the line between the two, "as far as their said respective territories extend in that direction." The English attack on the Chesapeake prevented the ratification of this projected agreement. After the war, and in the Treaty of Ghent, 1814, no notice was paid to the boundary west of the Lake of the Woods. As that treaty provided for the restoration of all possessions taken by either from the other during the war, Astoria was claimed by the United States. England declined to give it up, as never having been a national possession of the United States, but private property, and sold, as an individual enterprise, to English subjects before its formal capture. It was, however, restored as a piece of property, but the question of national title and sovereignty in it was kept in abeyance.

At the time of its restoration Astoria was a stockade post, 150 by 250 feet, with two bastions, twenty-one pieces of small artillery and sixty-five men, of whom twenty-three were white, and the rest half-breeds and Hawaiians. In 1818, the question of boundary again became a matter of negotiation at London, through Messrs. Rush and Gallatin. The English commissioners made an attempt to secure the right of navigating the Mississippi, but of course failed, and finally agreed to the 49° from the Lake of the Woods to the mountains. In discussing claims to territory beyond the mountains the American commissioners "did not assert that the United States had a perfect right to that country, but insisted that their claim was at least good against Great Britain." On the other hand the English commissioners did not propose any boundary, but intimated that the Columbia would best accommodate both, and said that England would insist on holding the mouth of it in common with the United States. In this mutual dissent and failure the plan of joint occupation for ten years was adopted and signed October 20, 1818.

The next year the Florida Treaty made the United States an heir to all Spanish claims and rights north of 42°. Early in 1820, the House of Representatives raised inquiries concerning the settlements on the Pacific, and the expediency of occupying the Columbia. A committee reported that the whole territory from 41° to 53°, if not to 60°, belonged of right to the United States, and they recommended "small trading guards" on the heads of the Missouri, and at the mouth of the Columbia to protect immigration and trade. The report, with estimates of cost, was laid on the table, and the business slept again till 1823.

That year a peculiar project was started by the United States, and it is thus stated by Mr. Benton: "That each of the three powers, Great Britain, Russia, and the United States, having claims on the northwest of America, should divide the country between them, each taking a third. In this plan of partition each was to receive a share of the continent from the sea to the Rocky Mountains, Russia taking the northern slice, the United States the southern, and Great Britain the centre, with 54° 40′ for her northern boundary, and 49° for her southern." The project was not acceptable to the other parties. In offering it Mr. Rush stipulated that the United States would not settle north of 49°, if the English would confine themselves between it and 54° 40′ In view of this offer by the United States in 1823, England must have looked with surprise on our claim to 54° 40′ in 1846, with the alternative of war.

Extracts from two letters of Mr. Adams, Secretary of State, will show how the United States regarded her rights over the mountains at that time: "The right of the United States from the 42d to the 49th parallels of latitude on the Pacific Ocean we consider as unquestionable." And again: "I mention the latitude of fifty-one as the bound within which we are willing to limit the future settlements of the United States. . . . As, however, the line is already run in latitude forty-nine to the Stony Mountains, should it be earnestly insisted upon by Great Britain, we will consent to carry it into continuance on the same parallel to the sea."[1]

When the proposal for a tripartite plan failed, the United States offered joint occupation for ten years, during which time the English were to make no settlements north of 55° or south of 49°. The English offered 49° to the Columbia, and thence to the sea by it, with freedom of settlement, navigation and travel, to both parties throughout the entire territory for ten years. Both offers were rejected, and the question rested till 1827.

When the convention of joint occupation was then expiring, negotiations were revived. Great Britain renewed her last offer, and the United States repeated the offer of 1818, which was substantially — the 49th to the sea, free and perpetual navigation of the Columbia, settlers of either nation outside these agreed boundaries could remain for ten years, but no more new ones. The proposals were mutually declined, and the policy of joint occupation was renewed to run indefinitely, with right to termination on notice of one year by either party. This was in 1827.

In 1831, Mr. Livingston, Secretary of State, informed

[1] Debates in Congress, vol. xv., 534.

Mr. Van Buren, minister to England, that " the subject is open for discussion, and until the rights of the parties can be settled by negotiation ours can suffer nothing by delay." The delay continued, without any prominent attention to the matter, till 1843. In that year Mr. Everett, our minister to England, was instructed that " the offer of the forty-ninth parallel of latitude, although it has once been rejected, may be again tendered, together with the right of navigating the Columbia upon equitable terms. Beyond this the President [Mr. Tyler] is not now prepared to go." But nothing was done of note or progress.[1] It was the year following in which Mr. Pakenham as minister plenipotentiary on the Oregon question, arrived at Washington, but he and Mr. Calhoun, our Secretary of State, only renewed the failure of all their predecessors.

When Mr. Polk gave his inaugural in 1845, negotiations had been merely prolonged without any visible progress. Yet it should be said that a gain was made in obtaining claims and the offer of limits, that were mutually rejected. In this way the area and scope of the controversy became narrower, and it gathered and concentrated information, showing to the studious and reflecting where the dividing line would probably run. It was a growth of public knowledge and of opinion, and this was as slow as it was indispensable. The President used the occasion to state that "our title to the country of the Oregon is clear and unquestionable," and he recommended that the jurisdiction of our laws and the benefits of our republican institutions be extended over the Americans there.

Matters then went on quietly till December, and nego-

[1] Senate Document, 489, 1st Session, 29th Congress, 1844.

tiation kept up a bare vitality through the summer, as the correspondence showed, when published. Mr. McLane, the American minister to England, was furnished by Mr. Buchanan, Secretary of State, with a *resumé* of previous negotiations and the views of the administration, since he might be able to use opportunities and influence the English ministry directly or indirectly in the matter. This was in July, 1845. In this communication of the Secretary it was made to appear, almost as if a discovery, that " the Straits of Fuca, Admiralty Inlet and Puget Sound, with their fine harbors and rich surrounding soil, are all south of this parallel," — 49°, while the country in dispute north of this was disparaged as comparatively worthless. Mr. Buchanan discarded arbitration, and showed that the United States were shut up to compromise on the much repeated offer of forty-nine, or to the exclusive claim of the whole of Oregon, with " war almost inevitable."

It was wisely concluded that the judgment of the civilized world would be adverse to the last resort, if Great Britain should yield all south of 49°. The President had offered this and free ports to England on Vancouver, south of it, but with no rights of navigation on the Columbia as previously proposed. This last offer, he affirmed, he could not make to any foreign power, and it was hoped that the offer now made of free ports on Vancouver would offset the withdrawal of that on the Columbia.

Mr. Pakenham refused this last offer without even referring it for home advice, and so, a month later, the last of August, the President formally withdrew it. He was the more ready to do this because, as he said, he would not have made so liberal an offer if he had not been entangled and constrained by the offers of his predecessors in a government that never dies. In a closing extremity he intimated through the secretary to Minister McLane, that he would concede the whole of Vancouver, but " will not renew his former offer, nor submit any other proposition." Then the next step must be taken by Great Britain. This was said as late as November 5, 1845. After this manner the summer passed in fruitless negotiation, except that the range of international debate was narrowed, and the points in it sharpened. Then, as I have shown in the preceding chapter, "the winter of our discontent" opened with the annual message of December 2d, on the ardent ultimatum of "Fifty-four Forty, or Fight."

Two things should be here noted. The Vancouver question was added as a new item in the struggle. While there was a growing tendency to compromise on the 49° on the main land, there was the grand island of Vancouver, about twice as large as Massachusetts, which this line, when continued, would divide.

As early as 1826, and for the first time, the proposal was made by Mr. Huskisson, an English plenipotentiary, to turn the boundary south from the 49th so much as to give all of Vancouver to Great Britain. Then the discovery was more and more obvious to the United States that Great Britain was but a proxy to the real party in interest with whom the American government had to do, — the Hudson Bay Company. This was the power back of the throne, a huge chartered and continental monopoly, too much for the English ministry as it was for the true English interest.

Only two days before Lord Aberdeen sent his draft of a treaty to minister Pakenham, which was adopted as the treaty of 1846, Sir John Pelley, then governor of the Hudson Bay Company, had an interview with his lordship, and pressed his theory of the water boundary. To make sure, if possible, the interests of his company, he immediately wrote out and forwarded his theory and wishes to Lord Aberdeen, that they might find place in the treaty. He assumes that Vancouver will be taken by Great Britain "upon the principle of mutual convenience." Thus, of the three possible channels from the 49th parallel in the Gulf of Georgia south into the Straits of Fuca, he proposes the one nearest to the continent, with the remark: "The only objection to this is giving to the United States the valuable Island of Whidbey; but I do not see how this can be avoided in an amicable adjustment."

As he could hardly run a yawl between the continent and this island, and so call that passage "the middle of the channel," he reluctantly concedes the loss of Whidbey. So grasping was this huge monopoly, whose next step might as reasonably have been to claim the kelp and seaweed on the mainland shores. Of course, when the machine becomes superior to the manufacturer, and the creature to be above the creator, the outlook is serious for the commonalty. It finally appeared that only a foreign power, and in its immigrating force, could handle that organized and embodied selfishness of pounds sterling.

It is devoutly to be wished that at this late day in monopolies, and early one in the rights of the people, a free government might profit by noted historic examples. Anthony Crozat, with imperial and solitary sway from the Alleghanies to the Rocky Mountains, and from the Great Gulf to the Great Lakes; the chartered

"Mississippi Bubble," to burst over the same domain in the hands of John Law; this Hudson Bay Company, with territory under its control one third larger than all Europe; the East India Company that wrestled oppressively with pagans and successfully with Parliament; and half a dozen railroad men who can set a price for the farmers on their five hundred million bushels of wheat, year by year, and fix the charge on the transfer of your trunk from Bangor to San Francisco — these illustrative cases should suggest to government to keep outside the ring of chartered monopolies, and inside the vastly more important ring of the people.

Sir Richard Pakenham hastily declined the last American offer, and President Polk as hastily withdrew it, and announced that he would not volunteer another. Earl Aberdeen expressed to Pakenham his regrets at this withdrawal; indeed he both lamented and condemned it; not that he was ready to accept the offer, but the withdrawal left nothing for diplomatic dignity to lean on and start from as a basis for continued negotiations. It embarrassed the English government by closing the door to compromise, and so forcing it to offer arbitration and abide answer, which the presidential message had declined in advance, or lie swinging in the current of events, which in some senses were drifting ominously in the direction of war.

The American Cabinet, alert in those critical and anxious times, was not insensible to the rumors floating across the Atlantic that Great Britain was making unusual warlike preparations. On official inquiry Aberdeen softened the anxieties, but did not entirely remove them. Just at the close of the year Minister Pakenham proposed arbitration, not on the title to the whole of

Oregon, but for "an equitable division," which as soon as decorous, or within six days, was declined.

So closed the year 1845. To the people under both governments it had been an anxious year, and it closed gloomily. For while tendencies within the screens of diplomacy were toward an amicable settlement by compromise, the citizens at large knew nothing of this positively. Later and bold assurances by leading men in the government that there would be no war, gave some buoyancy to drooping hopes, under the impression that these men had some inside views of the future. Before the first month of the new year had gone by Pakenham made a qualified renewal of arbitrators to the effect that they should first see whether either party had, of right, a title to the whole territory, and if not, they should then make an equitable division. To this Buchanan replied that the plan embodied too much temptation to the arbitrators to attempt to please both parties by dividing the territory between them. He added, "the continued conviction of the President that the United States hold the best title in existence to the whole of this territory," and "that he does not believe the territorial rights of this nation to be a proper subject for arbitration."

On the day preceding, February 3, Minister McLane writes hopefully to Secretary Buchanan. He expresses the opinion that a settlement could be effected by compromise, and that he could, if thought best, secure from the English Cabinet a reopening of negotiations. He thinks he can draw from it an offer similar to the one made by Mr. Polk, which Mr. Pakenham declined without reference to his government, that is, the forty-ninth parallel, with free ports on Vancouver south of it. And to save both American and English feeling he would vary it by offering to continue the privileges of the Hudson Bay Company, and the navigation of the Columbia for seven or ten years. There was hope in this dispatch, from the fact that our minister to England had been studying English sentiment, and seemed to have discovered regrets on their part that the offer in question was rejected, and that its renewal would be welcomed, if Great Britain could do it without compromising her dignity.

Our secretary replied promptly, and encouraged our minister to draw from that government the substance of the old offer, yet with such variations as to make it in a measure new, and so save each government from the humiliation of an apparent retraction. After Mr. McLane had informed Secretary Buchanan that he could not honorably draw from Lord Aberdeen an offer unless he " could officially know that the proposition would probably be acceptable at Washington," the secretary empowered the minister to secure, for substance, the offer in question.

By such careful and tedious and sensitive processes did this boundary question drag its slow length along. More than once these two great Christian powers verged on the edge of battlefields, under the pressure of punctilios. It is to be hoped that by and by, in the great scales of humanity and civilization, national pride and etiquette will not outweigh the horrors of war.

Another month passed, and diplomacy was hastened and made easier by the serving of notice on Great Britain that the joint occupation of Oregon would terminate in a twelvemonth. The passage of a resolution to this effect in Congress has already been detailed. Its passage was a practical declaration for closing the long controversy, and a broad confidence that it would be closed amicably. The vote in Congress and the notice in England were anticipated, and not only created no surprise, but were rather welcomed as an anticipated relief.

The delicate and tentative efforts of our minister to draw from the English government the offer mentioned were well timed with the approaching notice, as the offer left England on or very near to the time of the arrival of the notice. It was delivered to the Secretary of State on the 6th of June, in the draft of a new treaty. It was approved by the Senate, and at once matters hastened to a finality. The rapidity of action in the last stages of the Oregon question is worthy the momentum that it had gained in so many years of progress. The compacted dates and acts that rounded the grand period may be noted here. On the 6th of June the Secretary of State received from Mr. Packenham the English draft of a new treaty, covering the Oregon question; on the 10th the President submitted it to the Senate for advice; on the 12th the Senate advised its acceptance; on the 15th it was signed by Messrs. Packenham and Buchanan; on the 16th it went to the Senate for approval; on the 18th they ratified it; on the 22d it was sent to London to be exchanged for the English ratification; on the 17th of July the ratifications were exchanged at London; and on the 5th of August President Polk proclaimed the Oregon Treaty as the law of the land.

It is of importance to note here that the draft of this treaty was entirely, and word for word, from the pen of the English ministry. This should be remembered when we come to consider how obscure and complex and surprising the interpretation of it was made for twenty-five years afterward, by the English government. And in presenting the case finally to the Emperor William for arbitration, Mr. Bancroft aptly put the law of contracts as laid down by Grotius, that "where the contract is obscure the interpretation must be against the party who draughted it;" and by Vattel: "If he who could and should express himself plainly and freely has not done so, so much the worse for him. He cannot be permitted, subsequently, to introduce restrictions which he has not expressed." And this is old Roman law, that an obscure contract must harm him making it, if any one.

The worth and force of this treaty, fifty-four years in growth, are set forth in its first article, already quoted. Two subordinate yet important items should be here mentioned: The United States is put under obligation to regard all the property and possessory rights of the Hudson Bay Company south of the forty-ninth parallel. Also, the property of the Puget Sound Agricultural Company between the Columbia and the forty-ninth parallel is to be confirmed to that Company, and the United States may take it on an agreed valuation.

These two items are in reality one, for the Puget Sound Agricultural Company was only another form of the Hudson Bay Company, working in the line of agriculture, and somewhat of colonization. Surplus funds of the fur company were added to two stations or farms of the company, and used, under this new form and title, by an arrangement of the company, and the new "company," so called, was no separate chartered organization. It held the relations to the fur company that any trading factory had. It paid the company for supplies received, and charged it with supplies furnished, as any branch house in a large firm. When the fur company set it up it reserved the "supreme control of the Puget Sound Agricultural Company." This was five or six years before the treaty was made, and the policy served a good end. Two claimants instead of one could ask indemnity when the United States came in possession. The real Company, the Hudson Bay, filed a claim of $3,822,036.37, and the pretender, or quasi company, $1,168,000 more, a portion of which claims was allowed and paid. In a final settlement, November, 1864, the United States paid over to the Hudson Bay Company as indemnity $450,000, and to the other $200,000 — less than one seventh of the original claim.

So, therefore, at the last, as at the first, and always between, the United States had to do with this great monopoly. It was the second, yet greater self of Great Britain in North America. In the matters of the New World, the Hudson Bay Company was the secret providence of England, and it quietly foreordained. That magnificent and semicontinental monopoly stood squarely in opposition to the growth of British dominions in North America, and it did it by vigilantly and despotically preventing the growth of civilization on the northern half of the continent. The plough and saw-mill and anvil and the hum of village industries must not frighten the beaver.

It is on the authority of leading English authors that these strong statements are made, a few passages from which will close this chapter. "To say, then, that the trade of this country [England] has been fostered and extended by the monopoly enjoyed by the Company is exactly contrary to the truth." "If the Company were to be destroyed to-morrow, would England be poorer? Would there not rather be demanded from the hands of

our own manufacturers ten times the quantity of goods which is sent abroad, under the present system, to purchase skins? We boast that we make no slaves, none at least that can taint our soil, or fret our sight; but we take the child of the forest, whom God has given us to civilize, and commit him, bound hand and foot, to the most iron of despotisms — a commercial monopoly."
"Nor, turning from the results of our policy upon the native population to its effect upon the settlers and colonists, is there greater cause for congratulation." "The system which has made the native a slave is making the settler a rebel." It has "driven the best settlers into American territory, and left the rest, as it were, packing up their trunks for the journey." "The Hudson Bay Company has positive interests antagonistic to those of an important settlement." "It is a body whose history, tendency, traditions, and prospects are equally and utterly opposed to the existence within its hunting-grounds of an active, wealthy, independent, and flourishing colony."

CHAPTER XXIX.

WHAT DID THE TREATY MEAN?

THE Oregon Treaty was proclaimed as the law of the land, but it remained to run the lines. This would seem to be an easy work that could be promptly done, especially as the most of it was on a parallel of latitude. But there was an august delay. Nine years after the ratification of the treaty the President, in 1855, recommended that the survey be made. The next year Congress created a Boundary Commission; in 1857 commissioners were appointed to unite with English commissioners, and on June 27th of that year they held their first meeting. The head commissioners were, on the part of the United States, Archibald Campbell, Esq., and for the English government " our trusty and well-beloved James Charles Prevost, Esq., a captain in Our Royal Navy."

The Ashburton Treaty had fixed the boundary on the forty-ninth parallel to the Rocky Mountains, eight hundred to a thousand miles westward from the Lake of the Woods. One half of such a distance would prolong it to the Pacific. Thence it was to follow this parallel and take, as the treaty worded it, " the middle of the channel which separates the continent from Vancouver's Island," and follow it through the Straits of Fuca to the ocean. At the first meeting of the commissioners it appeared, though the reasons are not obvious, that Captain Prevost was limited to run and mark only the water line, from the Pacific coast to the open ocean — " so much of the line of boundary hereinbefore described as is to be traced from the point where the forty-ninth parallel of north latitude strikes the eastern shore of the Gulf of Georgia " — the Pacific coast. Perhaps this was best, for sooner or later the final struggle between the two governments was to come in dividing that archipelago between the mainland and Vancouver's.

Foot by foot, as I have traced the battle of diplomacy from the lost one of the sword at Yorktown, the retiring English had disputed the yielding ground. Starting on the forty-ninth parallel, to which the English and French fathers had agreed in the Treaty of Utrecht, in demarking Hudson Bay possessions from the ancient Louisiana, that boundary had now been prolonged to the Pacific. As an astronomical line, stated in astronomical terms in the treaty, it was hopelessly above the intermeddling and interrogations of state papers, signed " with the highest consideration." Astronomy was too strong for diplomacy, and so what could not be varied was left unfinished, between the mountains and the ocean, and Captain Prevost must begin his work on the coast, where, in the complexity of channels, there could be a forced ambiguity in the treaty.

It is a matter of regret that no map or chart was attached to the treaty of 1846 that would have insured a general agreement on its intent. When the treaty of 1783 was draughted, the joint commissioners, says Bancroft, " in the hope of preventing the possibility of a future dispute about boundaries " marked them on Mitchell's map. But in this case neither party had geographical knowledge enough of that breadth of archipelago to furnish a descriptive plan of it. In speaking of this Sir Richard Pakenham says: "It is my belief that neither Lord Aberdeen, nor Mr. McLane, nor Mr. Buchanan possessed at that time a sufficiently accurate knowledge of the geography or hydrography of the region in question to enable them to define more accurately what was the intended line of boundary than is expressed in the words of the treaty." The treaty of 1783, for the same reasons, entailed the same difficulties for the Ashburton Treaty to settle. Notably the prior treaty placed the boundary point on the Lake of the Woods many miles out of the way north, and guessed outside of a hundred on the sources of the Mississippi, and left the "true St. Croix" and "the highlands" on the Maine border for a hard search and final compromise in the Ashburton Treaty.

When the British Admiralty sent Vancouver to the northwest coast on a voyage of discovery, they instructed him to watch carefully for channels and rivers leading into the interior of the continent, with the hope that water communication might be discovered from the Pacific to the Lake of the Woods. As we have seen, he barely escaped the discovery of the Columbia that Captain Gray made soon after. So little was known of American geography, even after the Revolution.

Very few sections in this world could offer so good a field for diplomatic finesse in running an undetermined boundary as that medley of land and water between the continent and Vancouver, being about fifty miles in breadth, east and west, and having a length for its several channels of perhaps sixty, north and south. In these three thousand square miles there are thirty-nine islands that have come under name and description, that range from sixteen miles to less than one fourth of a mile in length, and from fifty-four to one half a square mile in area. Besides, there are very many unnamed smaller ones, and they all have more or less value for grazing, agriculture, and timber. Through these islands, a hundred or so, and in an area about twice as large as Rhode Island, there run ten channels southward, but combine in three as they empty into the Straits of Fuca; the eastern is the Rosario, the middle one is hardly worth a name for our purpose, and the western is the Canal de Haro. The scenery here is peculiarly grand and wild among bold shores and very deep waters, with mountain peaks as high as two thousand feet, and, in one instance, twenty-five hundred feet.

The two channels worthy of account are the Rosario and the De Haro, the latter being about one half wider and deeper than the former. It has six and a half miles maximum width to four of Rosario. Its greatest depth is one hundred and eighty-three fathoms to sixty in Rosario. Under the terms of the treaty the middle or President's channel is not entitled to notice. The least depth in the Canal de Haro is greater than the greatest in Rosario, while its average depths, widths, and volume of water are greatly superior. All these facts would mark the Canal de Haro as " the channel which separates the continent from Vancouver's Island," answering to these words of the treaty.

The marvel is that England should name any other than the Haro as separating the continent from Vancouver, since, when the treaty was made, none other was known to the negotiators in those waters. The term, Rosario Straits, was not then on any map — English, French, Spanish, or German — as a channel between that island and the mainland. In the Royal Library of Berlin, near to which the Court of Arbitration was held, a library rich in maps and charts, the Haro was the only channel named for the region where afterward the English rushed to locate the Rosario. When the treaty was negotiated, the "Rosario Straits" were north of the forty-ninth parallel, and these waters did not touch either Vancouver or the continent, and the Queen's geographer still located them there in 1848 — two years after the treaty was made. Afterward they appeared where the English could use them for their surprising interpretation of the treaty.

At the time when the treaty was made every map or chart shows "Rosario Straits" between Texada and the continent, which island is wholly north of forty-nine and a half degrees north. Thus the French map of Duflot de Mofras of 1844 places it. But the next year after the treaty the British Admiralty had new surveys made by Captain Kellett, and in their next map, 1849, they introduced these straits far below the forty-ninth parallel where they could serve their interpretation of the treaty.

But this complexity of islands and channels suits well the genius of a diplomacy that seeks an end by indirection, and delights, therefore, in curves and sinuosities and ambiguities. It will be seen that the liberal wording of a treaty, calling for a boundary across such region, would furnish strong temptation to evasion by those who may have come reluctantly to sign it. Had there been no Vancouver there would have been no question, and the forty-ninth parallel would have carried the boundary direct into the Pacific. But the United States conceded all of Vancouver, south of that parallel, for amity, and did not presume on giving up anything else of consequence south of that latitude. They conceded it only, and provided for taking the best channel that separated it from the continent. The main point was to leave Vancouver undivided to Great Britain. In 1826 Huskisson, the English plenipotentiary, proposed to Gallatin, the American minister, to run so far south of the forty-ninth parallel on Vancouver as to save all that island to Great Britain. This was the first appearance of the theory, and the deflection of the line of forty-nine was only to give all of that island, and no more, to Great Britain. Eminent justice, on this plan, was pleased finally to find the main channel to be the one nearest to the conceded island, thus giving, as was right, all the other principal islands south of that parallel to the conceding government.

But there were three channels possible for vessels, and between the best, which was near Vancouver, and an interior one near the continent, there lay about four hundred square miles, in which were several prominent islands, and many small ones, in land-area about one hundred and seventy square miles. The ownership and sovereignty of these were involved in the settlement of the channel question. The most valuable of all the islands between the mainland and Vancouver was San Juan, one of the above, containing fifty-five square miles, and the most of it good grazing land the larger part of the year.

It was not ominous of speedy and harmonious conclusion of the work of the Boundary Commission, when Captain Prevost informed Mr. Campbell that he had no authority to run the land line. His commission confined him to the water line. Over this water part of the northwestern boundary the two commissioners consumed much time and some feeling. They had seven official interviews in the fourteen months following the first, June 27, 1857, and fourteen letters from each passed between October 28, 1857, and July 19, 1859. But little was gained by the commissioners in the way of settlement, except a knowledge of the ground and of the intention of the two parties. Special skill and proficiency were shown by Captain Prevost how not to do the work.

Naturally, openly, and as the final arbitration showed, justly, Mr. Campbell claimed for the United States the Canal de Haro according to the intent of the treaty. The depth, breadth, and volume of this marked it as the channel from the Gulf of Georgia on the forty-ninth parallel to the Straits of Fuca. The facts of nature, developed in the hydrographic survey, left no other conclusion. The English advocate made the point that De Haro was seldom used by vessels, but Rosario ordinarily. But it appeared that the war of 1812 broke up all trade but English on that coast, and they used the Rosario as giving them the best access to their trading-posts. The Hudson Bay Company boasted that "they compelled the Americans one by one to withdraw from the contest;" and it does not appear that an American vessel visited those waters after 1810, till Commodore Wilkes entered them in 1841. This plea for Rosario against De Haro was not only painfully specious but provoking to Americans.

That the De Haro was the channel was the understanding at the time of the negotiation of the treaty. Sir Richard Pakenham quotes Mr. McLane, the United

States minister to England in the negotiations, as saying that the "boundary about to be proposed by her Majesty's government would 'probably be substantially to divide the territory by the extension of the line in the parallel of forty-nine degrees to the sea, that is to say, to the arm of the sea called Birch's Bay, thence by the Canal de Haro and Straits of Fuca to the ocean.'" Lord Russell indorses this by quoting its substance in a dispatch to Minister Lyons, and adds that Mr. Benton used similar language in the Senate, when the treaty came under discussion before that body. Mr. Bancroft, who was a member of President Polk's Cabinet when the treaty was concluded, says in a letter to Mr. Buchanan, Secretary of State: "It is not probable, however, that any claim of this character will be seriously preferred by her Britannic Majesty's government to any island lying to the eastward of the Canal de Arro." Elsewhere Mr. Bancroft writes: "Such was the understanding of everybody at the time of consummating the treaty in England and at Washington." He says this in a letter to Mr. Campbell in 1858. Mr. Buchanan, who signed the treaty for the United States, expressly mentions in a letter to Mr. McLane, our ambassador to England, and on the very day when Mr. Pakenham delivered to him the treaty, the Canal de Haro as the one intended by the treaty.

On the other hand, and in his first letter, Captain Prevost declares the Rosario Straits to be the channel of the treaty. By this claim he throws the four hundred square miles above mentioned and the important islands therein on the English side of the line. Among these was the island of San Juan, and occupied by the Hudson Bay Company as a sheep ranch, with animals selling at eight dollars a head. Albeit in the struggles to retain these they call them "islets of little or no value."

In his draught of instructions Captain Prevost was informed that his first duty, in connection with the United States Commissioner, "will be to determine with accuracy the point at which the forty-ninth parallel of north latitude strikes the eastern shore of the Gulf of Georgia, and to mark that point by a substantial monument." This point was astronomically and satisfactorily fixed by the chief astronomers and surveyors of the joint commission. It would be the point on the coast of the continent from which the land line of boundary would run off east, and the water line west on the forty-ninth parallel. Captain Prevost was willing to call the point a true and accurately taken one in latitude, and to mark the spot by a "substantial monument," but he would not consent to call it the initial or starting-point of the water line. No monument was set, and Mr. Campbell inferred that the English commissioner was under secret instructions not to fix, in that place, the eastern end of the water line, and that the English government attached considerable importance to this refusal. He appeared to be willing to fix the starting-point of the water boundary fifteen miles to the eastward on a bay. Mr. Campbell presumed that the secret theory of the English government was, after various delays and difficulties, in determining the intent of the word "channel" in the treaty, to gain the consent of the United States, in the way of compromise and peace, to the interpretation that it meant the entire body of water and islands between the continent and the shore of Vancouver. Then "the middle of the channel" would be a mathematical line crossing the forty-ninth parallel precisely half way between the continent and Vancouver. If, therefore, the starting-point of the water line had been previously carried inward and easterly fifteen miles, it would add to the English half a belt of this width.

In connection with this theory of Mr. Campbell two or three considerations should have place and weight. The Rosario Channel proposed by Captain Prevost would give to England not only all of Vancouver but the large archipelago between Rosario and Vancouver. The line of compromise and peace proposed by Lord Russell — the middle or equidistant channel — would also give to England the main island, San Juan. As to this island, it was now the splendid sheep ranch of the Hudson Bay Company, as already mentioned; moreover that company claimed it as corporation property. When, at a later date, the United States troops occupied it, the agent of the Company wrote to the American commander, "I have the honor to inform you that the island of San Juan, on which your camp is pitched, is the property and in the occupation of the Hudson Bay Company, and to request that you and the whole of the party who have landed from the American vessels will immediately cease to occupy the same."

Evidently the English government must save that island to the fur company, and some theory of interpretation of the treaty must be devised to hold it. The arrogance of the Company, in already claiming it as property, comports with their ordinary high tone in England and North America, since the treaty of joint occupation, 1818, made such an acquisition of right and title impossible for either party. Yet in violation of the compact of joint occupation, the Crown, in 1849, made a grant of Vancouver's Island to this company. The grant was recalled two years later.

The English government insisted that the Oregon Treaty must be so construed as to give San Juan to Great Britain. Lord Russell thus writes to Lord Lyons, the envoy to the United States: "Her Majesty's government must, under any circumstances, maintain the right of the British Crown to the island of San Juan. The interests at stake in connection with the retention of that island are too important to admit of compromise, and your lordship will consequently bear in mind that whatever arrangement as to the boundary line is finally arrived at, no settlement of the question will be accepted by Her Majesty's government which does not provide for the island of San Juan being reserved to the British Crown." "Your lordship will accordingly propose to the United States government that the boundary line shall be the middle channel between the continent of America and Vancouver's Island."

This claim and declaration were preceded by the high proclamation of Governor Douglas of Vancouver's Island: "The sovereignty of the island of San Juan and of the whole of the Haro archipelago has always been undeviatingly claimed to be in the Crown of Great Britain. Therefore, I, James Douglas, do hereby formally and solemnly protest against the occupation of the said island, or any part of the said archipelago, by any person whatsoever, for, or on behalf of any other power, hereby protesting and declaring that the sovereignty thereof by right now is, and always hath been, in Her Majesty, Queen Victoria, and her predecessors, kings of Great Britain. Given under my hand and seal," etc.

It is evident that the scheme of the English was to divide midway between the continent and Vancouver, and not on " the middle of the channel which separates the continent from Vancouver's Island," and it would seem to be evident why Captain Prevost would not mark by monument the initial point on the east of the dividing line, unless it was to be carried into the continent fifteen miles, on an intruding bay.

The tone of assumption and the spirit of dictation shown by the English in this affair are painfully obvious. The question was on the import of the phrase " the middle of the channel," yet they came to the conference arrogating sovereignty over a part of the territory in dispute, and declaring that " under any circumstances " they would maintain that sovereignty, and would accept no settlement that did not allow it to them. This left no ground for interpreting the treaty, or for argument, and the United States could no longer continue the conference with self-respect.

Mr. Cass, our Secretary of State, of course made reply that " if this declaration is to be insisted on, it must terminate the negotiation at its very threshold; because this government can permit itself to enter into no discussion with that of Great Britain or any other power, except upon terms of perfect equality." And three months later: " To declare that in no event will this island be conceded to the United States is, in effect, to close the discussion. . . . The discussion has been practically foreclosed by the declaration of Lord John Russell, that it can under no circumstances affect the British claim. . . . Since, therefore, Lord John Russell repeats with great frankness his original declaration that 'no settlement of the question will be accepted by Her Majesty's government which does not provide for the island of San Juan being reserved to the British Crown,' I am directed by the President to state with equal frankness that the United States will, under all circumstances, maintain their right to the island in controversy, until the question of title to it shall be determined by some amicable arrangement between the parties."

This was not an agreeable termination to the work of the joint boundary commission, and to diplomacy and ministerial correspondence. Of course those Pacific pioneers, fur men, and settlers of both governments became uneasy under the incomprehensible delays. They could not see why an agreement could not be executed and an agreed boundary line run in the course of twelve years. Such delays seemed manufactured rather than an inherent natural outgrowth of difficulties. It was no strange thing, therefore, that primitive and natural justice wearied of waiting for ministers of state, and that the pioneers pushed forward their personal rights and interests, as the original party in the affair.

This is characteristic of Americans who make the laws and the government, and was so on this occasion, when they thought the import of the treaty very plain. Border men are quick to detect any by-play by which the laws are made inoperative and rights are postponed or sacrificed, and then they are liable to become an irregular court, and make short work with the law's delay. They did this in the early days of San Francisco as a Vigilance Committee, and I found them strongly tempted to do the same in Leadville, when an officer reported to me two homicides a week for eight months, and the courts failed to convict and punish a single murderer.

The territory in dispute was under treaty for joint and

equal occupation, and now, after provoking delays of many years, uncivil and even belligerent collision was almost sure to take place between the settlers of the two nationalities, since their rival and mutually chafing interests covered the undivided territory through which the treaty line was to be run. It was most natural that the collision should come on the principal island in dispute — San Juan. For on this island twenty-five Americans, with their families, were living, and among and around them were the servants of the Hudson Bay Company, who assumed to be on their own territory, made over to them by the English government. This was against the spirit and letter of the agreement of joint occupation, which forbade any possessory or monopolizing rights in the soil to either party. Of this condition of things and the collisions which were imminent, Sir Robert Peel well spoke in the House of Commons : "differences which, unless speedily terminated, must probably involve both countries in the necessity of an appeal to arms."

It is not pleasant to think how near these two Christian nations came, several times, to the terrible struggles of war, on this Oregon question. The very air was charged with rumors and omens and anxieties, so that speeches and opinions, and even sentences, were powers. An eminent London merchant wrote about this time to a friend in the United States : "After the publication of Mr. Webster's speech here yesterday consols improved. The stock-jobbers say that the 49° is about right, and there can be no difficulty."

In the territorial legislature of Oregon, 1852–53, that government, weary of waiting for more stately and formal steps, included this island and all the Haro archipelago in one of its counties. Soon afterward the Hudson Bay Company took formal possession of it for a sheep ranch. Oregon levied taxes on the property of the Company, and payment was refused, when the Oregon sheriff sold sheep enough to pay the taxes. So the local conflict opened. Mutual trespasses and recriminations and personal conflicts followed and multiplied till 1859, when General Harney, Commander of the Department of Oregon, landed troops on the island, with instructions to Captain Pickett to protect Americans there from marauding Indians, and from personal violence and pecuniary damage to which they were exposed by the agents and workmen of the fur company. These American forces amounted to four hundred and sixty-one persons, who selected a good military position and made it defensible to the best of their ability. Meanwhile, in the same island, and under two governments, collisions were occuring in the matter of taxes and impost duties, and in civil and criminal cases for the courts.

In this threatening juncture of affairs, English naval forces were gathered near to the island, and in a menacing attitude, to the number of five ships, carrying one hundred and sixty-seven guns and one thousand nine hundred and forty men. Protests, both civil and military, were made against the occupation of the island by the American forces, and at the same time the Americans threatened to resist by force any attempted landing of English troops. The English commander proposed a joint military occupation of San Juan, but to this Captain Pickett replied that, "as a matter of course, I, being here under orders from my government, cannot allow any joint occupation until so ordered by my commanding general," and should resist any attempt to land English forces. In this direction he had the approval of his commander.

Blood was warm on both sides and liable to flow on the most trivial provocation. The spirit of those times and the critical poise in affairs may be judged from a passage in a report of General Harney to General Scott: " The senior officer of three British ships of war threatened to land an overpowering force upon Captain Pickett, who nobly replied that whether they landed fifty or five thousand men his conduct would not be affected by it; that he would open his fire, and, if compelled, take to the woods fighting; and so satisfied were the British officers that such would be his course, they hesitated in putting their threat into execution."

All this contrasts painfully with the satisfaction and confidence and happy augury of Sir Robert Peel, when he announced the consummation of the Oregon Treaty thirteen years before in the House of Commons. He was making his final speech for his retiring ministry : " The governments of two great nations, impelled, I believe, by the public opinion of each country in favor of peace — by that opinion which ought to guide and influence statesmen — have, by moderation, by mutual compromise, averted the dreadful calamity of war between two nations of kindred origin and common language, the breaking out of which might have involved the civilized world in general conflict. A single year, perhaps a single month, of such a war would have been more costly than the value of the whole territory that was the object of dispute. But this evil has been averted consistently with perfect honor on the part of the American government, and on the part of those who have at length closed, I trust, every cause of dissension between the two countries. . . . Sir, I do cordially rejoice that, in surrendering power at the feet of a majority of this House, I have the opportunity of giving them the official assurance that every cause of quarrel with that great country on the other side of the Atlantic is amicably terminated."

Mr. Campbell, the boundary commissioner for the United States, was quite embarrassed by the action of General Harney in occupying San Juan, and was made anxious for results when he ascertained that the General had acted without specific instructions from Washington. The President, also, withheld his approval of the commander in this act, and expressed the hope that he had taken possession of the island for the protection of American citizens and interests alone, and with no reference to territorial possession. The General asserted that the relative claims of the two governments to the title had nothing to do with his occupation of the island.

In the profound gravity of the crisis, when the two great nations might be plunged into war at any moment, General Scott was sent to the field of action, and arrived late in 1859. He went out with instructions to avert violent collision between the excited parties on the ground, and to bring about joint occupation of the island in dispute, till the boundary line could be run. This was simply an effort to carry out in good faith the conventions of 1818 and 1827, the intent and spirit of which rash men on both sides had disregarded.

The course of General Harney was peculiarly offensive to the English, but Lord Lyons expressed satisfaction in learning that he "did not act on that occasion upon any order from the United States government, but entirely on his own responsibility." It was thought best, however, to withdraw him from his command in the northwest, and he was assigned to another post. Some months prior to this, General Scott and Governor Douglas of Vancouver and its dependencies effected an arrangement for the joint occupation of San Juan by a hundred armed men of each party. Thus the local excitement subsided, and as the boundary commissioners had failed in their work, the Oregon boundary question reverted to the high officers of the two governments: Lord John Russell, the British Foreign Secretary of State, Lord Lyons, British Minister at Washington, and Lewis Cass, the American Secretary of State, and George M. Dallas, the Minister to England.

CHAPTER XXX.

THE EMPEROR WILLIAM AND ARBITRATION.

AFTER elaborate and exhaustive correspondence, ending in failure to interpret the treaty of 1846 and agree on a boundary, Minister Lyons wrote to Secretary Cass, that "the argument on both sides being nearly exhausted, and neither party having succeeded in producing conviction on the other, the question can only be settled by arbitration." Lord Lyons proposed the King of the Netherlands, or of Sweden and Norway, or the President of the Federal Council of Switzerland, as the arbiter. This was December 10, 1860.

This English proposal was declined by the government of the United States, and for various reasons that need not here be spread out in detail. For ten years more this vexing question had fitful slumbers and spasmodic wakings. Discussions in Congress and Parliament, conferences formal and informal, and diplomatic notes between high officials, extended the painful length of the struggle for another decade. The whole was narrowed to a finality, that apparently waited for only one move more. All hearts were at length lightened and all honor insured, when, May 8, 1871, the question was given for arbitration and finality, beyond appeal, to his Majesty the Emperor of Germany.

The question between the two nations was at last very single and separate, and exceedingly earnest. The issue, in its final shape, was between two channels. England claimed the Rosario, near the continent, and the United States claimed the De Haro, near Vancouver; and the treaty of arbitration stipulated that the Emperor William "shall decide thereupon finally and without appeal, which of these claims is most in accordance with the true interpretation of the treaty of June 15, 1846." That treaty called for "the middle of the channel which separates the Continent from Vancouver Island."

It will be noticed that this treaty had waited twenty-five years for its execution, under the *finesse* and delays which a possible ambiguity encouraged. The English hesitation over the final move in the game is not strange. Two hundred years, almost exactly, from the grant of the charter to the Hudson Bay Company by Charles II. in 1670, that huge monopoly of half a continent had been moving westward with the irresistible and grinding force of a glacier. It must stop on the Pacific, and in the end the narrow question arose: What islands must be yielded and what ones may be held? From claims for areas like England on the mainland, they had come down to islands and acres.

Around the conclusion, when it came, there was the gathering of the august and solemn and sad. The two leading nations of the world held their own wills in abeyance, and asked a third to put them under order and beyond appeal. There was a sublime humiliation in the act. For nearly a century these two nations had been in controversy over boundary questions. The younger was born into it and was not yet free. To crown the struggle of a hundred years, and thus sum up and conclude the work of three generations, and to do it peacefully, is an act for the gravest reflections and the most profound joy.

The final interpretation and execution of the treaty of 1846 had much of the sad to overshadow it. Twenty-five years had waited for that end. Sixteen members of the British Cabinet had framed it and offered it to the United States. Sir Robert Peel, Lord Aberdeen, and all that Cabinet, save one, were now dead. Of the American high officials who shared in its construction and adoption, the President and Vice-President, and Minister to England, and Secretary of State, and all the Cabinet, save one, were now gone. Upon the only survivor, the Honorable George Bancroft, historian, diplomatist, and scholar, and, when the treaty was formed, Secretary of the Navy, it was devolved to present the American case to the Emperor.

We note here what is too often forgotten in honoring single persons for single achievements. No one is great by himself. Greatness is an accumulation to which many contribute and one crowns it. In the total and final honor, therefore, the last actor is entitled to only a proportion, an undivided and indefinite moiety. Since 1783 many of the best statesmen and patriots in the United States had been preparing the way and the material for Mr. Bancroft's successful and concluding work. As Secretary of the Navy he was of the Cabinet of 1846 that advised the treaty, and was now the only one left to expound it to the German Emperor.

This he did in an exhaustive and admirable Memorial of one hundred and twenty octavo pages. After referring, in its graceful and beautiful exordium, to these changes which death had wrought in the ranks of the original laborers on the treaty, he says : —

"I alone remain, and after finishing the three score years and ten that are the days of our years, am selected by my country to uphold its rights. Six times the United States had received the offer of arbitration on their northwestern boundary, and six times had refused to refer a point where the importance was so great and the right so clear. But when consent was obtained to bring the question before your Majesty, my country resolved to change its policy, and in the heart of Europe, before a tribunal from which no judgment but a just one can emanate, to explain the solid foundation of our demand, and the principles of moderation and justice by which we have been governed."

Like all great works the process in arbitration was very simple. Each party submitted its case in print, with all documents and maps attached that were thought to be necessary. Then each party received the Memorial of the other, and put in a printed reply to it, so that each furnished two papers to the Emperor. These four papers his Majesty laid before three eminent jurists, also experts in such matters, on which they bestowed separate attention and gave separate opinion. The Emperor gave to the subject his personal attention, and most careful study and deliberation.

After a full and faithful examination of the case the Emperor decreed this award : " Most in accordance with the true interpretations of the treaty concluded on the 15th of June, 1846, between the Governments of Her Britannic Majesty and of the United States of America, is the claim of the Government of the United States, that the boundary line between the territories of Her Britannic Majesty and the United States should be drawn through the Haro Channel. Authenticated by our autograph signature, and the impression of the Imperial Great Seal. Given at Berlin, October the 21st, 1872."

So the end came, and an end to many things. Two great nations had divided North America between them and fixed the line of demarkation. For ninety years they had been in conference to put a treaty line of division on paper, and now they had marked it on the earth by the stars and an immutable ocean current. The end of boundary questions between the two nations was reached. Diplomacy, geography, anxieties, rivalries, and almost wars, were no more. Land and water, stretching across the continent from the Atlantic to the Pacific, were divided between the two governments.

From the Treaty of Paris, 1783, to the arbitration at Berlin, 1872, it would be quite difficult to state the number of diplomatic conferences between the two nations on this boundary question. Never before, apparently, or at other times, had the English language been so tested to embody agreements in inevitable words. What, in the last instance, the parties were four years in writing, they were twenty-six years in interpreting, and then they failed. But the march of rival empires across the New World came to an end at Berlin, when the Emperor William put his autograph to a few simple sentences of interpretation, and established a boundary.

CHAPTER XXXI.

THE WHITMAN MASSACRE.

This book is designed to be a history of the concession of Oregon, and not a history of Oregon. Yet it would seem to be incomplete if the tragic end of the man who saved Oregon to the United States were not outlined. It is an exceedingly painful record in human annals, and shows how much the benighted natives there needed the religion of " good will toward men."

Among the chapters of human tragedies this is one of the most tragic. The persons killed were the missionaries of Christ; they who killed them were the poor Indians whom they were instructing and lifting into the light and love and daily life of God's children; many who looked on, or stood afar off, knowing it and not interfering, were white people, and some of them the official servants of the church. The massacre ran riot through eight days, and Dr. Marcus Whitman and wife, of the American Board, and thirteen or more associates, were savagely killed on the 29th of November, 1847, and days following. It was the bloody baptism of Oregon, by the like of which the most of the American States have come to form the Union.

Lacking only the slow torture of hacking and flaying and burning, it stands among the most atrocious of Indian atrocities. The details, covering the dead and scarcely less unfortunate fifty captives, I will not relate, though spread out with painful and revolting minuteness before me. As I write the history of the massacre, and not a drama of it, I will not show the poor, dumb wounds, and the rent and bloody garments, as at Cæsar's funeral.

To understand this murderous assault on a Christian mission, and carry a well-balanced judgment about it, as a part of the history of Oregon, certain facts must be taken into account, especially concerning the two policies of the English and the Americans in regard to the Indian country. The former, under the Hudson Bay Company, desired to hold back the wilderness for a game preserve, and use it only for the production of furs. They, therefore, kept out of it the civilized grains and grasses, the plow and hoe, and water-wheel. All who came to settle the country and to develop it, and civilize the Indians, the Company kept back. No Europeans were admitted excepting their own servants. All schools for the Indians were opposed, and almost all Christian missions, except the Roman Catholic. These statements apply to the whole domain of that Company: the chartered part of it took in all the region whose waters drain into Hudson Bay, and the leased part took in all north and west of this to the Arctic and Pacific. They were hoping and planning for the valley of the Oregon. So their purpose was to hold forever for steel-traps an area one third larger than all Europe. This pleased the Indian, specially when intermarriage and an accommodated life met him half way.

On the other hand, the Americans wished to build the United States on Indian lands. The factory dam must take the place of the beaver dam; and wheat fields the place of buffalo ranges; mansions, of wigwams. This displeased the Indians, as they lost their lands and game and the pleasures of a wild life. One policy was to propagate wilderness and beaver, and Indians and half-breeds to catch them; the other, civilization in its highest type and thrift. No two policies could come more in contradiction, one fostering all the tastes and habits of the natives, and the other demanding a total change in the modes and grade of life. Hence the fact — so slow to be understood, coined into a reproachful criticism on the United States — that the English got along much better than the Americans with the Indians.

The English had their own way from 1670, when the fur company was chartered, till 1834, when they met our pioneer missionaries in the valley of the Columbia. As our missions meant plows and highways and factories, it meant less fur, and corn instead, and school books. From that date their jealousy of the Americans took a more active and violent form. At this time the Company held Oregon almost absolutely. No American interest could thrive there, and indeed the traders and trappers of the Company had come over the mountains and were holding the head waters of the Yellowstone and Missouri. Meanwhile the two nations were, by treaty, to have a joint occupation of Oregon. When the Company pleaded for a renewal of charter, one strong plea was that they had kept back the Americans. It would take a volume to tell how thoroughly they had done this.

At the time of the massacre the Indians had obtained from some source the conviction that the Americans wanted their lands, while the English did not. Moreover, they felt that the Americans wished to change the entire life of the Indian — his religious and civil life, and pursuits and pleasures, while the English wished only for fur, when a civilized Indian would be a hinderance. So it came to pass that the English had the territory and the Indians on their side when Americans began in 1834 to settle in Oregon. Diplomacy and trade, fraud and bloody violence, were used to keep them back, while the Company sought to hold Oregon by bringing in colonies from the Red River country. This aroused Dr. Whitman to that wonderful ride, already described, and he brought back to the Columbia 875 immigrants, with 200 wagons and 1,300 head of cattle, in 1843. The two policies now grappled in a final struggle. On the one hand it was beaver and Indians and wilderness for a huge corporation and so many pounds sterling dividends; on the other it was settlements, domestic animals, civilization, national wealth. The struggle was natural, as begun in the seventeenth century, the result inevitable, as ended in the nineteenth century.

The Oregon Treaty of 1846, which conceded the primitive American claim up to the forty-ninth parallel, brought disappointment and anger to the Hudson Bay Company. It left them as foreigners on the American side of the boundary, and with stipulations that they must leave. Their plans were a failure, as civilization had conquered the wilderness, and a State called Oregon was soon to enter the Union. Then, what was done to settle it would stimulate the settlement of the British Provinces over the line, and the fur trade must give way to a broad international commerce outside of their charter. The Canadian Pacific Railroad of to-day is confirmation of their well founded, yet poorly understood anticipations and fears. The thoughtful could foresee that the Hudson Bay Company must close its affairs. And American enterprise, pioneered by American missionaries, had done it.

The Oregon Treaty was proclaimed August 5, 1846. Three or four months would carry the news of their defeat up and down the Columbia. A year more intervened while they were removing and preparing to complete the transfer to their own proper limits, when the massacre took place.

Must we think it was planned by intelligent white people? Not necessarily. The general causes have been stated, which are enough to produce it, if Indian nature be taken into the account. He sympathized in this case with the fur-trader in his disappointment, and made it his own; also, he feared, and with the best of reasons, that the Americans would take his land. From colonial times such a condition of things has been followed by Indian raids. Every other state, as well as Oregon and Kentucky, has its "dark and bloody ground." It is true the Spanish, and French, and English, and Americans have each in turn used the Indians to destroy their enemies. Many American traders and trappers in the Indian country had been killed through the influence of the Hudson Bay men, though not perhaps by plot and contract. With the rivalry, monopoly, and bloody hostility of that company before they lost the Oregon country by treaty, the scant civilization of the border is enough to account for the massacre.

For twenty-five years and more after the Revolution, our emigrant border was made a reproach to civilization by the Indian raids that embittered Englishmen stimulated. Washington had painfully good reasons for writing this passage to Jay in August, 1794, "There does not remain a doubt in the mind of any well-informed person in this country, not shut against conviction, that all the difficulties we encounter with the Indians, their hostilities, the murders of helpless women and innocent children along our frontiers, result from the conduct of the agents of Great Britain in this country."

But the history of one period must not be reëdited as the history of a succeeding generation. Indian massacres have resulted from a variety of causes, and in the equitable writing of history this fact must be regarded. With the Indians, the powers of the physician and of the "medicine man," were conjoined under a thick veil of superstition. Such beliefs as come in this guise expose the "untutored mind" to the wildest fanaticism. In some instances an epidemic has visited a tribe, and its victims are beyond the saving power of the "medicine man." His inability to cure exposes him to death; he is given a test case, and under failure to heal he has sometimes been stoned or pounded to death.

This superstition in the Indian mind has been at times used as a great power in controlling him. In his "Astoria" Irving gives an illustration. McDougal, of Astor's company, who treacherously sold out Astoria to the English traders, found much difficulty in protecting his infant enterprise against the Indians. He showed them a small vial, and threatened to uncork it and sweep them all off with the small-pox that it contained, if they gave him more trouble. The chiefs, in alarm and horror, begged him to spare them, and they made all necessary promises.[1]

A case more in point is given by the Rev. Jedediah Morse, D. D. In speaking of the L'Arbre Croche Indians on Lake Michigan, he says: "They are afraid to have priests come among them, because it happened immediately after one had visited them, about the year 1799, that the small-pox was introduced among them from Canada, and carried off nearly half their number. They were made to believe, by the medicine men, that the Great Spirit "was angry with them for receiving this priest and his instructions, and that this fatal disease was sent among them to punish them for the offense." [2]

In the tenth chapter of this history a fact is stated, showing the amusing way in which a Hudson Bay officer worked on the superstition of the poor natives, and governed them by the combination of a music box, magic lantern, and galvanic battery. This mysterious power of the white man — and they put the power of medicine in the same class — the Indians connected, superstitiously, with divine and malignant spirits, and they feared and hated the white agent.

In defense against the suggestion of some, that the Indians were instigated to kill the missionaries because they were Protestant heretics, the Rev. J. B. A. Brouillet, Vicar-General, makes this statement: "The massacre at Waiilatpu has not been committed by the Indians in hatred of heretics. If Americans only have been killed, it is only because the war had been de-

---

[1] Chap. xii. p. 125.
[2] Report to the Secretary of War, 1820, on the Condition of the Indians. Appendix, p. 24.

clared against the Americans only, and not against foreigners, and it was in their quality as American citizens, and not as Protestants, that the Indians killed them." [1]

The Vicar would declare that they were killed as intruders, and the general impression among the Indians, that the Americans designed to possess the country, stimulated the act. To this agrees the statement of the Honorable Elwood Evans: "The history of the agency of Protestant missions in encouraging American settlement — the advent of settlers — the uniform first visit to the Whitman station — the treaty of 1846, which decided that the days of the occupancy, by the Company, of the territory were numbered, and that they had been baffled in getting Columbia River for the line — explain the causes of chagrin of the Company. The policy of the Company, pursued everywhere, of making the Indian subservient in time of peace, auxiliary in event of war, finishes the matter. There is no necessity to charge that the Indians who killed the inmates of Waiilatpu, on the specified occasion, were directly incited to that act." [2]

White encroachments had been a fruitful cause of Indian massacres, from Massachusetts Bay westward; it remains still a question whether it was mainly, partially, or not all the cause in this case. Other and strong causes ask for a consideration.

In 1836 a Cayuse chief lost three of his children by fever in a mission school. Other pupils sickened and died, which "created a prejudice against the school among the Indians, which it was not easy to overcome."

The American Board, in their Report for 1848, say:

[1] Thirty-Fifth Congress, 1859. House Document No. 38, p. 51.
[2] Evans's *History*, chap. xix.

"The immediate occasion of this outbreak of savage violence may probably be found in the prevailing sickness among the Indians."

The latest marked judgment on this most sad tragedy is, that "Probably the immediate cause was that immigrants brought the measles and other diseases into the country, which the Indians caught, and which, greatly aggravated by their imprudence, carried off a large number of them. Some pretended that Dr. Whitman was giving them poison, while others expressed their unabated confidence in him. To test the case it is said that three persons, who were sick, were selected, and he was asked to give them some medicine. Having done so, it is also said they all died, and that this so incensed the Indians that they began the work of death immediately." [1]

Studious and candid men have carefully weighed the mixed evidence as to the complicity of white men in the affair, but with no unanimous conclusion. After this lapse of time, and with the testimony filtered out of personal feelings and local pre-judgments, a change of venue to the extreme East may have advantages. Certainly these general facts following will be allowed all the weight to which they are entitled.

The rival nations held widely different policies — wilderness and civilization. The Indians made a tolerable comparison of the two, and had a decided preference for wilderness and its advocates. They recognized the imported diseases of white men, and were very superstitious as to their causes and cures. Disease and the healing art, and their connection with good and evil spirits, were

---

[1] *History of Indian Missions on the Pacific Coast.* By Rev. Myron Eells, 1882, pp. 21, 53, 54.

so blended in their religion as to make them susceptible of the most extravagant fanaticism. Therefore, the entangling circumstances of the Indians on the Columbia, under two rival peoples and conflicting policies, and their general character as uncivilized and superstitious, will be taken into account in assigning the causes of the Whitman Massacre.

CHAPTER XXXII.

THE OREGON OF TO-DAY.

It remains to give, in summary, the condition of the country whose concession to the United States has now been outlined. Properly and comprehensively this country was Oregon, and Washington and Idaho Territories. The three civil sections constitute a vast block in the American domain, with British Columbia on the north, Montana and Dakota on the east, Utah, Nevada, and California on the south, and the Pacific on the west. The area is 251,562 square miles — more than double that of Great Britain and Ireland, and thirty-two times the size of Massachusetts, whose citizen founded our claim to it in the discovery of its great river. Their total population was about 280,000, by the late census, of which Oregon had about 175,000. The three sections have, by nature and development, many characteristics in common, and as settlement and improvement go on, they will show increasing similarity, and the same general attractions to immigrants.

This region, the original Oregon of the treaty of 1846, is larger than three New Englands by the excess of six states like Massachusetts, and in most respects for human homes and national wealth, it is naturally superior to New England. In climate, soil, and mineral, both precious and practical, it leads promptly. In cereals, meats, fish, and vegetables, it is also naturally the leader of New

England, as its products and exports are steadily showing.

Its facilities for foreign commerce may not, at first, seem so favorable, from its westward outlook; but it is nearer, by the breadth of a continent, to the great market of the old East, while railways are treating water-commerce quite cavalierly, and shortening space and time in the exchange of goods. At Portland, Oregon, one in the Chinese, Australian, and general Pacific trade, is 10,000 miles nearer to his Asiatic markets than he would be at New York.

Had the same energy worked for two centuries on our northwest that has been expended on our northeast, the contrast between the two sections would now be extremely marked in favor of the former. Immigration and years only are wanting to show how highly nature has favored the country in question. The wide range of the Oregon block, about four hundred and seventy-five miles square, furnishes a great variety of natural qualities in its mingled mountains and valleys and prairies, and so a wide range in resources for human use and enjoyment. Probably few sections of the same area in the world bring the grand and sublime in mountain scenery so near to vast and rich prairie lawns and far-reaching slopes which invite to combined rural and city life.

The surprising climate of this section will show that no natural products can be denied it that may be elsewhere found in the United States farther north than the northern latitude of Virginia. For, the line of average heat or cold which passes through northern Virginia runs northerly and westerly by Pittsburg; forty miles south of Lake Erie, and sixty south of Chicago; a little north of Rock Island into Iowa; through southwestern Minnesota into Dakota; thence northwest through the upper and eastern corner of Montana, and about sixty miles over the line into British territory; thence by a great curve cutting northwestern Montana and the extreme north of Idaho; and, continuing midway and northerly, it passes through Washington Territory into British Columbia, and leaves the continent about two hundred miles north of the northern boundary of the United States. Along this line the mean or average annual temperature is fifty degrees, and sections cut by it have the average heat and cold of northern Virginia. It passes through the great wheat belt of North America. Other things being equal, therefore, the grains and fruits and vegetables which may be raised on this line in Virginia, or Ohio, or Illinois, or Iowa, may be raised in Dakota and Montana and Washington.

As to Oregon, it is left wholly on the south of this line. Says Hugh Small, in his "Oregon and Her Resources,"—"There is scarcely a grain, fruit, vegetable, grass, tree, plant, or flower, that grows in the United States, or in Europe, but some portions of the soil of Oregon will raise to perfection, with fair cultivation." The authority for this statement of climate is of 1870, and is based on "Blodgett's Tables." It may be added that in mountain elevations, one thousand feet in height are equal to three degrees of northing in latitude.

This fact as to the line of average temperature will prepare the way for other facts that otherwise might seem incredible. As a rule in both Oregon and Washington stock does well through the year in the open air, foraging on the abundant natural pasturage. The bunch grass matures in July, and is hayed by the sun uncut.

Horses and sheep may be trusted to it for good wintering, while it is good policy to provide some hay and shelter for horned cattle. The snow is light, and in some of the counties in Oregon it has not covered the ground for three consecutive days for a score of years.

The one third of Oregon west of the Cascade Mountains has a much milder climate and more productive soil than the eastern two thirds, as it has the warmth and rains and fogs thrown on it by the Pacific. On the coast the rainfall is about sixty-seven inches; in the Willamette valley about fifty; in the Columbia valley east of the Cascades about twenty; and in the great basin of the southeast, including the famous Lava Beds of the Modoc war, an average of twelve inches. In eastern Oregon much dependence must be placed on irrigation for agriculture.

The warmth of the coast belt is seen in the fact that the Columbia, as far up as the mouth of the Willamette, one hundred miles, and that river itself, have shown no ice thicker than window glass since 1862. The mouth of the Willamette is about two hundred miles farther north than Boston. Alexander Rattray, surgeon to the English navy at Esquimalt, Vancouver's Island, 1860–61, reports that "snow fell on twelve days only, . . . and the thermometer fell only eleven times below freezing during the year." [1]

[1] Surgeon Rattray gives the following table, made by himself, 1860–61: —

Place.	Latitude.	Mean annual temperature.
Victoria, Vancouver's Island.	48°24′	51.77°
New York.	40°23′	51.58°
Halifax.	44°39′	40.08°
Quebec.	46°48′	41.85°
Montreal.	45°31′	45.76°
Toronto.	43°40′	44.81°

The causes of this warm temperature, four and five hundred miles farther north than New York, are two. About seventy per cent. of the winds on that coast are from the southwest, and carry the heat from the tropics far inland, even to Dakota. Then the "black stream" — Kuro-siwo — starting off southeastern Asia, passes up by the Asiatic coast, and, dividing on the Aleutian Archipelago, the eastern half is forced down the Alaskan and northwest coast, carrying a large body of torrid water, which makes its warmth felt far into the interior. This warming force may be estimated somewhat by the fact that when fully formed off the coast of China and Japan this stream is four hundred miles wide, with a flow of four miles an hour in sections of it.

An illustrative fact may be here introduced from Europe, made by the effects of the Gulf Stream. Hammerfest, in Norway, is in latitude seventy-one, yet the warm waters of the Gulf Stream of the Atlantic have such an effect as to keep its harbor free from ice. That harbor, though 1,950 miles farther north than Boston, has never been known to be closed by ice. Also, on the Alaskan coast, the force of this torrid current is so great that at Sitka, a thousand miles farther north than Boston, ice cannot be found and stored for summer use, the average winter cold being two degrees above freezing.[1] Of the ability of a warm ocean stream to carry its heat, despite the cold of the ocean through which it flows, Professor Bache makes the statement that "at the very bottom of the Gulf Stream, when its waters at the surface were 80° in temperature, the instruments of

---

[1] Here it will be noticed that while Victoria, over against the northern portion of Washington, is 556 miles farther north than New York city, its average warmth for a year is greater than at New York.

the Coast Survey recorded a temperature as low as 35° Fahrenheit."

Sovereignty and organized government in Oregon were assumed by the American settlers in 1843. This was in anticipation of the great immigration of eight hundred and seventy-five persons under Dr. Whitman in the autumn. That overwhelming number, strengthening the government born of exigencies under natural and local rights, practically closed the question of possession, so long in dispute, for the United States, which became settled by treaty three years later.

A territorial government was granted in 1849, covering all of the original Oregon. In 1859 Oregon became a state in the Union, with its present limits. This left Washington, including Idaho then, under the territorial government, and so it remained till 1863, when Idaho received a government of its own.

The population of Oregon in 1850 was 13,294; in 1860, 52,465; in 1870, 90,923; and the census of 1880 gives it as 174,767. In the increase of population by immigration Oregon has not grown according to its merits and natural desirableness. Several causes conspired to this result. Except Alaska, it has been the most distant and inaccessible section of the Union. Prior to the opening of the Union and Central Pacific Railroad, it was three months off by land and very much more by Cape Horn, and tedious of access by the Isthmus. When emigrants could finally go by rail to San Francisco, a staging of four hundred miles, or steaming of anything but pacific waters offered a serious barrier, while the gold fields of California were more attractive than the slower but surer industries of Oregon.

Moreover, the productions of that distant region, however abundant, had but little commercial value, while markets were inaccessible. It was in the condition of the Middle States, before government roads and canals and railways offered purchasers to their burdens of produce, and wheat decayed in the stacks because it would not pay to haul and sell it for twenty-five cents a bushel. The through opening of the Northern Pacific Railroad will recreate Oregon, as earlier creative processes once came in upon the unfinished world, when it stood " out of the water and in the water," awkwardly waiting to be finished.

The agricultural products of Oregon have been named, but special mention should be made of its wheat crop. This is the leading staple, and is noted for its unusual weight, being often from five to nine pounds above the standard weight of sixty pounds to the bushel. Small gives the average for fair farming in the Willamette valley at thirty bushels to the acre, which is double the average for the United States. The harvest of 1881 gave a surplus for the general market of 10,000,000 of bushels, or 300,000 tons. Of this the region east of the Cascades produced 120,000 tons, and western Oregon and Washington the rest. The grains following wheat in quantity of product are oats, barley, corn, rye, and buckwheat, and in very satisfactory yield. The total product of the six has risen from about two millions of bushels in 1860 to about thirteen millions in 1880.

The amount of arable land will for a long time be a question of local option with the farmer of energy and thrift. Vast valleys stand assigned of nature to the plow, as truly as the unlimited wheat fields of Minnesota and Dakota. Leading among these is the Willamette, with its 5,000,000 of acres; then the Umpqua, one half as large; the Rogue River valley, a little smaller; the Umatilla; the Grande Ronde, about 275,000 acres; the Walla Walla, Klamath, John Day, Powder, Jordan, Palouse, Yakima, Spokan, and others. By the census of 1880 Oregon showed 16,217 farms, and their products are tabled at a cash value of $13,234,548. The stable wealth of Oregon shows one index in the estimated worth of these farms at $56,908,575.

Writers of compends and travelling observers speak of sections of our northwest as arid plains, desert region, lava beds, sage land, and otherwise condemned land. The man who says this, as well as the land of which it is said, must be regarded in any faithful statement about that country. The Swede, the Swiss, and the New Englander might look on the land most favorably, as also the man of will and work from any nationality or state.

But from our earliest geographical childhood the Great American Desert has been contracting and retreating. In 1806 Lieutenant Pike, in government explorations, swept over the prairies from St. Paul and the heads of the Mississippi to Colorado, and reported those magnificent plains as a desert barrier placed by Providence to restrain the American people from a thin diffusion and ruin! In 1819 Lieutenant Long, in similar service, crowded the "desert" into the country west of the meridian of Omaha, and made the region between it and the Rocky Mountains unfit for cultivation.

In the memorable Congressional debates in 1842, McDuffie had ascertained "that seven hundred miles this side of the Rocky Mountains is uninhabitable," and only a "tunnel through mountains five or six hundred miles in extent" would put us into Oregon. For agricultural purposes he would not "give a pinch of snuff for the whole territory."

Now, it would be difficult to find more magnificent farm lands than those in western Oregon and Washington, and the "desert" is shrinking on both sides before energetic settlers. On the Government Map of 1882, already referred to, "the Great American Desert" is located to the west of Salt Lake and adjoining it. It appears like a body crowded and cornered into a very irregular shape, with an area, possibly, one third larger than Rhode Island. In the days of our youth it must have occupied thousands of square miles just over the Missouri. It is believed that arable lands will increase as fast as the plows are offered to them for yet a long period. The basin of the Columbia is about one hundred and fifty by five hundred miles, and the fertility of it is a discovery of late years. Large tracts of it stood long on the maps of United States surveyors as "unfit for cultivation." The experiment of a thoughtful farmer brought the despised land to the front for wheat farms. Now it is well understood that where the bunch-grass grows wheat will flourish, and of such lands there are now boundless tracts devoted to stock-raising in Oregon and Washington.

Peaches, pears, apples, plums, cherries, grapes, and, indeed, generally, the fruits of the temperate zone, flourish in the lower lands. The smaller fruits of the garden are abundant and ready for the table early in May. It is expected that the exportation of dried fruits will become a leading item in the commerce of that country.

Of course where the cereals and fruits are in such quantity and quality, the vegetables keep them company in the homes of the settlers, as is usual elsewhere. Potato, cabbage, turnip, squash, onion, beet, carrot, parsnip, celery, tomato, and the varieties of melon are quite prolific. The last two do best in the drier and warmer soils east of the mountains.

As a timber and lumber country, with facilities for transportation, probably the region is not surpassed. The merchant marine of the world could be built and annually renewed there, without heavy drafts on the natural supplies. The timber distant from water transportation will wait as a proper reserve for the branch railroads. The majesty and beauty of these primitive forests can hardly be exaggerated, where the yellow fir stands two hundred and fifty feet, the pine, silver fir, and black spruce one hundred and fifty, and the white oak seventy. Cedars have been found there twenty feet in diameter. Nor does the demand allow these grand forests to stand uninvaded. A single mill has the capacity to cut out 200,000 feet of lumber a day, and in 1882 the aggregate cutting capacity of all the mills was 1,000,000 a day.

In this connection the extent of navigable waters is a first consideration. The Columbia drains a basin of 395,000 square miles, including its tributaries, which embrace twelve degrees of latitude and thirteen of longitude. The main stream is navigable for 725 miles from its mouth, with interruptions. This carries its navigation within 450 miles of the navigable Missouri, and within 350 of the navigable Yellowstone, at Huntley. Nothing nearer and better than this will ever answer to the " Straits of Anian," that chimerical passage for ships through America to Asia, in the vain search for which so much of the scholarly navigation of the world was wasted for two centuries and a half, with thousands of human lives and untold treasure.

Good steam vessels can go up the Columbia 300 miles, and light draught boats 725 miles. The Willamette is navigable for 138 miles, and the Snake for 150. Several navigable rivers empty into the Pacific on the Oregon coast, which allow much commerce for vessels of light draught. Tide water in Puget Sound and vicinity has a shore line of 1,800 miles in Washington, and such is its depth up to natural rock wharves, in sections, that the largest vessels can load and unload at them. For light draught steamers and for logging purposes the inland waters of Oregon and Washington furnish almost unlimited facilities.

The run by steamer from Portland to Sitka, 1,000 miles, is mostly in sight of the mainland, and through a perpetual archipelago. It would seem as if, on that far-away coast, the ocean and the continent once struggled for monopoly, and finally made a compromise. Hence the ocean runs up into the continent in an indefinite number of bays, inlets, creeks, and estuaries, while in and around these, as if to hold a full share, the continent has anchored her islands and peninsulas and bold headlands. Like spirited parties closing a controversy, the divide is quite on the perpendicular, with threatening depth of water and equal boldness and uprightness of shore land. In the interior are the sentinel mountains on picket, watching the invading ocean, while it makes constant and vain assaults on the boundary line. The wooded islands and main shores, with the heaviest of forest, add a beauty and a charm, which crown the scenery as picturesque and grand, perhaps beyond parallel; the sky and the water, meanwhile, rivaling each other in the deepest blue. The plain prose of all which is that that coast, inland and seaward, is unusually favorable to light and heavy commerce.

From what has been said of inland navigation it may be inferred that water power for mechanical purposes is abundant. It might be added that it is proximately unlimited, while there are vast natural stores for agricultural irrigation on the east of the mountain ranges. The water power of Oregon and Washington can be stated only briefly and in a general way.

The Cascades, on the Columbia, about 150 miles from its mouth, constitute a remarkable waterfall in this great river, where in the course of four miles its descent is 300 feet. The banks on both sides, to the extent of six miles, are susceptible of a double series of Lowells. Fifty miles above the Cascades are the Dalles, where the river is forced into a channel 175 feet wide, offering its full volume of water to canals and machinery. A hundred miles or so above the Dalles, Lewis' branch and Clark's branch unite, forming the Columbia, and the volume of water for these falls below may be judged from the fact that at the juncture, Lewis' River is 2,880 feet wide and Clark's is 1,725 feet.

Going up the Willamette to Oregon City we meet a water power estimated at 1,000,000 horse power, where the river makes a plunge of forty feet. Fifty miles above Oregon City is Salem, through which the waters of the Santiam, the main feeder of the Willamette, are emptied into that river by six falls, which aggregate 102 feet. Link River, that empties Upper Klamath Lake, offers manufacturing power equal to that of Oregon City. The Tualatin River, a west branch of the Willamette, furnishes rare opportunities. By falls of twenty-two feet it enters Sucker Lake, and by ninety more of fall it empties into the Willamette at Oswego. By an aqueduct eight miles, and with a descent of 136 feet, its waters could be brought into Portland.

All these falls are of course suggestive of manufacturing villages, and only a few of the whole are here mentioned. But a glance at the Government Map of the United States, compiled from the official surveys of the General Land Office, and issued late in 1882, will show one what abundant water facilities our Northwest possesses. The rivers are thickly laid, and the mountains among which they flow must give them a head and fall for an indefinite amount of power for human use.

The manufactures of Oregon can be compactly stated from the census returns for 1880, according to which it appears that at that date the state had 1,744 establishments, employing 6,056 hands on $12,474,019 of capital, with $6,155,560 of material and $2,016,311 in wages, and putting products on the market to the value of $13,342,130. Among the articles produced are agricultural implements, furniture, leather, and the various proceeds of it, the handiwork of wheelwrights, carpenters and blacksmiths, and of the most of the other trades that usually go with the above-mentioned.

The salmon fisheries constitute a leading commercial interest in Oregon. Professor Goode, Special Agent for Fisheries for the census of 1880, gives the number of cases of packed salmon from Oregon for that year as 538,587. As each case contains forty-eight one pound cans, here are nearly thirteen thousand tons of salmon for the trade of the world, at an estimated export value of $2,650,000. In 1866 this interest began with a product of $64,000, and has made this growth. The average salmon weighs twenty-two pounds, and three of them generally to a case, so that the catch for Oregon in 1880 was about sixteen hundred thousand of that prince of fishes.

Between Astoria and the Cascades are thirty-five canneries. The fish are taken with gill-nets, seines, and traps, and the fisherman receives about sixty-five cents per fish. In 1881 about 1,600 boats were engaged, each costing, with outfit, about $600. The seines are from 300 to 600 feet long, and the nets from 1,500 to 1,800, with depth of twelve feet. The head fishermen are generally Scandinavian and Italian.

There seems to be no decrease in the supply since this business opened seventeen years ago, and while the figures now given pertain mainly to the Columbia, it must be considered that the minor rivers, all the way from the California line to Frazer's River over the British border, are fairly stocked for local use, as well as for some foreign trade. Eminently this is true of the Puget Sound region, where the inland seas, estuaries, and small rivers are literally crowded with them.

Other varieties of fish on those coasts should not go unmentioned, as the several species of the salmo family, sturgeon, halibut, cod, herring, and smelt. The cod-fishing of the Northwest is said to rival that of the Banks, and especially in the quality of cod. Some English authors complain that Great Britain gave away Oregon, and the "London Times" explains, when it speaks of the Columbia salmon catch of 1875 as four times that of the whole United Kingdom.

Stock-raising was early tried in Oregon and Washington, and the success of the experiments has made that country a rival of even Texas, in the judgment of practical men. In 1880 it had 13,808,392 head of cattle in its 16,217 farms. Two or three things have favored this result. The native grasses are nutritious and abundant, and having been cured by the sun without cutting, they are constant and ample feed through the year. A tract east of the Cascade Mountains, 220 by 240 miles, embracing the entire eastern section of the state, abounds in these grasses, and while the rain-fall may be only from nine to twelve inches, the most of its lakes, rivers, creeks, and springs allow abundance of water for stock purposes. But for agriculture, irrigation must be adopted, and this necessity will keep back the region from farming, and leave the border unmolested for the present. Still the bunch-grass land is tempting as wheat land.

The mildness of the climate and the fair warmth of the winters, already mentioned, have made this an easy pursuit of wealth, since shelter and feeding in the cold season could be dispensed with. However, though milder there than in Illinois and New York, some disastrous storms, or unusually severe winters, have introduced changes in this regard; and cover of some kind, and feed for emergencies, are now regarded as the best financial policy, especially for horned cattle. Horses and sheep endure this neglect better.

The remarks of Mr. Hugh Small, made ten years ago, need qualifying under the experience of a decade: "The climate is fine: nine months of the year the climate is delightful. Snow falls in December, January, and February, but it is a dry snow: it never penetrates to the skin of the animals: they shake it off like dust. It seldom freezes, and all kinds of stock remain out all the year, and fatten as well in winter as in summer."

The intelligent and successful stock-raisers have devoted much interest and capital to the introduction of selected and approved bloods, even as in the East, and great changes have been wrought in that regard. The California steer, Mexican scrub sheep, and Indian pony have gone by with the early days and rough times of Oregon. Of cattle, about 150,000 head are annually driven to the Eastern markets.

In 1881, the clip of wool in Oregon was above 8,000,000 of pounds, and it is said to be ranking with the best fleeces that reach the Eastern factories.

It is too early to speak with much intelligence and authority on the minerals of Oregon. A thorough and unspeculative survey is yet waited for. Gold has been found in Jackson, Josephine, Grant, and Baker counties, and gold and silver have been mined to a million or so annually. What concerns more the interest and future history of Oregon is the fact that iron is abundant through the state, and that rich coal veins have been opened in several localities, as at Coos Bay, on the Umpqua and Yaquima rivers, at St. Helen and other places.

From what has been stated it will be seen that the inland navigation of Oregon is an important item in its commerce and growth. An efficient line of steamers is established on the Columbia for 300 miles from its mouth, while lighter crafts are used 425 miles farther up. First-class steamers run up to Portland on the Willamette twelve miles from its mouth on the Columbia. This river allows for the trade of small vessels for 138 miles, and the Snake for a greater distance. The navigable waters of the Columbia and Mississippi valleys approach within 350 miles of each other.

A system of packet steamers for travel and trade is quite inviting in this new state. Starting from Portland one has a charming run, past the Cascades, 65 miles, up to the Dalles, 110 miles; or the same distance down to old Astoria of earliest enterprise, and commercial romance and diplomatic history. Or one would vary with boat and rail as he runs up to Olympia, 120 miles, or yet farther into Washington to Seattle, 167 miles. If inland and Sound running be preferred the seaworthy and well equipped steamers will run down and over to Victoria on Vancouver, 260 miles.

Of course there are many small vessels, steam and sail, plying between the numerous ports, large and small, that give life and beauty to those inland waters, showing the energy, and thrift, and growth of that Pacific State. And what facilities for business and pleasure the navigable rivers of Oregon and Washington do not now furnish, the railroads are rapidly providing.

As these sheets are going through the press, the Northern Pacific Railroad, that herculean work, is laying its last connecting rails, and the grand ideal of its projectors is completed. Only by sections can its magnitude be realized. From Lake Superior into the Dakota Valley, 300 miles, to the Yellowstone, 300 more, and up and along that river, 400; then 300 through the Flathead Valley and a final 500 to Puget Sound. It is well that the ancients limited the wonders of the world to seven, else there would be a long catalogue. The scheme fills out the project and crowns the wonderful ride of the grand pioneer of it all. If the tomahawk could have spared him from the saddle of 1843 for the palace car and golden spike of 1883 !

This may be considered as a trunk road, to open by branches, two hundred miles of breadth on each side of it. The compass of such a belt, between Lake Superior and the Pacific, seems incredible. It would take in England and Scotland, and Ireland, France, Spain, and the thirty-five states of the old German Confederation.

And it is receiving, heavily, of these nations. A few hours of study at Castle Garden, watching the polyglot procession as it debarks, three thousand a day at one port only, and moves on, largely to the Northwest, will soon show how those magnificent areas are opening to overcrowded Europe. Since those prehistoric days, when Asia tilted toward Europe and spilled into it its Aryan hordes, there has not been such a column of the human race moving in one direction, as is now going out into our West and up into our Northwest. Heretofore such emigrations of mankind have served to divide up universal history into eras, and we are now opening for a new alcove in the historic library of the world.

We are better prepared now, in the completion of the Northern Pacific, to fill the words of Henry Wilson with their proper meaning. When this noble interoceanic enterprise was before Congress, he said, and with much of boldness for that day, " I give no grudging vote in giving away either money or land. I would sink $100,000,000 to build the road, and do it most cheerfully, and think I had done a great thing for my country."

In Oregon and Washington the branches of this trunk road are running out quite freely, in a new country, for its development. Not only do the connecting links go into the main line, but branches also are to be completed by midsummer of this year from Portland to Kalama; from Palouse Junction to Farmington and Moscow; from Riparia to Lewiston; and from Union to Baker City. The Oregon and California road is completed much south of Roseburg, and is progressing rapidly to a connection at the state line with the California and Oregon road.

That Northwest therefore, so far off till now, has become our next-door neighbor, and as near to New York as Monday is to Friday. Where were heard, mainly, only the dashings of her rivers in the primeval stillness of her wilderness, are now the puffing of steamers and whistle of locomotives, and clatter of mills and bustle of trade, and the glad sounds of farm life, and the winsome music of children. The Oregon question and the era of the beaver, one and the same thing, are ended.

CHAPTER XXXIII.

CONCLUSION.

It is with regrets that this monograph or study of a single line of thought and growth in American history is brought to a conclusion. In writing it not only a recreation and pleasure have been indulged, but a theory has been gratified that sometimes history is best studied and taught and mastered topically. In this instance a line of territorial growth to one termination has been carefully followed. It has proved a thread from which many lateral or side threads have sprung as we passed along. These have been allowed to extend, if we may illustrate by grape culture, till they have been pruned away, or set fruit in one or more historic clusters and then been headed off.

Wilderness traffic, nursed to the hinderance of civilization, has been traced, and the emigrant wagon followed from clearing to prairie, and on up the valleys and into the mountains. We have counted the cabins where government has since taken the city census. We have watched the scramble of nations for land with dubious titles or none at all, till hot blood and running blood prepared the way for diplomatists and civil engineers. Here we have seen that governments seem to be but immense business firms, ruinous to the smaller ones, by the laws of trade that the stronger enact and the weaker endure. In these struggles to possess a new country, or repossess a lost one, we look long for any national ethics or law of right except what is avoirdupois.

The inside view of high contracting parties shows us finesse, ambiguities, sinuosities, and misleading eddies in the grave current of the business in hand. Tricks that would shame a huckster have much lessened our childhood reverence for great names and nations, as we have followed these threads of history and lines of growth from York Factory and the St. Lawrence and from the Potomac to the Columbia.

While presenting the one topic, the concession of Oregon to the United States, it has been incidental and inevitable, and vastly instructive to see how wanting in honor and philanthropy and patriotism a huge chartered monopoly can sometimes become. It would require statesmen of the Bismarck and Webster and Gladstone type to show how much the British Empire was damaged when the Hudson Bay Company voted the northern half of our continent to be wilderness in perpetuity. What are the civilization of savages and fair fields and winsome homes to them in comparison with good dividends at the home office in Fenchurch Street, London?

By this detail of consecutive and fruitful incidents, all converging toward the Canal de Haro, policies of peace and war pass in review, and we note how difficult and how blessed it is for leading statesmen to be peacemakers. One secures popularity for to-day on a war-cry, while the broader patriot pacifies the excited populace, and cools popular ardor toward himself, and at Marshfield awaits honor from the ages.

While studying our national growth in one line we have incidentally and inevitably seen it on many lines.

To produce this result has been a leading aim in these historical tracings, that the reader might come to see the magnitude and magnificence of our country — what Gladstone has called "a natural base for the greatest continuous empire ever established by man."

In colonial and revolutionary days one of the best friends of the coming Republic was Thomas Pownall. He was early the Secretary of the Commission for Trade and Plantations. He negotiated for Massachusetts the expedition against Crown Point, and was afterward royal governor for Massachusetts, New Jersey, and South Carolina. Few men comprehended better the geographical character and natural worth of our country, and he studied the growth of our institutions both as a statesman and a traveler. He early saw and said, 1780, that such a people as the United States would become, would not "suffer in their borders such a monopoly as the European Hudson Bay Company."

In his letter of adieu to Franklin, who was about leaving Europe for home, he says: "You are going to a New World, formed to exhibit a scene which the Old World never yet saw." In an earlier letter to Franklin, and when referring to the planting and growth of the great nation he foresaw us to be, he expressed a wish to revisit America, saying: "If there was ever an object worth traveling to see, and worthy of the contemplation of a philosopher, it is that in which he may see the beginning of a great empire at its foundation."

Along our Oregon trail we have had one line of vision among these foundations. They have run off, right and left, from our path into magnificent distances, covering what we almost without meaning call "the West." To see and study the beginnings of these foundations of a great empire, as Governor Pownall wished to do, would turn provincial into continental men.

Our line of study and thought and feeling in this theme have, from the first, had a westward trend. Perhaps the readers will feel as Washington did, after returning from a "Western tour." While the army was lying in winter quarters at Newburg, under truce, and awaiting the treaty of peace, he made a journey with Governor Clinton, into the interior and as far west as the heads of the Susquehanna. Of this trip he writes: —

"Prompted by these actual observations, I could not help taking a more extensive view of the vast inland navigation of the United States, from maps, and the information of others, and could not but be struck with the immense extent and importance of it, and with the goodness of that Providence which has dealt its favors to us with so profuse a hand. Would to God we may have wisdom enough to improve them."

The treaty then pending was to concede to the United States about one fifth only of the territory she owns to-day. Yet Washington was "struck with the immense extent and importance" of that one fifth, and he continues his letter by saying, so like the statesman and American that he was: "I shall not be contented till I have explored the Western Country," — a noble and necessary sentiment for all who would be national Americans.

Map showing the last boundary in dispute between England and the United States.

INDEX.

ABERDEEN, Earl, regrets the haste of Pakenham, 290.
Adams, John Quincy, and the Russian claims on the Pacific, 23, 24; on and for Oregon, 275.
Agriculture discouraged by Hudson Bay Company, 88-90, 321-324.
Alaska, lower part, leased by Russia to Hudson Bay Company, 25.
Alexander VI., Pope, Bull of, 1, 5, 13.
American Board and "Whitman's Ride," 241-243.
American Desert, a popular and deceptive term, 192-197, 337, 338.
American domain, increase of, from Spain and France, 115.
American Fur Company, organized St. Louis, 1808, 58; rooms, St. Louis, remarkable scene in, 110.
Arbitration, proposed and declined, 315.
Ashburton Treaty, defended by Webster, 278; fixed boundary to the Rocky Mountains, 297.
Ashley opens trade on the heads of the Platte and Colorado, 79.
Astor, of Astoria, John Jacob, 58, 59; plans for fur trade on the Pacific, 59; founds Astoria by an overland expedition, and one by Cape Horn, 60, 61; sad fate of the Tonquin, 61; the war and other mishaps, 61; is treacherously sold out, 61, 62; the English take Astoria, 63; and decline to restore it according to the treaty of peace, 64, 65, 285; held by Northwest Fur Company till 1845, 66; what kind of a post, 66, 283; a settlement that constituted a claim, 219, 220.
"Atlantic Monthly" on the Whitman and Webster interview, 231.
Authorities used in compiling this volume, 353-356.

BAGOT, English plenipotentiary, opposes the reoccupation of Astoria, 64.
Balboa, claims of, to the Pacific Ocean, 2, 206.
Bancroft, George, manages the arbitration for the United States before the Emperor William, 317, 318.
Barrow, Sir John, and northwest passage, 45.
Beaver, abundance of, 34.
Bent, Charles, Governor, the hospitality of his fort, and his service to the Republic, 172, 173.
Bent's Fort, where and what, 172, 173.
Bent and St. Vrain lead the Santa Fé trade, 79, 173.
Benton, Hon. T. H., proposal to set the god Terminus on the Rocky Mountains, 19; to take Oregon with rifles, 259, 276; states a plan for dividing Pacific coast, 284.
Bering, his discoveries and death, 22.
Bible, sought by Indians in St. Louis, 103-113.
Black Hills, forbidden by Indians to white men, 28.
Black Hills, Carver's prophecy concerning, 28.
Bodega, Cal., Russian stockade post, 25.
Bonneville, and his romantic trade on the Colorado and Columbia, 81.
Boundary question between the United States and Great Britain, difficulties of, 53-56; finally settled by the Emperor William, 56, 315-319.
Bounty on marriage, 124.
Bridal tour of 3,500 miles, 129-139.
"British and Foreign Review," opinions of, 87, 192.
Brouillet, on the Whitman massacre, 326-328.
Buffalo, slaughter of, 99-101.

CALHOUN, JOHN C., on omission of Oregon from the Ashburton Treaty, 227; on war for Oregon, 278-280.

356 INDEX.

California, English scheme to seize, 273.
Campbell, Archibald, U. S. Commissioner, to run the Oregon Treaty line, 297.
Canada, a part of Florida under Spain, 5.
Canal de Haro, 300.
Cannon first taken into the mountains, 79.
Carver, Jonathan, explores the West, 1766-1768, 27-29, 31.
Cass, on war for Oregon, 280.
Catlin and the four Flat-Head Indians, 112, 113.
Cattle introduced from California, 89.
Chesapeake, frigate, attack on, destroys treaty of 1807, 67.
Chevalier de Poletica's bold claim for Russia on the northwest coast, 24.
Chief trader in the Hudson Bay Company, his domain of solitude, 95, 96.
Choate, Hon. Rufus, for watch and guard on Oregon, 65; for delay and peace, 259, 260; for occupation by immigration, 270.
Christian Missions on the northwest coast, their origin, 116, 117.
Christian work among the Indians, 88-91.
Clark, General George Rogers, saves St. Louis, 49.
Clark, General William, public life in upper Louisiana, etc., 106-113.
Clayton, on war for Oregon, 276.
Colonial [English] Magazine and missionaries, 91.
Colonists, criminal and immoral, shipped to the new world, 123-125.
Colonial [English] Magazine, the, 96.
Columbia River, all claimed by Rush, 73.
Columbia, such a river suspected by Meares, Vancouver, and others, 213; progressive discovery of, claimed by English. 215.
Conclusion, 349-352; American growth traced on one line, 349; national ethics, 349, 350; a monopoly studied and its lesson, 350; two kinds of popularity, 350; national growth, as a whole, 350, 351.
Cook, James, discoveries of, on northwest coast, 29, 30.
Council Bluffs, singular error as to location of, 73.
Crittenden, on war for Oregon, 274, 276.
Crozat and his Charter, 88, 289.
Cushing, Caleb, on the northern limits of Louisiana, 209, 210.

Davis, Jefferson, on war for Oregon, 275.
Dayton, on war for Oregon, 279.
De Tocqueville laments for France the loss of Louisiana, 21.
D'Iberville, energy and ambition of, 10.
Dinner in the Rocky Mountains, 136.
Discovery of the mouth of a river, gave its valley to the discoverer, 213, 216.
Distances in the "Lone Land," 39, 96.
Dobbs, opposed by Hudson Bay Company, in seeking the northwest passage, 45.
Dog-trains, 95-97.
Douglas, of Illinois, on war for Oregon, 275.
Drake, Sir Francis, ridiculous coronation of, 206.
Duflot de Mofras, map of, 301.
Duncan thwarted by the Hudson Bay Company in searching for the northwest passage, 46.
Dunn, John, on the monopoly of the Hudson Bay Company, 209.

East or West, for investment of benevolent donations? 77, 78, 197, 198.
"Edinburgh Review," opinions of, 150, 192, 194, 253, 264.
Elizabeth, of Russia, gains possession in North America, 3.
Ely Volume on the interview between Whitman and Webster, 231, 232, 242.
Emigration, examples of, 265, to Oregon, stimulated, 263, 264; early, on the Ohio, 240; early practice of, at St. Louis, 243-245; increased by Whitman, 251, 252.
England in the New World in 1607, 4; begins to explore her acquisitions from the French in 1763; struggles to retain the northwest territory after the revolution, 31; retains seven military posts against the treaty of 1783, 31, 32. 48; instigates the Indians to war on the frontier, 32; struggles to expel the French from the Ohio, 48; refuses to surrender Fort Albany to the French, according to the Treaty of Ryswick, 49; singular pretence to retain Oregon, 65; violates treaty of "joint occupation" of Oregon, 66, 67, 310; struggles to regain the West. 68; how England lost Oregon, 69; kept out of a magnificent country by the Hudson Bay Company, 99, 151, 152, 267, 295, 296; England's great mistake on Oregon, 87-102; her monopoly of Oregon strongly resented,

257-260; did not claim exclusive sovereignty, 223, 262; wished the Columbia for boundary in 1818, 283, 284; embarrassed by the haste of Pakenham, 290; damaged by the Hudson Bay Company, 295, 296.

English ambition for territory, 218.

English and American policies on the frontier, in two pictures, 99-101; in contrast, 114, 115, 117-119.

English, French, and Spanish mistake in colonizing America, 122-127.

European policy of colonization and failure in North America, 114, 115.

Evans on war for Oregon, 279; on Whitman massacre, 327.

FAMILY life indispensable to civilization, 122, 123, 126.

"Fifty-four forty, or Fight," 272-281; a six months question before the country and congress, 273; eminent debaters on, 274.

Florida Treaty, 1819, 222, 223, 284.

Floyd, the first of the House to move for legislation on Oregon, 198.

Fort Boisé, 143.

Fort Chartres founded 1720, 9; becomes French headquarter, and the Paris of Upper Louisiana, 9.

Fort Chipewayan, 33.

Fort Hall, its hostility to immigration, 142, 147-149, 152.

France in the New World in 1697, 2, 10, 17; discoveries of, 6-12; loss by Treaty of Utrecht, 18; by battle on the Plains of Abraham, 1759, 18; sells the Louisiana west of the Mississippi, 19; regrets for the same, 19-21; re-purchases, 20; defeated in occupying, and sells to the United States, 21.

Fraser Lake Settlement, the first beyond the mountains, 58.

Frémont and the Oregon trail, 133; as an escort, 249, 250; in California, 273.

Frobisher's trading post on Athabasca Lake, 33.

Frontier men, noble and neglected, 43; open the new country, 79.

GALLATIN, ALBERT, on the Oregon claims, 212.

Genet, the French Minister, intrigues for secession of the Southwest, 19.

Ghent, Treaty of, 64, 67, 68; does not notice Lake of the Woods, 283.

Gladstone on America's growth, 245, 351.

Government of Oregon, moral tone of, 265-268.

Gray's History of Oregon on the Whitman and Webster interview, 230.

Gray, Captain Robert, discovers the Columbia, 215-216.

Greenhow on the northern limits of Louisiana, 209.

Greenland in New Spain, 6.

HALF-BREEDS, 92, 94, 95, 125, 126, 149.

Hammerfest, Norway, and its climate, 334.

Harney, General, complicates the San Juan question, 311-315.

Harrison, General, and the Indian war of 1812, 52, 53.

Hearne, Samuel, discoveries by, 29.

Hines' History of Oregon, on the Whitman and Webster interview, 230.

Historic picture, 134, 135.

Hudson Bay Company explores the Northwest, 29; charter of, 33; leading force against the United States in possessing, 36; objects of the Charter, 36; scope of power and of territory, 36-39; monopoly of Indian trade in British North America, 37-39, 85; encroachment on United States territory, 37, 53; united in 1821 with Northwest Fur Company, 37; empowered in 1803 to adopt Canadian laws, 38, 84; unchanging sameness of business, 39, 40; why peace always with the Indians, 40, 41, 321; its trade six years in outfit and return to London, 41, 95; stock and profits of the Company, 42; ability of, 43-45; obstructed discoveries, 45-47; order filled for a wife, 69, 126; hostile to civilization, 69, 70, 88, 321; monopoly of, 74, 75, 84, 87, 198, 199, 269, 303; loneliness of the region, 88; hostile to missions, 88, 90; acquisition of property discouraged, 89; neat cattle kept out, 89; allows broken-down men to become farmers, 90; number of Europeans employed by, 94; mixed blood of the Company's employes, 94, 95; interior workings of, 95-102; amusements of employes, 97; trapping and hunting, methods of, 97, 98; amount of fur exported, 98; its policy in contrast with the American, 117, 119, 122, 123, 321, 322; officers and servants went out as single men, and married the natives, 125; opposition to wagons, 140-146; represents immigration over the mountains to Oregon impossible;

INDEX.

149-159; the managers men of great ability, 150; created international prejudice in their favor, 150, 151, 153-156; 191, 192; suppressed information, 153; power of the Company on the Pacific, 157, 269, 274: still turn back immigrants at Fort Hall, 158; plan to take and hold Oregon by settlement, 161; the plan revealed, 162; new policy of, 266; plan to hold by force and Jesuits, 268; grasping nature of, 288-289; damaging to Great Britain, 295, 296.

INDEMNITY, claimed and paid to Hudson Bay Company, 294, 295.
Indian and Traders' Fair, 135-139.
"Indian Countries," what, 87, 88; trading, 98.
Indian incident, thrilling, 107, 108; speech, eloquent, 110, 111; vain search for Bible, 103-113; Fair at Mus-ko-gee, 136, 137; Secession beyond the Alleghanies, danger of after the Revolution, 51.
Indian policy of the United States less peaceable than the English, and why, 40, 41.
Indian slavery in English Northwest, 91, 92.
Indians, Flat-Head, four, in St. Louis, 103-113; from Washington Territory, 104; had heard of white man's God and Book and came for the Book, 105; perils of the way, 105, 106; seek General Clark, known to their fathers, 106, 108; received kindly, 109, 110; fail to find the Book, 110; final audience and farewell speech, 110, 111; return to the mountains with Catlin, 112; their sad case reported by a clerk of the American Fur Company, 112; only one lives to reach his tribe, 113.
Indians, government of by imposition, 97; prejudiced against the Americans, 66, 67.
Indians, why the Whitman Massacre by, 320-329.
Irving, Washington, description of the half-breeds, 93, 94.

JACKSON, General, advising slow growth west, 199.
Jefferson's plan for northern boundary of Louisiana Purchase, 282, 283.
Jesuits, their zeal as discoverers, 7, 9, 30; to be used to exclude the Americans, 267, 268; no evident connection with the Whitman Massacre, 321-329.

"Joint occupation" of Oregon, terms of, 69; adopted 1818, 283; renewed 1827, 285; continued till 1843, 286.
Joliet explores the Mississippi, 1682, 8.
Journeying over the Plains and Rocky Mountains, 130-139.

KASKASKIA founded, 1705, 8; taken by United States in 1778, 9.
Kellett's surveys change an important map, 301.
Kelley, Hall J., aids emigration to Oregon, 81.
"Kuro-siwo," or "Black Stream" of the Pacific, 334.

LAKE OF THE WOODS, mistake in locating by treaty of 1783, 53, 55, 299.
L'Année du Coup of St. Louis, 49.
La Salle on the Mississippi, 1670, 7, 8.
Law, John, and the "Mississippi Bubble," 290.
Lee, Revs. Jason and Daniel, Missionaries to Oregon, 117, 121.
Lewis and Clark, Expedition of, 217, 218.
Linn, Senator for Missouri, fails to close "joint occupation," 255; calls for information, 256.
"London Examiner," opinions of, 192.
Long, Lieut. and a "Great American Desert," 337.
Louis XIV. proclaimed King of the Northwest, 7, 8; what his signature lost to France in the Treaty of Utrecht, 18.
Lovejoy, Amos Lawrence, with Dr. Whitman in his ride, 166; some account of the journey by him, 168, 169; left at Bent's Fort, 173.
Louisiana, secretly transferred to Spain, 1762, 12; exchanged with France for Tuscany, 20; southern boundary of, as conveyed to the United States, 71; annoying delays in running the southern boundary, 71, 72; and was never run, 72; extent of as affected by the Nootka Convention, 208; did the Louisiana extend to the Pacific, or beyond Lake of the Woods? 209, 216; transfer to the United States delayed, and guaranteed by Napoleon, 210; formal cession, 210, 211; the purchase of, 216; terms of reconveyance from Spain to France, 222; price of, 21.

MACKENZIE, ALEXANDER, excursion to the Arctic, 33; to the Pacific, 33-36; power of, 35.

MacNamara scheme to seize California, 273.
Madison on northern limits of Louisiana, 209.
Maine Historical Society, Collections of, on Ashburton Treaty, 235.
Manitoba, the home of the forest aristocracy, 94.
Marietta, founding of, 116.
Marquette explores the Mississippi, 1682, 8.
Marriage, how promoted in French, Spanish and English Colonies, 122-125; of Hudson Bay Company men, 92-94.
McDuffie, on war for Oregon, 274.
Meares fails to find the suspected Columbia, 213, 214.
Memorial of Bancroft to the Emperor William, 317, 318.
Mexican war made it unnecessary to run Southern boundary of Louisiana Purchase, 71, 72.
Middleton hindered by Hudson Bay Company in seeking the northwest passage, 46.
Military occupation of Oregon proposed, 72, 74, 76, 260, 261, 272, 284.
Mirabeau's adroit management in the Nootka Convention, 207.
Missionary explorers sent to Oregon, 117, 121; missions opened, 122.
"Missionary Herald" on the Whitman and Webster interview, 230-232.
Missionary party to Oregon, 129-139.
Mississippi, navigation of, sought by the English, 55, 68.
Mississippi River, English attempt to secure the navigation of, 55.
Monette on the English struggle for the Ohio, 48.
Monopoly, a warning example of, by the Hudson Bay Company, 102, 289.
Monroe Doctrine, its substance, urged by the United States, 24-26.
Monroe on the northern limits of Louisiana, 209.
Mule, singular case of instinct, 170, 171.

Napoleon guarantees the conveyance of Louisiana to the United States, against the delays of Spain, 210, 211; defeated in his plans for Louisiana, 20, 21.
New Caledonia, what, 58.
New England, idea of a new settlement, 115-117.
New Spain, boundary of, on the north never run, 12; quality of her colonists, 15, 16.

Newspapers in the Hudson Bay Company's regions, 41.
Nootka Convention of 1790. Causes of, 14, 15, outline facts of, 205-211; commercial and not territorial, 207, 210, 221; abrogated by war of 1795, 207, 208; commercial articles of, only renewed in 1814, 208; importance of, to the United States title, 220-223.
Notice, proposed to close "joint occupation" of Oregon, 274-281.

Ohio Company of 1751, and plans of, 48.
Ohio Company of Putnam, 116.
"Old Wagon" of Dr. Whitman, 140-146.
Oregon, first step of England into, 35; struggle for, opened, 58; pretense of Great Britain to hold, 65; treaty for "joint occupation" of, 68, 69; congressional action on, 72-76; "joint occupation" extended indefinitely, 75; falls of interest in the old states, 77, 78; is opened by Western men, 79; not included in the Ashburton Treaty, 179; Oregon disappointed, 185; a common question, was it worth having? 189-204; information scarce, 189-194; traders in, were not writers, 191; Oregon undervalued by Captain William Sturgis, 193; and by Benton and Winthrop, 193; by the "Edinburgh Review," 194; by McDuffie of South Carolina, 195; first congressional action on for legislation, 198; some willing Oregon should become a separate nation, 200, 201; boundaries and area of, 205, 212; title of, claimed by Spain, 205; title of, claimed by England through Drake, 206; Nootka Convention on titles, 207; this convention commercial and not territorial, 207, 210; abrogated by war of 1796, according to Lord Bathurst, 207, 208; reaffirmed, 1814, 208; claims of the United States from the Nootka Treaty, 208-210; Oregon question goes under discussion by the people, 255, 257; and by Congress, 256; call by Congress for information, 256, 257; strong feeling against "joint occupation," 258; state of the case December, 1845, 262; population of, 1846, 264; civil government inaugurated, 265, 266, 268; republican institutions in germ, 268, 269; immigration takes Oregon, 263-271; war for Oregon? a six month's question, 273; eminent debaters on,

360 INDEX.

274; notices to close "joint occupation" passed as a peace measure, 280, 281.

Oregon as a separate nation, favored by Jefferson, 200, 201; in Boston, 201; by Gallatin, 201.

Oregon Treaty, dates of progress in, 293; obscurity of, turned against the English writers of it, 293–294.

Oregon of to-day, 330–352; location, area, population, 330; as compared with New England for human homes, 330, 331; facilities for commerce, natural scenery, climate, and productions, 331–333; causes of warm temperature, 334; illustrated, 334; government organized, 335; population, 335; Northern Pacific Railroad creates a market, 336; wheat and other crops, 336; amount of arable land, 336–338; fruits and vegetables, 338, 339; timber and lumber, 339; navigable waters, marine and inland, 339, 340; water power, 341, 342; manufactures, 342; fisheries, 342, 343; stock-raising, 343–345; sheep and wool, 345; minerals, 345; inland steam navigation, 345, 346; Northern Pacific Railroad, 346, 347; immigration, 347; branch railroads in Oregon and Washington, 347, 348; Oregon and California railroad, 348; Oregon and New York five days apart, 348.

Oswald, in treaty of 1783, struggles to retain the northwest, 31.

"Out West" in old colony times, 144, 145.

Owen, of Indiana, on Oregon, 263, 264.

Pacific coast and United States ownership, 273.

Pacific coast, proposed division of, between United States, England, and Russia, 284.

Pakenham, English minister on the Oregon Question, arrives, 286.

Parker, Rev. Samuel, missionary to Oregon, 117, 121; exploring tour of, 121, 122.

Parma, Duke and Duchy of, in the retrocession of Louisiana to France, 20.

Pattie, J. O., and his travel for trade into New Mexico and Mexico, 80.

Pelley, Sir John, Governor of Hudson Bay Company, intercedes for Company interests, 289.

Peter the Great on the northwest coast, 3, 22–26.

Philadelphia, Mayor and Mr. Webster, 184.

Pickett, Captain, commanding American forces on San Juan, 311.

Pike, Lieutenant, and a "Great American Desert," 337.

Pilcher, and his important tour for furs, 80.

Pitt, the younger, shapes the Nootka Convention, 14.

Plains of Abraham, cost of battle there to France, 18, 19.

Polk, President, 260, 272.

Post Henry established, the first in valley of Columbia, 58.

Pownall, Governor, letters to Franklin and desire to see American foundations go in, 351, 352.

Prevost, James Charles, English Commissioner to run the Oregon Treaty line, 297.

Public buildings, the first in Oregon, 265.

Puget Sound Agricultural Company, 42.

Putnam, Rufus, and the Ohio Company, 116.

"Quart of seed wheat," 114–121.

Rabbits' Skins sold in London in one year, 43.

Railroads, when opened in New England, 143.

Rendezvous of trappers and traders in the mountains, 135–139.

Robinson's account of Indian government, 97.

Rocky Mountain Fair, 135–139.

Roman Catholic policy in withholding the Bible, 109; great zeal and sacrifice in missions, 109; no evident connection with the Whitman massacre, 324–329.

Rosario Straits, 300; location changed by English geographers, 301.

Rupert's Land, what, 33.

Rush, secures the reoccupation of Astoria, 64; on the Boundary Commission of 1818, 283.

Russell, Lord John, 307.

Russia in the New World, 3, 22–26.

Russian fur trade in North America, 22–26; colony in California, 23–26.

Ryswick, Treaty of, 1.

San Juan boundary, extent, islands, and channels of, etc., 299, 300; English finesse, 301, 302; amount of land involved in the San Juan controversy, 302; time and labor consumed by the commissioners, 303; de Haro marked by nature as "the channel which separates the continent from Vancouver's Island," 303; was understood by the makers of the treaty to be the channel, 303, 304; Prevost from the first claims Rosario, 304; Prevost refuses to mark by monument the point of contact between the land and the water line, 305; labors to carry that point fifteen miles too far east, 305; apparent English scheme, 305-308; San Juan had been conveyed to the Hudson Bay Company in violation of treaty of "joint occupation," 306, 307; refused absolutely to the United States, 307; English assumption, 308; apt reply of Secretary Cass, 308, 309; work of the commissioners ends suddenly and unsatisfactorily, 309; Americans and English occupy San Juan, 310, 311; civil conflict, 311; American and English forces near to fighting, 311-313; General Scott arrives and restores peace, 313, 314; Minister Lyons, 1860, proposes an arbitrator to interpret the treaty, the King of the Netherlands, or of Sweden and Norway, or the Swiss President, and Secretary Cass declines, 315; in 1871 the Emperor of Germany is made arbitrator and accepts, 315, 316; august and sad tribunal, 316, 317; the finality of the boundary question after ninety years, 319.

Santa Fé, what; receives Dr. Whitman, 172.

Scott, General, quiets the San Juan parties, 313-315.

Secession, early, proposed, 19, 50-52.

Selkirk settlement, 94, 161.

Semple, of Illinois, estimate of emigration, 264.

Settlements, mercantile and civilizing in contrast, 122-127.

Settlement of a country is more than occupation, 219.

Seward, W. H., Secretary, anticipated by Carver, at St. Paul, 28.

Seward, W. H., Secretary, and his prophesy of Seat of Empire, 28.

Silence, painful, of the Great Fur Land, 41.

Simpson, Sir George, tours and observations of, 153-158; he speaks discouragingly of distances, soil, great deserts, etc., 154; assumes validity of the English claims, and defies the United States to take possession, 115; proposes to divide the vacant parts of the world with Russia, 156; shows how England may take California, 157.

Sixty years' struggle of England for the Ohio region, 48.

Slavery in English northwest, 91, 92.

Slocum's Report to Congress on slavery in Indian countries, 91, 92.

Small, on the products of Oregon, 332.

Spain, in the New World, 1, 5-16; shrinkage of, 11-16; expels the English from West Florida, 1779, 49; tempts a secession of the southwest, 51; the Nootka Convention, 205-211.

Spalding, Rev. H. H., engages as missionary, 127-129; misapprehends Webster on the Oregon question, 229-238; testimony to the work of Dr. Whitman, 263.

Spalding, Mrs., heroism of, 133.

State House, a primitive one, 265.

St. Croix, what river is it? 54.

St. George, English name for Astoria, 63-65.

St. Louis, attacked by the English and Indians, 1780, 49, old centre of the fur trade, 79.

St. Lusson on Lake Superior, 1671, takes the northwest for Louis XIV., 7, 8.

Straits of Anian, 6, 7; search for, 27, 28, by Carver, by Hearne, 29, Hudson Bay Company to search for, 33; neglect of, 45; Vancouver instructed, 299.

Sublette and the Rocky Mountain Company, 80.

Tartary in New Spain, 6.

Testimony for Dr. Whitman, by his emigrants, 246-7.

Tecumseh and General Harrison, 52, 53.

Texas taken by the French, 1685-1689.

"The Divide" what, 132, two women open it for Frémont, 133.

The trapper and a civilized woman again, 138.

The West tardily appreciated by the East, 60, 77, 78, 196-198, 200, 224.

Tippecanoe, battle of, 52, 53.

Trappers of the Hudson Bay Company everywhere, 43, 44.

Trappers' festival at Fort Walla Walla, 160.

Treaty of Fort Stanwix, Indian boundary fixed by, 32.

Treaty of 1783, American struggle in, to save the northwest, 31; unfortunately expressed, 180.

Treaty of 1794 and English surrender of the seven posts, 48.

Treaty at last for Oregon, 282-296; main article of, 282; time required

to write it, 282 ; steps taken to run the line, 297 ; English commissioner not empowered to run the continental part of the line, 297-298, 302, 303 ; still diplomacy, 298 ; the treaty without a map, 298, 299.
Tuscany exchanged for Louisiana, 20.
Twiss, Professor, on discovery of the Columbia, 216.
Tyler, President, urges the settlement of the Oregon question, 256 ; announces negotiations as begun, 260.

UNITED STATES, claims of, to Oregon, 212, 223, 284 ; tedious settlement of, through sixty years, 212 ; claim by prior discovery, 213-216 ; by the Louisiana Purchase, 216, 217 ; by prior explorations, 217-219 ; by prior settlements, 219, 220 ; no English claim possible between Spanish ownership and the American purchase, 216, 217, 222 ; openly explored by the United States as purchased property, 217, 218 ; England enters no protest, 218 ; explorations continued without protest, 219 ; the first settlement in Oregon was American, Astor's, 219, 220 ; continuous life of civilization afterward, 220 ; Florida Treaty conveyed to the United States all Spain claimed north of latitude forty-two, 222, 223 ; Great Britain makes important concession, 223 ; other claims of, 262 ; not perfect claim, 283 ; as stated by J. Q. Adams, 285 ; offer of forty-nine vainly renewed by Mr. Everett, 286 ; President Polk in his inaugural, 1845, asserts the American claim to be "clear and unquestionable," 286 ; a new offer and rejected by Minister Pakenham, 287 ; policy of "notice" and probable war discussed for months, 287, 288 ; United States discovers the Hudson Bay Company as the real power in negotiation, 288 ; gloomy anxieties of the people, 296 ; proposal of arbitration declined, 290 ; renewed and declined, 291 ; hopes of settlement, 291, 292 ; "notice" served on Great Britain, 292, 293 ; draft of a treaty obtained, approved, ratified, and proclaimed, 293 ; United States agree to protect the rights of the Hudson Bay Company, and Puget Sound Agricultural Company, south of forty-nine, 294 ; amount of indemnity, 295.
Utrecht Treaty of 1713, 18.

VANCOUVER barely fails to discover the Columbia, 214.
Vancouver Island and deflected boundary offered, 1826, 288 ; free ports on, offered, 287 ; offer of island renewed, 288.
Vergennes, secret agent of France to recover Louisiana, 19.
Virginia, population of, 1650, 6.

WAGONS first taken into the mountains, 79.
Wagons for Oregon, 140-146 ; two hundred, 239-254.
War of 1812 stimulated by the English through the Indians, 52, 53.
War, almost, for Oregon, 310-314.
War of 1812, and one object of, 50.
Washington on danger of early secession, 51 ; obligation of the United States to divine providence, 135 ; on Indian wars, as instigated by the English, 324, 325.
Washington, discontent of, till he could explore the Western country, 352.
Webster, Daniel, offers memorandum for settling the Boundary Question, 180, 225 ; becomes Secretary of State in 1841 and proposes negotiation, 180, 181 ; state of the case, 181 ; concludes the treaty in 1842 with Lord Ashburton, 181, 182 ; accumulated perplexities of the case, 182 ; impossible to include Oregon, 182 ; treaty and author criticised, 183 ; delicate and difficult work in the temper of the times, 183-185 ; misunderstood and blamed in the Oregon interest, 224 ; did not indulge the war spirit, 224 ; adopted Whitman's theory and plan to save Oregon, 225 ; omitted Oregon from the Ashburton theory, as impossible, 226, 227, 255 ; made full claim up to forty-nine, 226 ; times not ripe for inserting it in the Ashburton Treaty, 226 ; Sustained by Calhoun, 227 ; injustice has been done in attributing to Webster the neglect of Oregon, 228 ; this impression traditional and unhistoric, 228 ; published by Rev. H. H. Spalding and copied by Gray, Hines, "Missionary Herald," "Atlantic Monthly," and "Ely Volume." of the American Board of Missions, 229-232 ; the published statements are contrary to the official documents, 232-234 ; contrary to the policy of the United States since 1814, 234 ; various reasons for the error, 235-237 ; on war for Ore-

gon, 276–278, 280; expounds the Ashburton Treaty, 278.
Whitman, Marcus, M. D., missionary to Oregon, 117, 121; exploring tour of, 121, 122; engages as missionary, 127; finds an associate, 127–129; his "Old Wagon," 140–146; left at Fort Boisé temporarily, 143; discovers a project of the Hudson Bay Company, and lays a plan, 162; hasty preparation for a daring ride to Washington to carry intelligence, 163; perils of the trip, 163; his deep determination, 164; the great issues involved, 164, 165; opposition of his friends gives way, 165; ready to start in twenty-four hours, 165, 166; general course of route, 167, 168; lost in the mountain storms and swimming the rivers, and arrival at Santa Fé, 168–172; arrival in St. Louis, 174; his appearance, 175, 176; his reception, and his haste to be gone, 174–177; arrival at Washington, 177; some other wonderful rides, 177, 178; Ashburton Treaty closed months before, with Oregon left out, 179; no evidence of his dissatisfaction with the policy of the treaty, 187; the omission of Oregon created his opportunity, 187, 188, 228, 237, 238, 256; was not slighted at Washington, 201, 202; satisfied with the omission, 227; gave notice as he came over the plains, of taking back emigrants, 239, 240; visits Boston and is reproved for leaving his mission, 241; suffered for being in advance of the times, 242, 243; great caravan prepares for Oregon, 243; growth of settlement by emigration, 244, 245; activity of Dr. Whitman on the march, 245; testimonials, 246; usual troubles at Fort Hall, 247–249; Frémont as an escort, 249, 250; a wide rally for Oregon, 250–252; happy arrival of Dr. Whitman, 253, 254; report of, in Congress a stimulus, 257, 258, and on the country, 263.
Whitman Massacre, 320–329; thirteen or more savagely murdered, and fifty made captive, 320; English policy of occupation, 321; American policy of settlement, 321, 322; conflict of English and American policies, 322, 323; Indian view of the two policies, 322, 323; treaty of 1846 disappointed and alarmed the Hudson Bay Company, 323; massacre not necessarily planned by whites, 324; Indian nature sufficient cause, 324, 325; Indian superstition about medicine, and cases illustrative, 325, 326; statement of Brouillet, Vicar-General, 326, 327; statement of Evans, 327; of the American Board, 327, 328; of Eells, 328; general causes operating to produce the massacre, 328, 329.
Westcott, warmth of, on war for Oregon, 275.
"Westminster Review," opinions of, 194, 196, 267.
Western men saved the farther West, 79, 198.
Westward movement of the nation, 144, 145; not favored by Jackson, Winthrop, and Webster, 199, 200.
White, Elijah, government agent, leads first emigrant band to Oregon, 190.
Wild animals, different estimates of, by the thirteen colonies and the Hudson Bay Company, 98, 99.
William, Emperor of Germany, settles the San Juan boundary, in favor of the United States, 318, 319.
Wilkinson, General, suspected of promoting secession of the Southwest, 51.
Winthrop, John, his theory of a home, 115, 116, 120.
Winthrop, Robert C., warm claims of, for Oregon, 258, 259, against notice to close "joint occupation," 274.
"Wolf Meeting," the beginning of civil government in Oregon, 265.
Wolf steals Dr. Whitman's axe, 172.
Womanly heroism, 127–139.
Women, unworthy, sent to New World for marriage, 123–125.
Women, white, first to cross the Rocky Mountains, 121–139.
Wyeth, Nathaniel J., and singular outfit and excursion, and failure, 81–84.

XAVIER, promptness of, 165.

YANCEY, on war for Oregon.
Yazoo, Washita, Arkansas, Missouri, and Mississippi explored by D'Iberville, 10.

ZACHREY, one of Whitman's emigrants, 150, 151.
Zachrey of Texas and misrepresentations of the Hudson Bay Company, 150, 151.

American Commonwealths.

EDITED BY

HORACE E. SCUDDER.

A series of volumes narrating the history of such States of the Union as have exerted a positive influence in the shaping of the national government, or have a striking political, social, or economical history.

The commonwealth has always been a positive force in American history, and it is believed that no better time could be found for a statement of the life inherent in the States than when the unity of the nation has been assured; and it is hoped by this means to throw new light upon the development of the country, and to give a fresh point of view for the study of American history.

This series is under the editorial care of Mr. Horace E. Scudder, who is well known both as a student of American history and as a writer.

The aim of the Editor will be to secure trustworthy and graphic narratives, which shall have substantial value as historical monographs and at the same time do full justice to the picturesque elements of the subjects. The volumes are uniform in size and general style with the series of "American Statesmen" and "American Men of Letters," and are furnished with maps, indexes, and such brief critical apparatus as add to the thoroughness of the work.

Speaking of the series, the *Boston Journal* says: "It is clear that this series will occupy an entirely new place in our historical literature. Written by competent and aptly chosen authors, from fresh materials, in convenient form, and with a due regard to proportion and proper emphasis, they promise to supply most satisfactorily a positive want."

The series, so far as arranged, comprises the following volumes: —

NOW READY.

Virginia. A History of the People. By JOHN ESTEN COOKE, author of "The Virginia Comedians," "Life of Stonewall Jackson," "Life of General Robert E. Lee," etc.

Oregon. The Struggle for Possession. By WILLIAM BARROWS, D. D.

Maryland. By WILLIAM HAND BROWNE, Associate of Johns Hopkins University.

Kentucky. By NATHANIEL SOUTHGATE SHALER, S. D., Professor of Palæontology, Harvard University, recently Director of the Kentucky State Survey.

IN PREPARATION.

Tennessee. By JAMES PHELAN, Ph. D. (Leipsic).

Kansas. By LEVERETT W. SPRING, Professor in English Literature in the University of Kansas.

California. By JOSIAH ROYCE, Instructor in Philosophy in Harvard University.

Connecticut. By ALEXANDER JOHNSTON, author of a "Handbook of American Politics," Professor of Jurisprudence and Political Economy in the College of New Jersey.

Pennsylvania. By Hon. WAYNE MCVEAGH, late Attorney-General of the United States.

South Carolina. By Hon. WILLIAM H. TRESCOT, author of "The Diplomacy of the American Revolution."

New York. By Hon. ELLIS H. ROBERTS.

Michigan. By Hon. T. M. COOLEY, LL. D.

Missouri. By LUCIEN CARR, M. A., Assistant Curator of the Peabody Museum of Archæology.

Massachusetts. By BROOKS ADAMS.

Others to be announced hereafter. Each volume, with Maps, 16mo, gilt top, $1.25.

PRESS NOTICES.

"VIRGINIA."

Mr. Cooke has made a fascinating volume — one which it will be very difficult to surpass either in method or interest. If all the volumes of the series ["American Commonwealths"] come up to the level of this one — in interest, in broad tolerance of spirit, and in a thorough comprehension of what is best worth telling — a very great service will have been done to the reading public. True historic insight appears through all these pages, and an earnest desire to do all parties and religions perfect justice. The story of the settlement of Virginia is told in full. ... It is made as interesting as a romance. — *The Critic* (New York).

It need not be said that it is written in a fascinating style, and animated by a spirit of strong love for the author's native State, and pride in its history. It should be said further that it brings out many an obscure or forgotten bit of history, and makes real an epoch which is familiar to very few. — *New York Evening Post.*

No more acceptable writer could have been selected to tell the story of Virginia's history. Mr. Cooke is a graceful writer, and thoroughly informed in reference to his subject. ... He has mastered his subject, and tells the story in a delightful way. — *Educational Journal of Virginia* (Richmond, Va.).

"OREGON."

The long and interesting story of the struggle of five nations for the possession of Oregon is told in the graphic and reliable narrative of William Barrows. ... A more fascinating record has seldom been written. ... Careful research and pictorial skill of narrative commend this book of antecedent history to all interested in the rapid march and wonderful development of our American civilization upon the Pacific coast. — *Springfield Republican.*

There is so much that is new and informing to the reading world embodied in this little volume that we commend it with enthusiasm. It is written with great ability and in a pleasing style, a vein of humor rippling along its pages and imparting an agreeable and appetizing flavor to the varied descriptions. ... The book is worthy of careful perusal by all who claim to be intelligent concerning the rich and progressive country beyond the Rocky Mountains. — *Magazine of American History* (New York).

"MARYLAND."

In the choice of Mr. William Hand Browne as an author for a trustworthy and graphic account of the rise and development of Maryland, the editor of this valuable series of historical volumes has made a very strong point. Mr. Browne's familiarity with the political and material development of the Province as well as the State has enabled him to produce a work of more than usual excellence. . . . Much that has been hitherto obscure is now presented to the reader in a clear light. The book is well written in simple, straightforward, vigorous English, and is a substantial contribution to the history of America. — *Magazine of American History.*

In every way an admirable and most useful contribution to American history. . . . Mr. Browne has done his work with rare skill, thoroughness, and the moderation that of all things befits historical writing. His narrative, he tells us, has been written almost entirely "from the original manuscript records and archives." He has certainly made the subject his own, and the result is a volume of such interest that the reader cannot afford to skip a line. — *New York Graphic.*

"KENTUCKY."

Professor Shaler has made use of much valuable existing material, and by a patient, discriminating, and judicious choice has given us a complete and impartial record of the various stages through which this State has passed from its first settlement to the present time. No one will read this story of the building of one of the great commonwealths of this Union without feelings of deep interest, and that the author has done his work well and impartially will be the general verdict. — *Christian at Work* (New York).

Professor Shaler has prepared a succinct, well-balanced, and readable sketch of this "pioneer Commonwealth." Himself a native of Kentucky, he writes with the natural affection which a man of loyal impulses feels for his State, and yet with no apparent bias. . . . The volume is in every way a worthy addition to a series which possesses unique value and interest. — *Boston Journal.*

A capital example of what a short State history should be. — *Hartford Courant.*

*** *For sale by all Booksellers. Sent by mail, post-paid, on receipt of price by the Publishers,*

HOUGHTON, MIFFLIN & CO., BOSTON, MASS.

www.ingramcontent.com/pod-product-compliance
Lightning Source LLC
Chambersburg PA
CBHW030346230426
43664CB00007BB/551